50 Hikes in the Mountains of North Carolina

50 Hikes

In the Mountains of North Carolina

**Walks and Hikes from the Blue Ridge Mountains
to the Great Smokies**

ROBERT L. WILLIAMS, ELIZABETH W. WILLIAMS,
ROBERT L. WILLIAMS III

Second Edition

Backcountry Guides
Woodstock, Vermont

An Invitation to the Reader

Over time trails can be rerouted and signs and landmarks altered. If you find that changes have occurred on the routes described in this book, please let us know so that corrections may be made in future editions. The author and publisher also welcome other comments and suggestions. Address all correspondence to:

Editor
Fifty Hikes Series
Backcountry Guides
P.O. Box 748
Woodstock, VT 05091

Library of Congress Cataloging-in-Publication Data

Williams, Robert Leonard, 1932–
    50 hikes in the mountains of North Carolina : walks and hikes from the Blue Ridge Mountains to the Great Smokies / Robert L. Williams, Elizabeth W. Williams, and Robert L. Williams III.–2nd ed.
        p. cm.–(Fifty hikes series)
    ISBN 0-88150-449-1 (alk. paper)
    1. Hiking–North Carolina–Guidebooks.
    2. Trails–North Carolina–Guidebooks. 3. North Carolina–Guidebooks. I. Title: Fifty hikes in the mountains of North Carolina. II. Williams, Elizabeth, 1942– III. Williams, Robert L. (Robert Leonard), 1976– IV. Title. V. Series.
    GV199.42.N66 WS55 2001
    917.56–dc21
                                    00-037880

Published by Backcountry Guides, a division of The Countryman Press
P.O. Box 748, Woodstock, Vermont 05091

Distributed by W.W. Norton & Company, Inc., 500 Fifth Avenue, New York, New York 10110

Series design by Glenn Suokko
Text composition by Janice Moore
Maps by Mapping Specialists Limited, Madison, WI, © 2001 The Countryman Press
Cover photograph by Jim Hargan

Printed in the United States of America

10 9 8 7 6 5 4

This book is dedicated to the memory of Steven Wise and Johnny Williams, both of whom found the world of nature to be a constant friend and unfailing source of comfort and joy.

50 Hikes at a Glance

HIKE	REGION
1. Crowders Mountain Trail and Rocktop Trail	The Foothills
2. The Reed Gold Mine Trail	The Foothills
3. Alder Trail	The Foothills
4. Lakeshore Trail	The Foothills
5. The South Mountains: A Sampler	The Foothills
6. Skyline Trail and Cliff Trail	The Foothills
7. Broad River Greenway Trail	The Foothills
8. Pilot Mountain State Park Corridor Trail	The Mountains
9. Pilot Mountain	The Mountains
10. Hanging Rock State Park	The Mountains
11. Hanging Rock State Park Indian Creek Trail	The Mountains
12. Stone Mountain Trail	The Mountains
13. Stone Mountain Middle and Lower Falls Trails	The Mountains
14. Basin Creek Trail	Blue Ridge Area
15. Bluff Mountain Trail	Blue Ridge Area
16. Boone Fork Loop Trail	Blue Ridge Area
17. Price Lake Loop Trail	Blue Ridge Area
18. Richland Balsam	Blue Ridge Area
19. Moses Cone Memorial Park Trails	Blue Ridge Area
20. Crabtree Falls Loop Trail	Blue Ridge Area
21. Craggy Garden Trails	Blue Ridge Area
22. Green Knob Trail	Blue Ridge Area
23. E. B. Jeffress Park Trails	Blue Ridge Area
24. Tanawa Trail	Blue Ridge Area
25. Grandfather Trail and Daniel Boone Scout Trail	Blue Ridge Area

DISTANCE (IN MILES)	VERTICAL RISE	RATING	GOOD FOR KIDS	VIEWS	WATERFALLS	NOTES
4.9	4,520	M/S		★		View of Kings Mountain, Gastonia, and Kings Pinnacle
0.5	300	E	★			Site of the first US gold strike
1.2	480	E	★			Picnic areas; fishing
6.3	1,560	E/M	★	★		View of Lake Norman, largest body of water in state
9.2	1,694	M/S		★	★	Good views with waterfalls
1.5	1,060	M		★	★	Beautiful waterfalls, distant views
5.0	440	E	★			Picnic areas, fishing
6.1	885	M/S		★		Canoe camping along the Yadkin River
6.9	1,200	M/S		★		Best trail in NC, lots of lookouts
3.6 9.5	925	E/M	★	★	★	Lake fishing, swimming, boating, camping
7.4	4,040	M/S		★	★	Many short trails, camping
3.8	1,200	M		★	★	Granite monadnock, waterfalls
4	1,920	E	★	★	★	Many waterfalls
10.9	1,560	M	★	★		Trout streams, wildlife, scenic views
7.5	2,160	M	★	★		Views of Stone Mountain
4.9	2,920	M			★	Waterfall, stream crossings
2.5	200	E	★			Boating, camping, fishing
1.5	540	M		★		Significant woolly adelgid devastation
5.7	1,220	M		★		Miles of graded carriage roads; manor house
2.5	1,920	M/S		★	★	Waterfalls, camping, picnicking
4.9	3,640	M		★		Rhododendrons & wildflowers in June
2.4	2,040	M		★		Pond and wildlife; pasture land
2.2	600	E	★	★	★	Picnic area, waterfalls
13.5	6,920	M/S		★	★	Spectular view, waterfalls, unusual wildlife
6.7	3,720	S		★		Nature museum, wildlife habitats, swinging bridge

50 Hikes at a Glance

DISTANCE (IN MILES)	VERTICAL RISE	RATING	GOOD FOR KIDS	VIEWS	WATERFALLS	NOTES
3.2	1,920	M		★	★	Falls, beautiful rock formations, spectacular views
1.0/1.7	400/960	E	★	★		Wildlife, picnic areas, naturalist's paradise
8.9	1,360	M		★	★	Spectular views, camping, wilderness area
0.8	1,400	S		★		Site of Cherokee legend
1.5	960	M	★	★	★	Handicapped accessible; waterfalls
2.4	880	M	★	★	★	4 different trails, gorges and waterfalls
12–15.9	7,960	S		★		Most rugged wilderness east of the Mississippi
10.4	5,120	M		★		Picnic, camping, trout fishing
1.6	880	M		★		Mysterious Brown Mountain lights
6.3	2,520	M			★	Wildlife, creek crossing, 100' waterfalls
2.4	1,640	M				Views of Linville Gorge
5.6	3,720	S				Highest peak in the East
5.4	3,540	S		★		Camping, picnic area, 360° views
2.7	820	E	★	★		Handicapped accessible; picnicking & camping
5.0	800	E		★		Handicapped accessible; rhododendron gardens
7.8	5,400	S		★		Varied scenic trails
6.4	2,600	M				Abundant wild birds, brooks, rock formations
3.0	540	M/S		★		Rhododendron and mountain laurel
3.0	2,240	S		★		Former Biltmore estate lands; panoramic views
5.0	480	M/S		★		Three 400-foot waterfalls
3.1	1,280	M			★	Fascinating series of waterfalls
1.0	5,760	M/S		★		Clingmans Dome observation tower
10	6,240	M/S		★	★	Camping, creeks, wildlife
1.5	480	E				Handicapped accessible, variety of hikes
6.0	2,720	M		★		Camping, nature trails

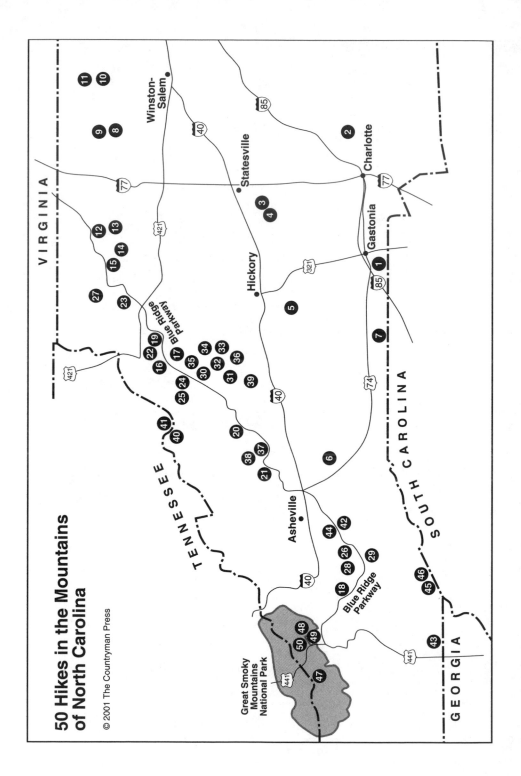

50 Hikes in the Mountains of North Carolina

© 2001 The Countryman Press

CONTENTS

IV. SOUTHERN HIGHLANDS

V. THE GREAT SMOKIES

Introduction

Selecting 50 hikes out of all the hiking trails in North Carolina was no easy task. In truth, selecting the hikes required more time than making many of the hikes.

When it was time to prepare a second edition of this book, we found that the task was no easier. However, after reviewing the contents of the first edition carefully, we decided that several hikes should be added in order to provide more variety to the hiking experiences. So, among other changes, we included an *underground* hike; at least, the major part of the hike is underground, in an old gold mine that is now a state historic site. This hike is both fun and educational, particularly for the young hikers in the group. We also added one hike that follows the Broad River for the entire duration of the hike, and this hike is great during every month of the year. Other changes include hiking along the ridge of one of the legendary mountains in the state, climbing to the top of the highest peak along the Blue Ridge Parkway, and hiking along the highest waterfall east of the Mississippi.

The Tar Heel State offers more than 750 hiking trails, providing a total of nearly 2,500 miles of outdoor recreation. Imagine this distance in terms of hiking from the mountains of North Carolina closest to the Atlantic Ocean to the Grand Canyon in Arizona, and you will have a rather impressive concept of the trail system. These many hikes range in distance from ten-minute walks of only a hundred yards or even less to one trail that traverses the entire width of North Carolina. The Mountains-to-Sea Trail covers about 475 miles of North Carolina terrain and crosses the highest mountains and the flattest farming territory in the state.

This book began as a hiking sampler of the entire state, but rather quickly we decided that the mountains of North Carolina would provide the best sampling of hiking trails. While there are trails from one end of the state to the other, many of them in totally urban areas and others in the Sandhills part of the Tar Heel State, the mountains provide the greatest variety in scenery, animal life, wildflowers, nature study, and photographic opportunities available.

About the North Carolina Mountains

Even by limiting the hikes to the North Carolina mountains, the selection was still awesome and difficult. Some people may think of North Carolina as a rather small state; however, it is the sixth largest state east of the Mississippi. The greatest width of the state is 187.5 miles, while the greatest length is 503.4 miles.

Lying completely within the warmer part of the northern temperate zone, North Carolina has a mean elevation of about 700 feet above sea level; however, in the western mountains there are more than 40 peaks with an elevation of greater than 6,000 feet and 80 peaks between 5,000 feet and 6,000 feet. There are literally hundreds of peaks between 4,000 and 5,000 feet in elevation.

Avery County in the North Carolina mountains is the county with the highest elevation east of the Mississippi. It was also the 100th and final county to become recognized in the state.

The state has a series of mountain ranges, the best known of which are the Blue Ridge, Great Smokies, Uwharries, Black, Balsam, Nantahala, and Unakas. The average elevation of the Blue Ridge Mountains is about 4,000 feet. The highest peaks in the state are Mount Mitchell, at 6,684 feet, and Clingman's Dome, 6,642 feet.

Not only is the state impressive in terms of size and elevation, it is one of the most beautiful states in the Union, and the western mountains provide some of the most scenic vistas to be found in the South.

These same mountains are also rich in resources, with great numbers of deer, quail, bears, wild turkeys, and other large animals in abundance. Of the 33 species of oaks identified in the nation, 25 grow in North Carolina. Other trees in great numbers include several species of pine, hickory, elm, maple, dogwood, fir, hemlock, walnut, pecan, magnolia, birch, beech, basswood, ash, and poplar. Laurel and rhododendron are virtually everywhere throughout the mountains.

The state at one point led the nation in gold production, and some of the mountains produce amazing emeralds and other precious stones. One of the finest emeralds ever discovered was the 13.2-carat Carolina Emerald; in recent months another enormous stone, this one 112 carats, was found in the Carolina mountains.

But for the outdoorsman, the leading attractions of the Tar Heel State are fishing, hunting, hiking, skiing, and sight-seeing, all of which are generously available in North Carolina. Several national forests, including the Nantahala and Pisgah, are located in the state.

Organization of the Book

Our trail selections were made with the convenience of the hiker in mind (as much as possible and within reason). Therefore, we have included two or even three hikes from the same geographic part of the state and, at times, within the same state park. For instance, we supposed that if you are traveling in the area of Hanging Rock, which is a good day's drive from hiking trails in the far western part of the state, you would prefer to enjoy hikes that can be reached within a few minutes rather than spend an inordinate amount of time in driving from one point to another.

We've included groups of trails from five distinct parts of the mountains of North Carolina: the foothills, the "mountains away from the mountains," the Blue Ridge Parkway area, the Great Smokies, and the southern Highlands, or the Land of the Waterfalls.

We tried to include something for every taste: the strenuous hikes of Grandfather Mountain and Mount Mitchell, the easy hikes at some of the Blue Ridge Parkway areas, the hikes that follow leading area rivers or streams, hikes that are picturesque in nature, those that have interesting historical or natural backgrounds, and hikes of widely varying lengths. We have included hikes that are handicapped accessible. These include hikes 18, 40, 43, and 49. Some parts of hikes 5, 19, 30 (the Erwin's View leg), and 47 are handicapped accessible; see the hike descriptions for further detail.

Some of the trails included in this book are less than a mile in length; these shorter hikes are ideal for leg-stretching or warm-up walking prior to undertaking a long trail. They are perfect for concluding a day's hiking when there is not enough daylight left for a full-scale hike but too much left to stop hiking for the day. If you choose, you can map out your own loops so that the shorter hikes can be expanded into hikes of 15 to

20 miles or almost any distance in between.

Some trails emphasize waterfalls, of which North Carolina has hundreds (Transylvania County alone has more than 200 waterfalls), others stress interesting and varied flora and fauna. Still others are "busy" hikes, while others are so isolated that you are not likely to meet another person in a full day of hiking.

Only two hiking areas require an admission price or fee. These are Chimney Rock Park and Grandfather Mountain.

In two instances we have "expanded" state boundaries to include trails that are just across the border or lie in part in two states. These trails include the Kings Mountain Battleground Trail and the Clingman's Dome trails. The first lies in South Carolina and the other, in part, in Tennessee.

One major trail may be striking by its omission. We did not include the Mountains-to-Sea Trail because the trail itself is largely a linking of dozens of other trails that existed long before the Mountains-to-Sea Trail was begun. So if you hike some of the many trails suggested in this book, you will be hiking a Mountains-to-Sea sampler.

We did include one segment of the Appalachian Trail, simply because this particular trail is among the most beautiful in the entire state of North Carolina.

In several instances we hiked trails in reverse order; that is, we started at what is generally recognized as the terminus of the trail and ended at the trailhead. We did so because certain trails are either easier to hike in the less common direction and others allow for better vehicle shuttle operations.

For example, many if not most hikers traverse the Grandfather Trail so that they end their hike at the mile-high swinging bridge. However, if you leave a car parked there after the gate closes and you have not made prior arrangements, park authorities may consider you lost and begin a search. On the other hand, if you start there and someone drives the vehicle to the terminal point, there is no problem.

Rating the Hikes

In calculating distances we used a traditional pedometer. We know that this is not a totally accurate way to measure a trail, because in rough terrain there is a tendency to take either longer or shorter steps than usual. But we are assuming that other hikers will take similarly longer or shorter steps and that the final distance is accurate in terms of time and energy needed if not exact in distance covered.

We used our own judgments in rating the hikes as easy, moderate, or strenuous. Ratings were based in part on our own physical traits: the three of us included a 61-year-old man with a healing broken leg, a 51-year-old woman, and a 16-year-old man in superb physical condition. At the end of each hike we compared notes and estimates and reached a conclusion for the rating of the hike.

"Vertical rise" in this book refers to the total amount of climbing on a trail. The rise may occur in one single climb or it may be spread among several climbs.

"Hiking time" includes time for walking the trail at an average pace, with occasional breaks.

"Total distance" at the beginning of a chapter will refer only to the mileage of the main hike described. Many chapters describe optional side trips and extended loops; therefore, shorter or longer hikes may be planned easily by reading the text and looking at the trail map.

Equipment Needed

For any hikes in the rugged mountain area, the very minimum equipment required includes the following items: good, sturdy hiking shoes or boots, flashlight, whistle, notebook and pencil, a copy of the trail map or topo map of the area, basic first-aid equipment, pocketknife, proper clothing, and adequate food and water. Remember that in 5,000-foot altitudes and higher, the weather may change within minutes. It is not uncommon for a day to begin with warm sunshine and end with snow. In the summertime there are rain showers virtually every afternoon in parts of the state. In Ashe County in the western mountains there is an average of 47 inches of snowfall each winter. In Macon County the rainfall averages more than 82 inches per year, while at Marshall, 60 miles away, the lowest average rainfall in the state, 39.08 inches, occurs. Thus rain gear is absolutely necessary.

Remember, too, that in higher elevations the temperature even in summer can be as much as 40 degrees cooler than that of the foothills only an hour's drive away. The best months to hike, typically, in the North Carolina mountains are April through October. In the foothills hiking is good all year except in inclement weather.

Maps

Trail maps are included in this book. For more detailed information you can consult either United States Geological Survey (USGS) maps or United States Forest Service (USFS) maps.

Maps of individual state parks often contain far more information than either of the two types of maps mentioned earlier, but for trails outside the state park system the USGS or USFS maps are helpful. You can obtain USFS maps from ranger district offices (listed at the end of this introduction); state park maps may be obtained from the Division of Parks and Recreation (addresses listed below), or you can write or call the individual

parks. Addresses and telephone numbers are also included at the end of this section.

USGS maps may be purchased at many sporting goods stores, and they can be ordered from Timely Discount Topos by calling 1-800-821-7609.

Backpacking or Overnighting

Keep in mind that no overnight camping is permitted on Blue Ridge Parkway trails; however, in national forests and selected other territory there are many camping areas along the trails. Permits are usually necessary, and you should make arrangements for permits before you arrive at the trail sites. Trail maps of all backpacking and overnight areas show the locations of campsites, many of which are on a first-come first-served basis. Others require reservations. This is particularly true of crowded areas like the Great Smoky Mountains National Park.

As with all hiking and camping, your obligation is to observe all of the rules of etiquette and ecology and to take the responsibility for caring for the land. Many mountain trails are located in ecologically fragile areas, and you are urged to stay on the trails and to observe conservation and protection measures at all times.

Safety

When you are hiking in any wilderness area, far from telephone or transportation, you need to be aware of the need for personal safety. Be aware of the presence of poisonous snakes or animals that may represent a threat to your health (if such creatures are present). Insects can also be a threat, particularly if you are allergic to bee stings or bites of certain insects.

Thunderstorms or snow and sleet storms can be very dangerous if you are hiking in areas where sudden changes in weather are common. Be prepared for sudden drops in temperature and for prolonged or heavy rainfall. Carry with you rain gear, extra clothing, and first-aid kits.

When you are caught in a thunderstorm, stay off ridges and exposed areas if possible. Seek shelter in lower elevations, and stay away from solitary trees in fields or meadows.

Hypothermia can be a problem at all times of the year. Be alert for such symptoms as disorientation, loss of muscular control, difficulty in speaking, and confusion. Dress warmly in all seasons.

Information Sources

Stone Mountain State Park
Star Route 1, Box 17
Roaring Gap, NC 28668
(336) 957-8185

Crowders Mountain State Park
Route 1, Box 159
Kings Mountain, NC 28086
(704) 867-1181

Duke Power State Park
Route 2, Box 224M
Troutman, NC 28166
(704) 528-6350

Lake James State Park
PO Box 40
Nebo, NC 28761
(828) 652-5047

Mount Mitchell State Park
Route 5, Box 700
Burnsville, NC 28714
(828) 675-4611

New River State Park
PO Box 48
Jefferson, NC 28640
(828) 982-2587

Pilot Mountain State Park
Route 1, Box 21
Pinnacle, NC 27043
(336) 325-2355

Mount Jefferson State Park
PO Box 48
Jefferson, NC 28640
(910) 246-9653

South Mountains State Park
Route 1, Box 206C
Connelly Springs, NC 28612
(828) 433-4772

National Park Service/
    Oconaluftee Visitor Center
150 Highway 441 North
Cherokee, NC 28719
(704) 497-9146

Pisgah Ranger District
District Ranger
USDA Forest Service
1001 Pisgah Highway
Pisgah Forest, NC 28768
(828) 877-3265

Backcountry Manager
Grandfather Mountain
PO Box 128
Linville, NC 28646
(828) 733-2013

Chimney Rock Park
PO Box 39
Chimney Rock, NC 28720
(828) 625-9611

Kings Mountain National
    Military Park
PO Box 40
Kings Mountain, NC 28086

Forest Supervisor
National Forests in North Carolina
Post and Otis Streets
Asheville, NC 28802

District Ranger
USDA Forest Service
Library Building
Logan Street
Marion, NC 28753

For other state parks, write to:
Division of Parks and Recreation
PO Box 27687
Raleigh, NC 27611
(910) 733-PARK

Other Resources

You may wish to contact hiking clubs or other outdoor organizations that share your interest in the outdoors. Such organizations include the North Carolina Chapter of the Sierra Club (for the state chapters contact the Sierra Club, 730 Polk Street, San Francisco, CA 94109, or telephone (415) 776-2211). Several organizations similarly interested in enjoying and preserving wilderness areas are listed below.

Friends of State Parks
4204 Randleman Road
Greensboro, NC 27406

North Carolina Recreation and Park Society
436 North Harrington Street
Raleigh, NC 27603

North Carolina Wildlife Federation
PO Box 10626
Raleigh, NC 27605

Piedmont Appalachian Trail Hikers
PO Box 945
Greensboro, NC 27402-0945

Carolina Mountain Club
PO Box 68
Asheville, NC 28802

Nantahala Hiking Club
31 Carl Slagle Road
Franklin, NC 28734

Key to Map Symbols

— — — main trail

• • • • • alternate or side trail

Ⓟ parking

⇤ view

⚲ Appalachian Trail

△ campground

Ⴖ shelter

I

The Foothills

Jim Hargan

1

Crowders Mountain Trail and Rocktop Trail

Total distance (loop): 4.9 miles

Hiking time: 4 hours

Vertical rise: 4,520 feet

Rating: Moderate to strenuous

Map: USGS 7.5' Kings Mountain (NC/SC)

In 1846, when Ulrick Crowder arrived in the part of North Carolina that would become Gaston County, he obtained a vast amount of land and planned to build, on part of it, an ideal city. When completed, "Ulricksburg" would extend for 36 square miles, making it one of the largest cities in land area anywhere in the South.

But Crowder wasn't concerned with numbers as much as he was with quality of life, and he deliberately planned his city so that there would be 34 families, each owning one square mile. The other two square miles would be devoted to educational buildings and municipal government buildings, each to have one square mile of space in which to grow.

The dream died when ill health forced Ulrick Crowder to move south to a warmer climate, but meanwhile several houses had been built in the vast forest that came to be known as Crowders Mountain. Even today a visitor can occasionally stumble across the foundation walls or remains of an outbuilding that was once part of the dream city of Ulrick Crowder.

After Crowder's death the land passed through many hands until, in the 1960s, a group of citizens reacted with outrage when they learned that the beautiful mountain would be strip-mined, totally destroying it in terms of ecology, beauty, and usefulness.

The citizens appealed to owners, to state officials, to county administrators, and to anyone else who, they felt, could help them. And they won. Within months the owners had agreed to donate the land to the state of North Carolina for use as a state park, and shortly afterward Crowders Mountain State Park became a reality.

Today the park has been designated a National Heritage Area, and it can boast of 2,551 acres and an environmentally sound recreation area that annually attracts some 165,000 visitors who come to fish, sightsee, photograph, but primarily to hike some of the trails which range in length from 0.9 miles to 5.5 miles.

Crowders Mountain is believed by geologists to have once been higher than the Rockies; before that time period, the area was under water, they claim. They point to the discovery of a tiny sea creature named *Pentrimites obesus*, a marine invertebrate known to be from 480 million to 500 million years old.

Alan Stout of the Schiele Museum in nearby Gastonia explains that the Crowders Mountain terrain is perhaps the oldest land mass on the continent of North America. The *obesus*, incidentally, is on display at the museum.

The area around Crowders Mountain was once home to Catawba Indians, and the Cherokee Indians established trade routes through the region. At present a large number of Catawbas live on a reservation across the border of South Carolina.

To reach the park, take I-85 south of Gastonia or north of Shelby and Kings Mountain. The turnoff to the park is 8 miles south of Gastonia or 4 miles north of Kings Mountain.

When you see the signs on either I-85 or US 74 north of Kings Mountain, turn right onto Freedom Mill Road. At 2.5 miles turn right onto Sparrow Springs Road and watch for a right turn into the park at 0.7 mile. After the turn into the park, the next right (0.3 mile) leads to the park office, where the Pinnacle Trail begins.

When you leave the park office, take a gravel trail 20 yards to the entrance to a hardwood forest north of the office. At the beginning of the trail you will see a chestnut tree (not one of the original native American trees) and signs directing you to the trails. Take the right trail and follow it through the hardwood forest 0.4 mile until you leave the forest and cross a paved state highway, one of the roads you drove in on as you arrived at the park.

Cross the highway and walk, to the right, alongside the highway, for 25 yards, and then take an abrupt left, following the clearly visible trail, up the hill and into another hardwood forest. You will climb 0.2 mile before you reach a huge rock cliff on the right side of the trail.

Follow the trail as it leads around the rock cliff and along the side of the mountain. Minor switchbacks help reduce the strain of the climb. At 1.7 miles you will reach the crest of Crowders Mountain. The rocks along the edge of the peak are "rotten" and can be very treacherous, so stick to the trail.

Interesting rock formations can be seen at nearly every point along the trail, and you can spot vultures soaring over the mountain on almost any given day and hour of daylight. A wide array of other birds, including hawks, songbirds, and the almost ubiquitous crows, enliven the terrain.

From the crest of the mountain you can see the cities of Kings Mountain, Gastonia, and even the skyline of Charlotte, to the east. To the west you can see a huge factory under construction: the old Loray Mill (site of one of the fiercest labor disputes in the nation's history and cause of a sensational courtroom trial) stood in Gastonia but is being transferred, under recent ownership and name, to the area south of the mountain.

To the south and southwest you can also see other mountains that jut up alarmingly from the flat Piedmont farmland. These include Kings Pinnacle and Kings Mountain, the latter the scene of the Revo-

A late autumn view of Kings Pinnacle over Short Lake.

lutionary War battle that was, to Thomas Jefferson and other Founding Fathers, the turning point in the war.

As you hike along the crest of the mountain, you will meet, on almost any weekend in which the weather is suitable, hikers and sight-seers who park at the base of the mountain and take the short and more direct walk to the top. You may also see rock climbers, who have found the area to be an excellent place for them to practice their craft.

Note the markings on the rock beds that form the base for the majority of the crest hike. The rocks are grooved, scored, and carved as if by water currents.

At miles 3.5 through 3.7 you will move from rock cliff areas to hardwood forests, alternating. At mile 3.8 you will reach a tower that was constructed for telephone and other electronic communications. Hike alongside the mesh wire fence that surrounds the tower and descend the gradual trail that leads you back to the park office.

The final 1.1 miles of the trail will be a gradual and easy descent through more hardwood forests. In wet weather you may find part of the descent to be slippery because of erosion and exposed mud that washes across the trail. When you reach the paved state road that you crossed on the way up the trail, you have a choice of returning through the forest trail which started the hike or hiking the paved road that veers off the main road.

You will emerge from the forest at the turn-off of the road to the state park. The paved road is not crowned exaggeratedly and the walking is comfortable. Follow the paved road 0.4 mile to the signs indicating the park offices.

Conclude the hike by walking up the state park road to the point where you started. If you want to do additional hiking in the Crowders Mountain area, you can take a short hike (one mile) around the lake.

There are other trails that intersect with the Pinnacle Trail you completed. These vary in distance from 0.9 mile to 3 miles. These trails are Backside Trail (0.9 mile), Tower Trail (2 miles), Pinnacle Trail (1.7 miles), Turnback Trail (1.2 miles), Fern Nature Trail, (0.7 mile), and Lake Trail (1.0 mile). You may also drive a short distance (15 miles) to the Kings Mountain area, just across the state line and into South Carolina, in order to hike the Kings Mountain Battleground trails. This area is described in chapter 2 in this book.

The Reed Gold Mine Trail

Total distance (loop) 0.5 mile

Hiking time: 1 hour

Vertical rise: 300 feet

Rating: Easy

Map: USGS 7.5' Locust

This hike is extremely short, but it is as interesting as most long trails are. It is, in fact, unique among the trails described in this book in that a large part of the trail is underground, and the part of the trail that is above ground is a hike through history.

The Upper Hill portion of this trail is just that: a hill, not a mountain. However, when you realize that you start the climb from far below the earth's surface and then hike to the top, the walk is more impressive. The trail itself needs nothing to embellish it; it is one of the most interesting places in all of North Carolina. You hike not just along a gentle trail through a thick forest but also through the site of the first documented gold strike in the United States.

Perhaps one of the major attractions of this short hike is that it is a superb place to get the younger members of the family interested in hiking. There is an abundance of attractions to interest them and encourage them to want to see and hear (and learn) more. Here, in brief, is the story. On one sunny Sunday in 1799, several children, the offspring of Johannes Reith (later Anglicized to John Reed) were arrow-fishing in the Little Meadow Creek, which flows through land that was once Reed's property but is now owned by the State of North Carolina. Reed was a Hessian soldier sent by the British to fight for the Crown during the Revolutionary War. He had deserted and settled near what is now the tiny town of Locust, North Carolina, a short drive east of Charlotte.

During the afternoon's recreation, young Conrad Reed was watching for fish

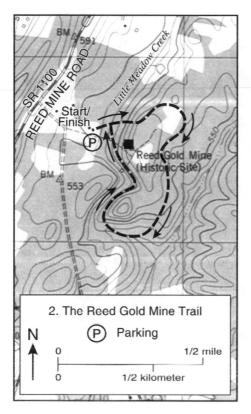

2. The Reed Gold Mine Trail

N

(P) Parking

0 — 1/2 mile

0 — 1/2 kilometer

1803 one of his workers located a nugget weighing 28 pounds. Soon the Reed family and associates sank a mine deep into the rocky hillside near Little Meadow Creek. Months and years later more huge nuggets appeared, and the gold fever that caused foreign countries to explore North America hit the Locust and Stanfield area and then spread westward into the mountains of North Carolina. The gold rush expanded to such an extent that in the first half of the 19th-century gold mining was second only to farming as the leading form of employment.

The North Carolina gold rush ended when prospectors found gold at Sutter's Mill in California. The Reed Gold Mine ceased to operate at a profit and was soon sold. Eventually the state of North Carolina restored the mine, but instead of a working gold mine it is now a tourist and recreational area.

To get to the Reed Gold Mine, take I-85 from Charlotte to Concord. Exit onto Highway 601 through Concord (about a 15-minute drive), and 10 miles south of Concord you will see a sign indicating that the Reed Gold Mine is 10 miles away. After 7 miles on Highway 601, you will reach a junction with NC 200. You must turn left (it's the only way you can turn) and you will see another sign indicating that the mine is 4 miles away. After driving 4 miles, you'll see the Reed Gold Mine road. Turn right and drive 0.75 mile. The Reed Gold Mine is on the left.

When you arrive you will see a parking lot on your right and the Visitors Center on the left. Start your day with a tour of the Visitors Center and spend a few minutes watching the short film about the history and the operations of the Reed Gold Mine. If you choose to take the underground tour, you must be accompanied by a guide. No one is permitted inside the tunnels alone.

You will start the brief hike by walking along a wide pathway that crosses Little

in the deeper pools of the creek when he saw a shiny object that was too interesting to neglect. Conrad Reed picked up the stone, which was extremely heavy for its size, and took it home to show to his parents, who liked the stone so much they decided to use it for a doorstop. For three years the stone remained in the Reed house, and in 1802, at the urging of friends, Reed took the stone with him on a trip to Fayetteville, North Carolina, where he learned to his shock and delight that the stone was a seventeen-pound gold nugget. The jeweler who identified the "stone" offered to buy it on the spot, and Reed asked for what was to him a princely sum: $3.50! The sale price was one-thousandth of the nugget's total value at the time.

Reed returned to his home and immediately began making plans to mine for gold. In

---

The Reed Gold Mine Trail

Panning for gold on Little Meadow Creek

Meadow Creek. As you stand on the bridge and look at the clear, shallow water, you will realize that in this creek, near where you are standing, the son of John Reed spotted the "rock" that launched the first documented discovery of gold in this country and gave impetus to the first gold rush. On both sides of the path you can see boggy terrain where gold was unearthed many years ago. The path continues until you reach a cutaway hillside where a large and strong door guards the entrance to the mine. As you enter the mine, you will be struck first by the chill in the air, no matter what the season, so take along a light jacket or at least a long-sleeved shirt or sweatshirt. The hike moves along as an easy pace, suitable for all ages and for people in or out of good shape. As you walk, you will pause often as the guide explains the more technical aspects of the gold mining processes used at the Reed Gold Mine. Please note that if you are prone to claustrophobia, you may find the mine uncomfortable.

Persons in wheelchairs or on crutches will be able to handle almost the entire tour easily, and young children will be able to keep up the pace. It is only when you come to the steep stairway that there will be problems. At this point those who cannot climb the stairs must return to the entrance of the mine.

You will climb the stairs and emerge at the crest of the Upper Hill, and from there you can hike at your own pace around the hillside, unless you choose to remain with the group for a look at the stamp mill and other points of interest with the informative talk given by the guide. When you leave the tour you can hike back down to the creek by way of the Middle Hill (where the stamp mill is located) and to the lower hill. If you feel that you have not walked enough, you can repeat the hill hike as often as you wish. You will bypass the mine itself on the repeat hikes and stay on the heavily wooded path back to the top of the hill. The youngsters in your party will want to listen to the "talking rocks," where hidden speakers can be activated to present a brief and informative history of the area.

Or you can try your hand at panning for gold. You can buy a panful of soil for $2 and wash or pan the soil at the site adjacent to the creek. You can actually find tiny flecks of gold in some of the pans or scoops. In fact, one of every six buckets of soil contains at least some gold.

Hours of operation at the Reed Gold Mine are as follows: During the months of April through October, Monday through Saturday 9–5, Sunday 1–5. From November 1 through March 31, Tuesday through Saturday, hours are 10–4, Sunday 1–4.

To contact the site before your visit, write to Reed Gold Mine, 9621 Reed Mine Road, Stanfield, NC 28163. You can call (704) 721-GOLD (4657) or fax (704) 721-4657.

3

Alder Trail

Total distance (loop): 1.2 miles

Hiking time: 0.5 hour

Vertical rise: 480 feet

Rating: Easy

Map: USGS 7.5' Troutman

During the Great Depression years and continuing until the early fifties, East Monbo was a thriving mill village that perched on a hilltop just above the dam across the Catawba River and above the mill that supported the village. Along the banks of the river there was the East Monbo baseball park, a Depression-era version of the Field of Dreams ideal that popularized the Iowa-set movie starring Kevin Costner.

The park was among the most naturally scenic baseball fields in the South. The outfield fence was not man-made: in fact, a low mountain circled half the field, starting at the right-field foul line and continuing around the outfield until it stopped abruptly near the Catawba River.

The mill itself was one of the most enchanting versions of pre-World War II nostalgia imaginable. In the early morning hours workers hiked down the steep and spiraling road to the mill, which stood among the fog and mist rising from the river. Huge bass leaped and splashed near the pilings of the mill itself and fed along the honeysuckle-laced banks.

The workers carried with them their lunch buckets and their fishing rods or poles. When they started their machines, they also cast their lines out of the mill windows and then worked while they waited for the first fish to bite. Work rules permitted any employee to stop his machine long enough to take a hooked fish off the line.

At the end of the day the workers trudged back up the hill to their homes. This time they carried their lunch buckets, their fishing gear,

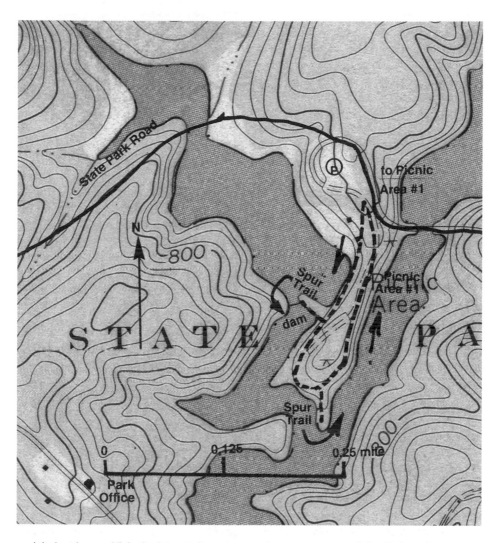

and their stringer of fish, the latter to become their evening meal.

When the East Monbo baseball team played a home game, the workers were permitted to leave their machines and sit outside and watch the game. The only regulation was that someone had to keep an eye on the machines.

One day, according to the story, the boss stormed toward the field where every worker from the mill was engrossed in the local baseball contest. The boss demanded to know why someone wasn't inside keeping an eye on the machinery.

"You didn't tell us we had to be inside," one of the workers said. "We thought all we had to do was keep an eye on the machines."

When the boss insisted on learning how they could keep an eye on the machines without being inside the mill, one of the workers led the boss into the weave room where a one-eyed worker was usually employed. There, glistening in the dim light, a glass eye lay on top of one of the machines.

The East Monbo village, mill, dam, and baseball field are now gone. When Duke Power Company constructed the Cowan's Ford Dam and created the massive impoundment known today as Lake Norman, the entire East Monbo area was flooded. Fishermen may now catch bass where once second base was located, and hikers may enjoy a superior walk along the peninsula of Duke Power State Park and enjoy the shoreline that was once the baseline for the ball field.

Before the arrival of Europeans, the Catawba Indians, once a tribe of more than 5,000, lived in the area. Disease and battle reduced the numbers in the tribe to only 60 men plus some number of women, and eventually the remainder of the tribe settled a few miles south, in South Carolina.

In 1959 Duke Power Company began construction of the Cowan's Ford Dam near the site where Revolutionary soldiers engaged Lord Cornwallis in the Cowan's Ford skirmish. The dam was completed in 1964, and when the water levels reached their peak, Lake Norman had become a reality. It is the largest lake in North Carolina and its shoreline, if stretched into a straight line, would reach from Cowan's Ford Dam to Florida.

Lake Norman itself covers more than 32,000 acres, and as of this writing Duke Power State Park includes 1,458 acres, including 33 acres of the lake inside the park. A dam and spillway maintain the lake at a constant level year-round.

Alder Trail begins at picnic area #1 and creates a loop that provides a superb view of the eastern peninsula and the wildflowers, wildlife, and marine life present in this section of the park.

To get to Duke Power State Park, take I-77 north of Charlotte or south of Statesville. Turn west off I-77 onto NC 150. Drive west for 3 miles and then turn right, or north, on the Perth Church Road in the tiny community of Doolie.

Continue on NC 150 and you will cross over a bridge 0.9 mile from Doolie. In 4.2 more miles you will cross a second bridge, and at 5.9 miles from Doolie you will turn left or west onto Duke Power State Park Road.

At 1.8 miles from the start of Duke Power State Park Road you will enter the park itself. Pass through the gates and cross a bridge 0.4 mile from the gate. Near the top of the hill after you cross the bridge you will see signs (0.1 mile from the bridge) directing you into picnic area #1. Here you will find abundant parking space, as well as picnic tables, rest rooms, and park information. The swimming area can be seen from the picnic area.

At the picnic area, signs indicate the start of Alder Trail, which leads from the picnic ground and along a heavily timbered ridge from which you can see Lake Norman on both sides of the narrow peninsula.

You will hike through a forest of huge oak, poplar, pine, and hickory trees. Smaller tree species such as dogwood and sourwood are also abundant.

This is a great part of the park in which to watch for any of the approximately 130 species of birds that either live in the park or spend part of the year there.

From the picnic area you can leave the trail and follow fishermen's trails close to the water. Perhaps you'll catch sight of some of the larger birds: osprey, great blue heron, snowy egret, little blue heron, green-backed heron, Canada goose, wood duck, green-winged teal, Mandarin duck, mallard, American black duck, canvasback, merganser, black vulture, turkey vulture, and other striking species of fowl.

The main trail leads from the picnic area

down a hardwood-forest hillside to the dam for the swimming area impoundment. You can hike (from mile-point 0.1) out to the spillway and then return to the main trail. The spur trail to the dam is 0.1 mile long.

When you rejoin the main trail, hike south through the hardwood forest for 0.5 mile and reach another 0.1-mile (one way) spur trail to the point where Hicks Creek and Norwood Creek joined before the lake was formed. Backtrack to the main trail.

You can return to the parking lot when you reach the point where the trail veers left and up a thickly wooded hill or continue straight ahead and follow the shoreline of the lake. While this extra jaunt is not part of the Alder Trail, you can follow the trails made by fishermen for 0.1 mile to a bridge over a narrow neck of the lake.

Be careful to watch for copperhead snakes in this part of the park. You will also have a wonderful opportunity to view turtles, huge carp, and bass in the shallow waters. Ospreys feed in this part of the lake. Turtles include snappers, eastern box turtles, and eastern painted turtles. You will find a wide variety of salamanders as well as water snakes.

From the bridge follow the paved road as it curves up the hill and leads to the parking lot at picnic area #1.

Watch for snakes as you hike along the paved road, especially in cooler weather when the reptiles like to bask in the warmth of the pavement. Among the snakes in the park you may see one or more of the following: northern water snake, queen snake, red-bellied water snake, brown snake, eastern garter snake, eastern hognose snake, southern ringneck snake, northern black racer, rough green snake, corn snake, black rat snake, eastern kingsnake, scarlet kingsnake, and perhaps others.

No rattlesnakes have been sighted by park officials during the time that the park has been in existence. However, rattlers have been seen and killed in Iredell County as well as in neighboring counties on the lake.

Another longer loop hike at Duke Power State Park is the Lakeshore Trail found in chapter 4.

4

Lakeshore Trail

Total distance (loop): 6.3 miles

Hiking time: 3.5 hours

Vertical rise: 1,560 feet

Rating: Easy to moderate

Map: USGS 7.5' Troutman

When you arrive at Duke Power State Park, one of the first sights you will notice is the wide expanse of water along the park entrance road. The second thing you will notice is the vast number of fallen trees that can be seen throughout the land area of the park.

These trees were uprooted and broken in 1989, during the night that Hurricane Hugo surprised nearly everyone and turned inland at South Carolina. Rather than continuing up the coast, the hurricane headed toward the Piedmont region of North Carolina and left a path of near-total wreckage in many parts of the Carolinas.

At Duke Power State Park, which includes part of Lake Norman (the largest body of water in North Carolina), approximately 50 percent of the forest was hit by the storm. Of that half that was hit, one of every four trees, it is estimated, was either blown over or damaged severely by the high winds.

As you enjoy the Lakeshore Trail, you will walk very close to the fallen trees. It is wise to remember that fallen trees and underbrush attract birds and rodents which, in turn, attract snakes in many varieties. The number of snakes includes a large population of copperhead snakes which, while normally not life-threatening, can cause severe pain if they bite a human being. Medical care is virtually essential in all bites, particularly if a hyperallergenic reaction results.

Because of the snakes, underbrush, and sometimes uncertain footing, it is best to hike in the middle of the day when the light

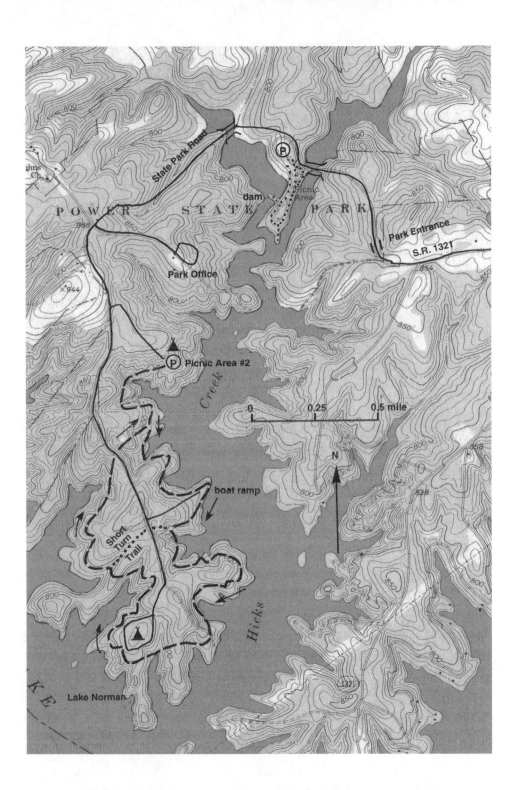

is good. Plan to complete the hike before dusk.

To reach Duke Power State Park, drive I-77 north of Charlotte or south of Statesville. Turn west off I-77 onto NC 150. Drive west for 3 miles and then turn right, or north, on the Perth Church Road in the tiny community of Doolie.

Continue on NC 150 and you will cross over a bridge 0.9 mile from Doolie. In 4.2 more miles you will cross a second bridge, and at 5.9 miles from Doolie you will turn left, or west, onto Duke Power State Park Road.

At 1.8 miles from the start of Duke Power State Park Road you will enter the park itself. When you arrive at the park, drive past two bridges (3.9 miles from the entrance to Duke Power State Park Road) and turn left into the parking lot for picnic area #2. The entrance or head of the trail is on your right, 75 feet after you enter the parking area.

Hike down the clearly marked trail until you reach an information board with maps and park data. The trail is blazed with white diamonds and is to your left as you read the information board.

You will note that the posted information states that the trail is 5.5 miles long. Some printed materials in outdoor recreation books also provide the same distance.

The trail is actually 6.3 miles long, and you should keep the extra distance and necessary hiking time in mind as you prepare to start the hike. There is a shortcut you can take that will reduce the distance to 3.2 miles if you decide that you are running too late or are becoming too tired.

If you plan to take the shortcut, or Short Turn Trail, as it is labeled on park maps, you should take it when you are at mile 2.8. Do not plan to take the Short Turn Trail at a later point, because it will increase rather than reduce your distance.

The Short Turn Trail is blazed in red; other trail markers are blazed in white. These diamond shapes are not painted to trees but are fastened with nails in most instances.

As you begin the trail, you will pass through a hardwood forest that is made up of huge oaks, many of them fallen as a result of the September 22, 1989, hurricane. In addition to the oaks, both red and black, you will see large hickories, pines (both Virginia and loblolly), dogwoods, cedars (usually small and stunted), and an occasional sourwood.

At the beginning of the trail there is a rich patch of creeping cedar that covers the forest floor. Along the hike you will encounter many other such growths.

The dogwoods will be in full bloom in early May. Because of the loss of so many of the larger trees, blooming may be accelerated by as much as two weeks. Small wildflower growth, such as violets, will be best in mid-April to June 1.

At 0.2 mile you will descend into a shallow valley with a small stream at the bottom. The stream can be crossed easily without stepping stones. The trail steepens considerably as you leave the valley, but by 0.3 mile, you will reach the densely forested crest where the trail flattens and you will have very easy hiking for the next two miles.

When you reach mile 0.4 you will be in the heart of the hurricane damage. Fallen trees surround you, and you can take a close-up look at the power of Nature and the fragility of the forest. You will also see that the apparent fragility is yet another way for the natural world to heal itself.

When you are 0.8 mile into the forest, another information board tells you that you can return to the trailhead (a 30-minute walk), hike ahead to the boat-launch area (a 1-hour hike), or continue the Lakeshore Trail west (hiking time 1.5 hours). Both the boat-launch area and the Lakeshore Trail use the same trail to continue from this point.

Be wary of the time schedule. Unless you are in better-than-average shape, you will be pushed to make the hike in 1.5 hours, particularly if you pause to enjoy the wildflowers, trees, grape or muscadine vines, water, and possible wildlife.

Among the animals that have been spotted inside the park are opossums, shrews, silver-haired bats, red bats, black bears, raccoons, minks, striped skunks, red and gray foxes, bobcats, woodchucks, eastern chipmunks, gray squirrels and southern flying squirrels, several types of mice and rats, muskrats, white-tailed deer, and cottontail rabbits.

If you travel toward the boat-launch area on the Lakeshore Trail, you will continue to have a superior hike ahead of you. At times the trail leads to the very edge of the lake, where you can observe wildlife or fishermen or boaters.

You will cross several small bridges early in the hike, the third at 0.9 mile. As you reach the 1.0-mile point, you will be in a forest of huge pines. Hurricane damage is not so noticeable at this point.

At 1.0 mile you will also reach another beautiful growth of creeping cedar. At 1.1 miles you will cross the fourth bridge, which is near a modest growth of ferns and mayapple. This latter plant, which grows profusely in North Carolina, has recently been recognized as the source of a chemical that may prove beneficial in the treatment of certain types of cancer.

One hundred feet ahead of you is a fifth bridge and a ravine where watershed flow has washed out a gaping gully 15 feet deep and equally wide. Here you will begin another fairly steep ascent that is only 205 feet long.

At 1.2 miles you will begin a gentle descent that leads again to the edge of the water. The trail is particularly beautiful and enjoyable at this point. Another tenth of a mile and you will be across the neck of water where the boat-launch area is located. You may wish to rest and watch the boats being launched and hauled out from the water. You will find boaters launching their boats virtually any hour of the day in good weather.

At 1.7 miles you will begin a series of hills and hollows, all easy walking and all relaxing and interesting. More dogwoods grow along this stretch of the trail; you will also see beech, pine, hickory, and holly, with a groundcover of wildflowers in profusion.

You will be at mile 1.9 when you reach the paved road leading to the boat-launch area. You will find rest rooms at the launch ramp.

When you return to the trail (the slight detour to the launch adds 0.2 mile to the trail) you will find another information board a short distance (600 feet) into the forest. Here you can elect to take the Short Turn Trail (which is blazed in red) or stick to the longer Lakeshore Trail. This is your only opportunity to select the shorter version of the trail.

If you stay on the Lakeshore Trail, you will arrive at mile 2.9 and find a point of land clear of underbrush and trees and affording a clear view of the lake. For the next 0.6 mile you will have magnificent views of the water, and at the tip of the peninsula you will enter a thick growth of pines, with a heavy covering of pine needles as a walking surface.

The remainder of the hike is a continuation of the rolling hills and lakeside walking. Several banks have been undercut by the water and you are dangerously close to deep water. You will want to take extra caution at these points.

At the 5.0-mile point you will skirt the edge of the family campground. Tents and trailers may be visible, but you do not hike into the campground. At 6.1 miles you will see an immense beech tree along the trail. This tree is 11 feet in circumference 5 feet from the ground.

Almost immediately you will arrive at the paved road leading to the boat-launch area, but you are a considerable distance from the water at this point. Cross the road and hike the remainder of the trail, returning to the information board at the starting point. The parking lot is 0.1 mile straight ahead.

5

The South Mountains: A Sampler

Total distance: 9.2 miles (4.0-mile loop; 5.2-mile backtrack)

Hiking time: 2–4.5 hours

Vertical rise: 1,694 feet

Rating: Moderate to strenuous

Maps: USGS 7.5' Casar and USGS 7.5' Benn Knob

The South Mountains, which are described as eroded outlines of the Blue Ridge Mountains, cover about 100,000 acres in Burke, Rutherford, and Cleveland counties in western North Carolina. Lowest elevation in the South Mountains area is 1,200 feet along the Jacobs Fork River; the highest point is Benn Knob with an elevation of 2,894 feet.

The South Mountains are located between I-85 and I-40 in the western part of North Carolina. The hiking trails are essentially located between Benn Knob and Old Highway 18. The entire area falls about midway between the cities of Morganton (on I-40) and Shelby (just off I-85), which is only a 15-minute drive from the South Carolina border. To get to the area, leave I-40 at Morganton and take NC 18 south until you see signs directing you to South Mountains State Park. Or leave I-85 at the Gaffney, South Carolina, exit for NC 18. Drive north through Shelby and continue on NC 18 until you reach the sign indicating the park, which is 10 miles from the highway. Signs direct you to Old NC 18, and you will follow the old highway until you reach Ward Gap Road. Turn left (if you are driving north) and head in a westerly direction for 3 miles. You will be on a gravel road for this last leg of the trip.

The state park includes 7,225 acres, all located in southwestern Burke County. The park is open all year, seven days a week, except for Christmas Day. Park hours vary, with opening time set at 8 A.M. but closing times ranging from 6 P.M. in winter to 9 P.M. during the summer season.

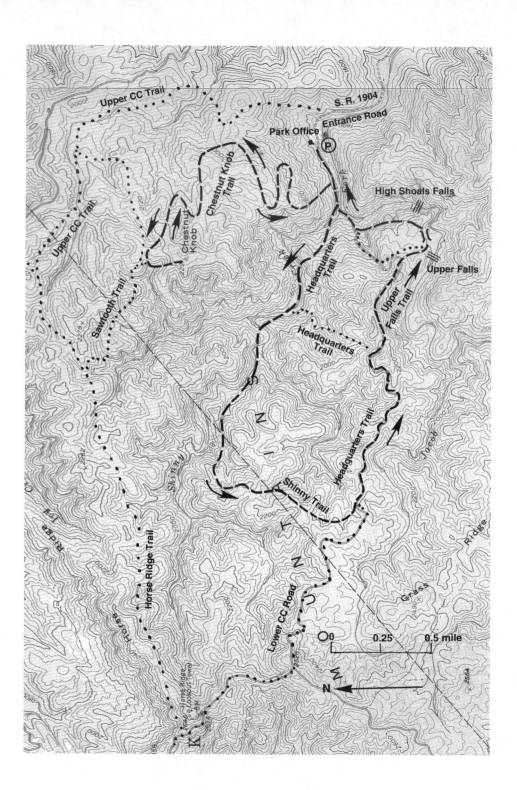

At the South Mountains State Park, a parking area is on the left when you reach the ranger's office. From the parking lot the Headquarters Trail, a hard-surfaced trail, leads into the forest. On the left near the trail entrance are the Jacobs Fork Picnic Area and restrooms.

The Headquarters Trail is extremely easy for the first 0.5-mile leg of the hike. Then it leads sharply upward as the trail leaves the macadam. A footbridge crosses Shinny Creek (pronounced "shiny") and in 0.6 mile you see trail markers directing you to the Upper Falls and the Lower Falls (High Shoals Falls).

A good way to see as much terrain as possible is to continue to hike the Headquarters Trail until it joins the Shinny Trail, which leads back in 2.6 miles to the Headquarters Trail.

The Shinny Trail follows Shinny Creek all the way to the top of the ridge, where in 1.1 miles it turns left, or southward. As you climb the slope to the ridge, the trail at times hugs the creek and at other times will round a knoll and leave the stream for a tenth of a mile or less. The trail rises rapidly, with a series of rock steps or alternating wood-framed steps.

The forest through which you hike is hardwood and pine mixed. Major forms of hardwood are oak, hickory, dogwood, fire cherry, locust, and poplar. White pine, cedar, and yellow pine are abundant.

Rhododendron and laurel mark the banks of streams (and there are several beautiful streams in the park and along the hiking trails).

Copperheads and timber rattlers are seen occasionally, and hikers should exercise caution.

As you hike, listen to the forest around you. During all times of the year you can hear the furtive or careful crackle of dead leaves as the numerous deer that inhabit the park move through the underbrush. If you stop and wait quietly, chances are excellent that you will see a huge buck or several does moving and foraging peacefully on the acorns and other forms of mast that is plentiful in the park.

When you turn left at the top of the rise, you leave the Shinny Trail and continue the hike by rejoining the Headquarters Trail until it intersects with the Upper Falls Trail. You will see trail markers directing you to take the right fork for the Upper Falls Trail.

Hike 0.8 mile from the fork to reach the Upper Falls area. There are pack-in campsites near the Upper Falls. You must pay a fee and register if you plan to spend the night at the top of the falls.

A bridge connecting the Upper Falls and the High Shoals Falls, sometimes referred to as Lower Falls, creates a loop trail for the waterfalls trails.

Cross the bridge and follow the trail to join, in a short distance, the High Shoals Falls Trail. On the left is a wide wooden platform for viewing the High Shoals Falls, which plunge more than 80 feet into a deep pool where you can see trout at almost any time of day.

As you hike down the High Shoals Falls Trail, which rises from the parking area to an elevation of 2,894 feet, you will find the going much easier. Since 1990 there have been footbridges constructed so that hikers no longer have to wade the river or step from rock to rock.

At 0.8 mile from the falls you reach a fork where you must turn right onto the Headquarters Trail to return to your vehicle.

On your way back to the parking area you will pass the Chestnut Knob Trail, a 2.6-mile trip (one way) that is very easy, except for the rapid gain in altitude for the first 0.3-mile stretch of the hike. Quickly the

The Lower, or High Shoals, Falls at South Mountains State Park

Robert L. Williams

trail levels, and you can walk out to undeveloped overlooks from which you can see the skyline of Charlotte 65 miles to the east, and Kings Mountain and Kings Pinnacle, both southeast.

From several points along the Chestnut Knob Trail you can see the Shoals Falls across the valley. Hawks soar overhead almost constantly as you hike, and you can hear their screams piercing the forest quietness. At dusk owls of several varieties add their voices to the chorus.

At the end of the Chestnut Knob Trail the elevation is 2,291 feet. The final 0.2 mile of the trail is rugged and marked by difficult footing at times.

The South Mountains trails are excellent hiking during any part of the year. Rainfall over the centuries has cut away the slopes until some exceed 60 degrees, creating rather strenuous hiking on some sections of trails. But rarely is the weather bad enough (except during rains and summer thunderstorms) to create emergency situations. There are usually no more than three or four snowfalls of any significant accumulations. There may be an equal number of days when light rains and mist freeze on tree limbs, but the trails generally remain easily passable.

The best time to hike these trails is October, with late September and early November providing nearly the same plea-sures. In the fall the insects have largely disappeared and the heat of the summer has passed. You can expect high temperatures in the 70s and lows in the 30s at this time of year.

There is almost no chance of snow or ice until after New Year's Day in this part of the country, and usually a light sweater or sweatshirt will provide adequate warmth in autumn.

Early spring hikes are also excellent. As in autumn, the haze is minimal at this time of year and you will have far more rewarding views of the peaks and valleys of the South Mountains.

One delightful aspect of the South Mountains trails is that they are never crowded. Even on a "busy" day you may encounter no more than three or four people during each hour of hiking. If you hike during the week rather than on weekends you may hike all day and never see another person.

Most of the trails here can become loops that return you to the parking area. The hikes offer splendid scenery as the Jacobs Fork River and Shinny Creek flow over and around huge stones in the riverbed and create countless smaller waterfalls and rapids. If time permits, try to spend one night camping in the park and get in two days of hiking, during which time you can hike several of the trails with ease.

6

Skyline Trail and Cliff Trail

Total distance (loop): 1.5 miles

Hiking time: 1.5 hours

Vertical rise: 1,060 feet

Rating: Moderate

Maps: USGS 7.5' Bat Cave and USGS 7.5' Lake Lure

Reach the trailhead to the Chimney Rock Skyline Trail from US 64/74 by car, via the paved Chimney Rock Park Road. (At this writing the admission fee is $8 for adults and $4 for children.) Three miles up the park road you will reach a paved parking area, a nature center, rest rooms, the tunnel entrance to the elevator that climbs to the top of the chimney itself, and the termination point of the annual Chimney Rock Hill Climb race up the mountain. The elevation here is 1,965 feet.

From the parking area near the base of Chimney Rock, walk down the 198-foot tunnel carved into the solid mass of rock that forms the mountain. On a hot day the 60-degree temperature inside the tunnel is wonderfully refreshing; on a cold day the warmth of the 60-degree temperature is comforting and delightful.

At the end of the tunnel there is an elevator that takes you up a shaft equivalent to a 26-floor building. When you emerge from the elevator, you are in the Sky Lounge and near the Chimney itself. Outside the lounge, follow the paved walk to the steps up to the clear-span bridge that leads to the top of the Chimney. From the Chimney you have a spectacular view of Lake Lure as well as the entire length of Hickory Nut Gorge. On a clear day you can see all the way to Kings Mountain on the North Carolina-South Carolina border—a distance of 75 miles.

At the Sky Lounge, free self-guiding hiking brochures are available; these will help you locate and enjoy some of the best views and most interesting points along the two trails. The park consists of 1,000 acres

The Foothills

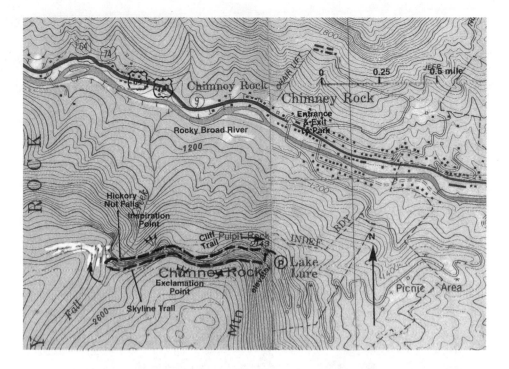

of rugged mountain land and scenic hiking trails in addition to a number of other attractions.

From the Chimney, after you have enjoyed the view fully and crossed the bridge back to the pavement, you will see some flights of stairs built against the granite. To hike the Skyline Trail, climb these steps and follow the clearly marked trail leading to a steep stairway consisting of several flights of steps and landings.

The trail then leads around the mountain through a dense hardwood forest mixed with evergreens. At Exclamation Point (0.3 mile into the hike), the highest point on the trails, you have another spectacular view.

You may be able to see, across US 64/ 74, a series of primitive structures built on the hillside opposite that of the mountain you are on. These dwellings are the buildings of the Huron village that was built as one of the sets for the movie *The Last of the*

Mohicans. The set area is not open to the public, but you can view it from your vantage height on Exclamation Point.

At 0.7 mile you will come to the end of Skyline Trail. Cross Falls Creek on the footbridge to continue the hike by joining the Cliff Trail, or turn back to the Chimney.

If you proceed down the Cliff Trail, you will pass several points where you have a breathtaking view of Hickory Nut Falls as the Falls Creek plunges more than 400 feet to the rocks below. As you wind your way down the trail you will reach (at mile 0.1) Nature's Shower Bath, where water finding its way through the tiny fissures in the rocks sprays a faint mist (sometimes more than a mist!) across the trail.

At Inspiration Point (0.2 mile) you have the first of the exceptional views of Hickory Nut Falls. Other special points along the trail include Groundhog Slide and Wildcat Trap, unique rock formations.

Hickory Nut Falls as seen from Cliff Trail

At 0.5 mile you will reach a spiral staircase built into the rock or, if you take the alternate route (the two routes merge within a few feet) you will pass (or squeeze) through several narrow fissures and reach the Grotto, a natural cave carved into the rock face.

A series of trail spurs lead to the stairway back to the Chimney, to a moonshiner's cave, complete with a real moonshine still, picnic tables, and other attractions created to supplement the work of Nature.

As you hike, you may have the opportunity to observe a black vulture, turkey vulture, osprey, sharp-shinned hawk, broad-winged hawk, red-tailed hawk, or a rare peregrine falcon. Since 1990 a pair of peregrine falcons have been nesting in the park and have produced their offspring there.

Common birds in the park include the ruby-throated hummingbird, red-bellied woodpecker, yellow-bellied sapsucker, downy woodpecker, eastern wood peewee, eastern phoebe, Carolina chickadee, tufted titmouse, Carolina wren, blue-gray gnatcatcher, wood thrush, robin, solitary vireo, yellow-throated vireo, red-eyed vireo, Cape May warbler, scarlet tanager, rose-breasted grosbeak, rufous-sided towhee, and a variety of finches.

Four-footed animal life in the park includes deer, foxes, raccoons, groundhogs, chipmunks, and squirrels.

Some of the notable vegetation in the park includes the wineberry, tulip tree, red oak, cucumber tree, wild hydrangea, giant chickweed, toothwort, rock cress, little sweet Betsy, purple Phacelia, bloodroot, Jack-in-the-pulpit, Solomon's seal, mayapple, false goatsbeard, broad-leaved tickseed, and numerous other wildflowers.

Along the trail you can enjoy information markers that explain the significance or characteristics of some of the plants or rock formations seen in other parts of the trail complex. At one point, for instance, you will see the stump remains of an American chestnut tree, a tragic reminder of the blight that virtually wiped out one of the most valuable trees in the American forests. In addition to the information on the marker, you may be interested and heartened to know that not far from the gorge there is an authentic American chestnut tree that has miraculously survived for about 40 years. Even more heartening is the fact that the tree had been hit by the blight and had somehow "cured" itself and managed to regain its health. The tree is being used to pollinate another American chestnut tree found nearby, with the hope that the nuts produced by the trees will in turn produce a blight-resistant tree that is authentically American.

Along the higher elevations of the upper trails, you can look down on a superb example of what geologists call a "hanging valley," a tributary valley that drops off sharply into the main valley. The hanging valley that produced Hickory Nut Falls was cut by Falls Creek, which worked much more slowly than did the Rocky Broad River in the larger valley below. Because of slower erosion, the hanging valley is more shallow than the gorge itself, and when the river below cut down the valley sharply, the awesome cliffs on the hanging valley side were left, creating the waterfall.

If you time your visit to the Chimney Rock Park carefully, you can be on hand for some of the special demonstrations and events that are sponsored by the park. Sunrise Easter services are held in the park annually. Other events, such as the Chimney Rock Photo Contest, rock-climbing demonstrations, bird-watching tours, wildflower study and identification, rhododendron walks, slide presentations, the Chimney Rock Hill climb (pitting sports cars against each other), a vintage car rally, cave study programs, and similar events are held on a regular basis.

Across from Chimney Rock is a mountain called Round Top Mountain where, according to local legend, several Englishmen who had struck it rich in the gold-producing hills of Rutherford County were preparing to haul their gold away—their future secure—when Indians attacked and killed all but one of the party.

Before the Indians could complete the massacre, so the story goes, the men had managed to cache their gold inside one of the natural caves on the mountain. The man who survived the attack made his way back to civilization. He lost his sight before he died, but he drew a map, from memory, of the area and pinpointed the gold location.

During the Civil War a Confederate general, Collett Leventhorpe, dispatched 50 men in a fruitless search of the mountain for the elusive gold which, according to the folktale, remains there to this day.

When the hike is completed, you emerge from the trail at the parking lot.

7

Broad River Greenway Trail

Total distance: 5.0 miles

Hiking time: 2 hours

Vertical rise: 440 feet

Rating: Easy

Map USGS 7.5' Boiling Springs South

At this writing, this hike is one of the newest, in North Carolina, and it is one of the most delightful anywhere in the state. On this trail it is impossible to get lost, because the trail follows the Broad River for several miles; in fact, you are seldom, if ever, out of sight of the river. The Broad River Greenway is a superb walk along the Broad River. The Greenway is a recreational area that features nature study and informative programs about the wildlife in the area, the history of Cleveland County, bluegrass music, and folklore and crafts. When there are no programs in session, you can enjoy a splendid hike through the forest along the banks of the river.

Another wonderful attribute of this trail is that it is impeccably clean, neat, well-ordered, and focused entirely on the river and the forest. In winter the weather is warm enough during the coldest days in December and January that you can hike this trail in relative comfort. In the spring and autumn the walking conditions are near-perfect. It is only in summer that you'll encounter heat, insects, and occasionally reptiles. You may see harmless black snakes, perhaps a king snake, a garter snake, or a rare copperhead. You will see water snakes of several varieties, but do not jump to the conclusion, as many people do, that any snake that lives in water is a water moccasin. Most water snakes in this part of the country are harmless, and they slip into the water as soon as they are disturbed. The cottonmouth water moccasin is indeed a poisonous snake that can inflict serious harm to pets and humans. The safest bet is to stay on the trails (and this is

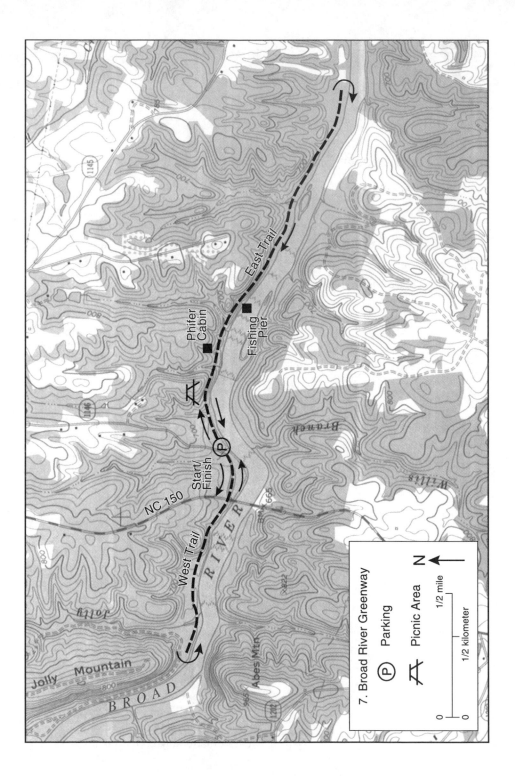

7. Broad River Greenway

Ⓟ Parking

⚷ Picnic Area

N

0 ———— 1/2 mile
0 ———— 1/2 kilometer

good advice for all hikes) and not molest or try to pet any animals you encounter. Incidentally, human encounters with larger animals are rare.

Do not misunderstand: this is not to say that the hike is not a good one during the dog days of August. But you may enjoy it even more at other times of year, and for several reasons.

In May the laurel and rhododendron are at their richest colors, and other early wildflowers bloom between late February and late May. The fall wildflowers stay in bloom until the first killing frost, which can occur as late as the end of October. In all seasons, however, there is something interesting to be enjoyed along the trails.

To get to the Broad River Greenway, follow NC 150 from Boiling Springs (west of Shelby), about three miles south of town. You will see the bridge over the Broad River before you see the sign directing you to the Greenway, which is to the left of the highway. You will see a parking area almost as soon as you enter the Greenway, and as a rule there is never a scarcity of parking spaces.

When you park and visit the information boards, you will see maps of several trails, but two hikes stand out as the most interesting and satisfying. The east trail continues along the north side of the river and heads eastward. The west trail goes under the bridge and continues westward to Jolly Mountain. You are still on the north side of the Broad River.

After you hike 100 yards east, you will pass neat and attractive shelters and a walkway, and you will reach an information board that shows you where the trails lead. Note that no distances are given. The west trail is roughly 2 miles long, one way, with the second mile beginning once the formal trail ends at the one-mile mark. The east trail is slightly more than 3 miles long.

You will quickly find that this is a wonderful trail for the entire family. Children who are able to walk 2 or 3 miles can handle this trail without difficulty, and there is far more than simply walking. Not far into the hike you will find picnic tables, but if you're not ready to stop yet, you can wait. There are many other tables further down the trail.

At about 0.2 mile you will reach a neat and striking footbridge (and other bridges are located down the trail). At 0.3 mile you reach the Phifer Cabin, a log structure built about 1850. Stop to enjoy the cabin and examine its structure. Notice the V-notch technique incorporated into the corners. Most old cabins use the dovetail notch or the butt-and-pass technique. The V-joint technique was brought to this country by northern European immigrants who came to this part of the United States two centuries ago. The cabin itself was built nearby and was moved to its present site in 1998.

At just under half a mile you reach the fishing pier, which is equipped with safety rails and benches on the pier itself and other benches within a few feet of the pier. From here both children and adults (with proper licenses) may fish for bream, bluegill, bass, perch, catfish, and the occasional crappie. There are facilities nearby where you can cook your catch if you wish. At the pier you have a great view of the river, which is surprisingly large. The river surface is broken irregularly by rocks that jut upward, and in warm weather you may see huge turtles sunning themselves on virtually every one of these rocks. You may see as many as a dozen large turtles on each of the broader rocks.

As you pass the pier, you are on a combination horse and bike trail as well as a hiking trail. There is not a great deal of evidence of horseback riders on the trails, and bikes are few.

A log cabin near the trailhead

In another 250 yards you'll reach a wide opening in the trees where you can enjoy a great view of the river. Often there are wild ducks, Canada geese, or other waterfowl enjoying the river. Soon you'll cross a small and very clear stream via stepping stones. The woods from the beginning of the hike are dense and rich, and you hike among huge trees that completely obliterate the sun, including tulip poplar, hickory, oak, and maple. In fact, you will not see the sun for more than a few steps at a time during the entire hike.

You will begin to see growths of laurel and rhododendron at around ¾ mile. After you cross a footbridge the laurel growth becomes denser, and in May the blossoms are overwhelmingly beautiful.

One of the most interesting points of the hike comes at 1.5 miles, where you will find a "beach" of coarse sand and a small pool of water separated from the river by a dozen feet of soil. This beach is roughly the size of a room in a house, and the pool is the size of a Volkswagen Beetle. But if you wait patiently for a few minutes, you will see aquatic life in many forms begin to stir in the water or in the growth alongside the pool. You can see tadpoles, frogs, small fish, salamanders, tiny water snakes (and perhaps some larger ones), and other animals.

You can turn back at this point, because in many ways you have already seen the most interesting parts of the hike, or you can continue. The trail is very sandy and your progress will be somewhat impeded. The trail narrows, too, at this juncture. If you turn back, you will have hiked a little more than 16,000 feet, or slightly more than 3 miles, by the time you are back at the parking lot.

II

"The Mountains Away from the Mountains"

Jim Hargan

8

Pilot Mountain State Park: Corridor Trail

Total distance (one way): 6.1 miles; optional 1-mile side trip

Hiking time: 4.5 hours

Vertical rise: 885 feet

Rating: Moderate to strenuous

Maps: USGS 7.5' Pinnacle and USGS 7.5' Siloam

The Corridor Trail, as its name suggests, traverses a narrow corridor of land that connects the two distinct properties that make up Pilot Mountain State Park. The northern portion of the park includes the mountain peak itself and surrounding terrain. The southern portion is separated from the larger part of the park by private lands, and the trail starts in the upper portion and crosses these lands to reach the second part of the park, the land alongside the Yadkin River.

To hike this trail you will most likely want to have a second vehicle to serve as shuttle transportation, unless you are willing to face a very long backtrack hike. Park your second vehicle in the state park parking area at the end of the Bean Shoals Canal Trail (see below) and then drive to where the Corridor Trail begins at the junction of State Road 2061 (Pinnacle Hotel Road) and State Road 2063. This is also where the Mountain Trail and the Grassy Ridge Trail emerge from the south slope of Pilot Mountain.

To reach this junction from I-40, take the I-77 exit and follow it to Exit 85, also known as the CCC Camp Road, until it intersects with NC 268. Follow NC 268 for 25 miles until it intersects with US 52 in the town of Pilot Mountain.

At the junction of the two highways, take US 52 south until you turn right onto State Road 2063.

Note that the Corridor Trail is blazed with yellow dots on trees. You can park at the unpaved area where the two roads junction. The trail leads south through a small growth of pine trees.

Almost immediately you will cross a pair

of footbridges and through a field studded with wildflowers. These flowers (listed in more detail later in this trail description) are in bloom at almost any time from early April through the first killing frost, usually in late October.

Whenever you enter a clearing, you may wish to turn and look back at the pinnacle of Pilot Mountain, also known as "Jomeokee" (see chapter 9 for more on the history of Pilot Mountain's name), which is clearly visible for 50 miles and which can be seen on a clear day from as much as 100 miles away.

A series of streams, all but one of them small and easily fordable via stepping stones, cross the trail. Within 1.7 miles you will cross State Road 2064 (Mount Zion Road), and you will reach State Road 2048 (Shoals Road) 3.3 miles into the hike. Between the two roads the trail will cross farmland, fields, and stands of immature timber and wild hardwood forests.

At mile 5.2 you will leave the forest stands and cross Stoney Ridge Church Road (State Road 2072), entering mature stands of pine and hardwoods.

As you cross State Road 2072 you will enter uncut forest where the terrain is generally smooth and the hiking is easy. About 300 feet into the forest the trail veers sharply to the east and continues for 0.4 mile before turning south again. You will cross several streams and near the end of the trail you will reach an old and rarely used Southern Railroad spur. This railroad line is still considered active, although train traffic may occur no more than once or twice each month.

As you cross the tracks you will descend from the forest down a steep embankment and emerge from high weeds and wildflower growth onto the railroad cut. Immediately after you reenter the woods you will hear the sounds of the Yadkin River. As you reach the river you will see two islands, which do not look like islands at all but seem to be part of the river's bank because they are so large for a river the size of the Yadkin.

One of the islands is 15 acres and the other is 45 acres. The trail actually crosses the river, but the fording is usually done by horseback riders. The islands can also be used for canoe camping. In wet months, usually late winter and early spring, the river is prone to flooding, and hikers should exercise great care when hiking along the riverbank.

In dry conditions the trail often approaches within one or two feet of the water, and in flood conditions parts of the trail may be under water.

At the river itself you can hike alongside and enjoy the vast array of wildflowers. Among the flowers found in Pilot Mountain State Park are the butterfly weed, fairy wand, dwarf iris, bird-foot violet, wild geranium, trailing arbutus, white turtlehead, round-leaf hepatica, bee balm or wild bergamot, yellow-flag iris, goat's rue, wild columbine, turkey beard, foamflower, black cohosh, starry campion, closed gentian, orange-fringed orchid, goat's beard, false Solomon's seal, ox-eye daisy, fire pink, Queen Anne's lace, pink lady's slipper, sand myrtle, bristly locust, hearts-a-bustin', and many others.

When you reach the river, the trail leads down the banks in both directions. Turn to the left, so that the river is on your right and you are traveling in the same direction as the current. Within 0.5 mile you will reach Bean Shoals Canal Trail, which is often considered a part of the Yadkin River Trail. (The Yadkin River Trail, not part of this hike, continues eastward along the river before looping north to the service road and parking area.)

The Bean Shoals Canal Trail leads past the remains of an effort decades ago to dig a canal in order to rechannel the river for improved shipping. Bankruptcy closed the effort before any real progress was made.

As you follow this trail, you will curve north

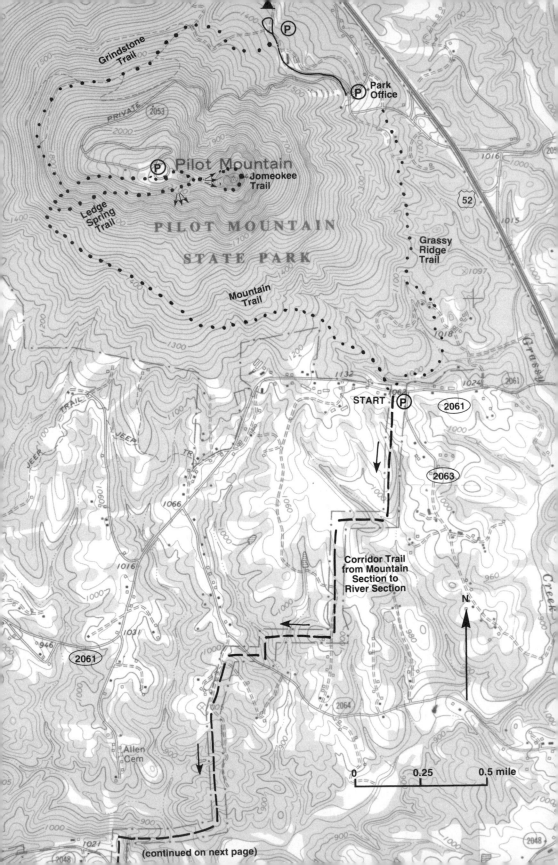

Grindstone Trail

PRIVATE

2053

Pilot Mountain

Jomeokee Trail

Ledge Spring Trail

PILOT MOUNTAIN

STATE PARK

Mountain Trail

Grassy Ridge Trail

Grassy Creek

Park Office

52

US 52

START

2061

2063

2061

2064

Corridor Trail from Mountain Section to River Section

JEEP TRAIL

JEEP TRAIL

Allen Cem

N

0   0.25   0.5 mile

(continued on next page)

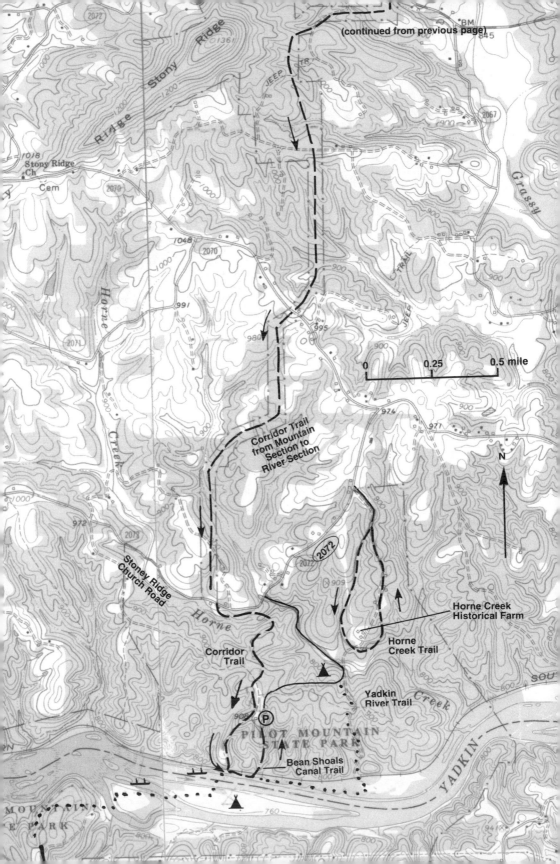

(continued from previous page)

Corridor Trail
from Mountain
Section to
River Section

0   0.25   0.5 mile

N

Stoney Ridge
Church Road

Horne Creek
Historical Farm

Corridor
Trail

Horne
Creek Trail

Yadkin
River Trail

PILOT MOUNTAIN
STATE PARK

Bean Shoals
Canal Trail

Stony Ridge
Ch

Cem

YADKIN

MOUNTAIN

E PARK

On the Yadkin River Trail

ward and hike near the camping area just off the state park road at the round-out or turnaround. This is the place to leave the second vehicle before you start the hike.

If you wish, you can now drive a very short distance to the Horne Creek Historical Farm, which is located just off State Road 2072.

Drive out of the park and turn right onto State Road 2072, and within a half-mile you will see signs directing you to Horne Creek Historical Farm. The farm is closed on Mondays and major holidays. There is no admission charge.

Follow the driveway into the farm and park in the small parking lot. The Horne Creek Trail, an easy 1-mile loop, starts here.

The farm is a state-operated living-history farm; the farmhouse itself is currently under renovation. When completed, the farm will be a tribute to the rural heritage of late 19th-century and early 20th-century North Carolina.

The farmhouse was built in 1847 and was added to in 1887. The Hauser farm (pronounced Hoozer), as it was known at that time, consisted of 100 acres. Adjacent to the Hauser farm is the Solomon Sawyers farm; Sawyers, a free African American, bought the property in 1842. The site will be used to interpret the story of African American farm families who lived in the area at the turn of the century.

The Horne Creek Trail takes you to the old Hauser house, and then to the barn, corncrib, orchard, tobacco patch, fruit house, well house, smokehouse, and other parts of the typical farm.

When the hike is completed, you are ready to drive to the beginning of the Corridor Trail and pick up the first vehicle.

9

Pilot Mountain

Total distance (one way): 6.9 miles

Hiking time: 6.5 hours

Vertical rise: 1,200 feet

Rating: Moderate to strenuous

Maps: USGS 7.5' Pinnacle and USGS 7.5' Siloam

Pilot Mountain State Park, which includes one of the most impressive landmarks in the South, has some of the finest trails in the mountains of North Carolina and, indeed, some of the very finest to be found anywhere. The four trails described here can be hiked in a modified loop form that will permit hikers to add or subtract distance from the total hike as desired and conditions warrant.

Pilot Mountain is one of the three major peaks—along with Sauratown Mountain and Hanging Rock—located in what is known as the Sauratown Mountains. Pilot Mountain and Hanging Rock are included in the state park system of North Carolina.

The three peaks, all of which have fine hiking trails, are virtually aligned in an east-to-west manner. Pilot Mountain stands at the westernmost position, Sauratown Mountain is in the center, and Hanging Rock is on the far eastern limits of the so-called "mountains away from the mountains." The expression is used because the three peaks are almost totally separated from the Blue Ridge chain about 30 miles to the north and west.

Pilot Mountain is located in the northwest Piedmont of North Carolina. Piedmont literally means "foot of the mountain," and this region extends for 1,000 miles from the Hudson River in New York to central Alabama. In North Carolina the Piedmont is bounded on the east by the coastal plain area and on the west by the Blue Ridge Mountains.

Originally the area known as the Sauratown Mountains was part of the huge Iapetus

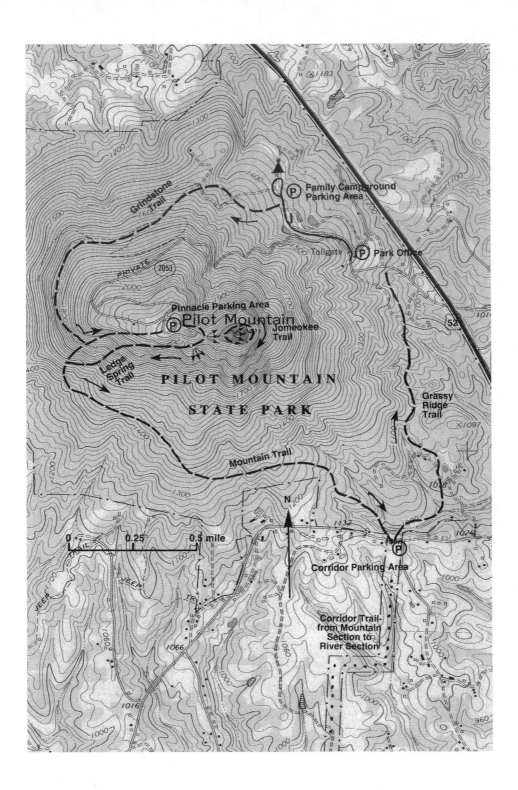

Sea, which at one point in history covered all of the Piedmont. A billion years ago silt, sand, and clay washed into the sea and thick layers of sediment accumulated. As intense heat and pressure acted upon the sediment, a metamorphic rock known as quartzite was formed.

Continued pressure forced the rocks upward. The harder stone remained as layers of sediment were washed away and the softer materials eroded, leaving the mountain peaks jutting about 2,500 feet above sea level and 1,550 feet above the valley area surrounding the three peaks.

The most striking of the three peaks was called "Jomeokee," which means "Great Guide" or "Pilot," by the Saura Indians. At their peak population, the Saura Indians probably numbered around 2,000, and they hunted, fished, and created their forms of civilization around the three peaks that form the Sauratown mountains.

The more aggressive Cherokee Indians gradually pushed the Saura out of the area and settled the territory themselves. But both tribes of Indians used the huge monolith called Jomeokee as their basic guide and landmark. So did the white settlers and traders who moved into the territory in the 1700s.

Among the newcomers to the area in pre-Revolutionary times were the Moravians. In 1751 Pilot Mountain was mapped by Joshua Fry and Peter Jefferson, whose more famous son Thomas wrote the Declaration of Independence and served as president of the United States.

In 1968 Pilot Mountain became the 14th state park in North Carolina. In 1970 the state acquired an additional 1,000 acres of land along the Yadkin River, and small tracts were added later to bring the total acreage of Pilot Mountain State Park to 3,703. To get to Pilot Mountain State Park

from I-40, take the I-77 exit and follow it to Exit 85, also known as the CCC Camp Road. Follow the CCC Camp Road until it intersects with NC 268.

Follow NC 268 for 25 miles until it intersects with US 52 in the town of Pilot Mountain.

At the junction of the two highways, take US 52 south for about 2.9 miles until you see the signs directing traffic to Pilot Mountain State Park. Follow the signs; you will reach the park office within 2 miles. A shuttle arrangement of vehicles is best for those who want to hike as much of the park as possible without backtracking. If you wish to take the extended hike described here (6.9 miles), leave one vehicle at the parking area of this park office. Then drive to the family campground to start the hike.

You will see adjacent to Campsite 16 a broad grassy lane leading up the mountain toward an area overgrown with underbrush. The grassy lane is the trailhead for the Grindstone Trail. Signs are prominently visible. Follow the grassy lane up the mountain for 200 feet and note that the trail cuts into the thick hardwood forest just before you reach the underbrush.

The trail heads south at the outset and then at 500 feet begins a gentle swing first west, then north for 600 feet before circling west and again south and starting a steep ascent up a very rocky trail. You will hike among oaks, dogwoods, huge poplars, hickories, and other hardwoods until you climb into a forest of hemlocks and other evergreens.

After 0.7 mile the trail is almost constant rocks. There are low rock cliffs along the trail, and as you continue to climb the cliffs grow higher and higher. Soon you will be walking near very high cliffs; so, be very careful at all times.

From the initial series of curves at the

outset of the trail, the trail proceeds for 1.4 miles in an almost straight but constantly elevating hike. At 1.5 miles from the camping area you cross a footbridge over a small stream. In this area you will find thick growths of laurel and rhododendron.

At 1.6 miles your trail merges with the Ledge Spring Trail, and your path leads through the picnic area and into the pinnacle parking lot.

Cross the paved parking area to a wide paved walk that leads to three overlooks. The first overlook provides a superb view of the Yadkin River valley and, to the left, to the sheer cliffs that you will pass later on the Ledge Spring Trail.

The second overlook provides a glimpse of Jomeokee and more of the cliffs and valley. The third overlook leads to the greatest view of—and the greatest opportunity to photograph—the 200-foot pinnacle known as Jomeokee.

In late September and early October (the best times to hike the trails) you will see, from the overlook, huge numbers of broad-winged hawks in the migratory flight patterns that will take them to the Gulf of Mexico and into South America where they will winter.

The hawks pass in clusters, called "kettles" because of the manner in which the air currents seem to "percolate" the hawks up and down as they ride the currents. In the early afternoons you may be able to see as many as 40 to 60 hawks in a single "kettle."

At other times, when the hawks are not migrating, you can see black vultures, turkey vultures, and ravens that nest on the craggy pinnacle.

Leave the overlook and turn right, or northeast, and follow the paved walk until you reach the Jomeokee Trail. This 0.8-mile loop trail will lead down an extremely rocky

trail to the base and around the pinnacle. At times, as you circle Jomeokee pinnacle, you will be 50 feet from the rock. At other times you are within touching distance. At all times you have an excellent view of the rock formation, complete with water-erosion marks that cause sections of the pinnacle to resemble the rocky coast of Maine.

These erosion marks were created when the sea was receding and the Dan and Yadkin rivers were carving out the valley.

After circling the pinnacle on the Jomeokee Trail, take the Ledge Spring Trail below the picnic area and 0.2 mile from the pinnacle.

Follow the Ledge Spring Trail, which opens to magnificent vistas of the Yadkin River valley, as it first descends and then begins to climb sharply. After 0.9 mile, you join the Mountain Trail, which leads south to the Corridor Trail and to the Pinnacle Hotel Road (State Road 2061).

At the Mountain Trail, you will be leaving the Ledge Spring Trail with 0.5 mile of it unhiked. The part you miss consists largely of a very strenuous climb as the trail loops back to the pinnacle parking area.

The Mountain Trail will descend sharply as it follows the contour of the mountain. There will be huge boulders on each side of you as you hike, and often you will walk for considerable distances on solid rock.

Along the trail are pines, rare cedars, occasional hardwoods, and hemlocks. Ravens and crows thickly populate the forest area. The trail begins by heading south from the Ledge Spring Trail and then at 0.3 mile swinging east. In 0.4 mile it veers north briefly as it circles around an outcropping and then heads southeast.

As the trail descends it moderates in its level of difficulty, and by the time it drops to 1,300 feet above sea level the trail is easily hiked. At 1.1 miles the trail again swings

Jomeokee Trail, Pilot Mountain

northeast and for 0.3 mile it becomes rougher and more difficult. It climbs about 300 feet within a short distance, and then it curves downward to junction with the Corridor Trail which connects with the Grassy Ridge Trail.

When you leave the forest area, you emerge onto State Road 2061, near the Corridor Trail parking area. Take the Grassy Ridge Trail and follow it along the state road (at times so closely that you can see clearly a residence across the highway).

Follow the trail along a thick forest area and emerge at 0.2 mile into a field with weeds and grass nearly three feet high. Then join an old maintenance road that winds downward to a small stream. From this point upward the trail meanders through a hardwood forest and climbs steadily until you reach the park office where you left the shuttle vehicle for an extended hike.

10

Hanging Rock State Park

Total distance: 3.6–9.5 miles

Hiking time: 1.5–4.5 hours

Vertical rise: 925 feet

Rating: Easy to strenuous

Map: USGS 7.5' Hanging Rock

Hanging Rock State Park is located in Stokes County, four miles northwest of Danbury in the far northern part of North Carolina's Piedmont plateau. More than 300 species of mountain flora can be found along the park's trails and around its 12-acre lake, which serves for both swimming and fishing in addition to boating. The park also has family and group camping facilities.

To reach the park, which has 18 miles of hiking trails, leave I-77 at Exit 85 (CCC Camp Road) and follow the road east until it intersects with NC 262. Follow NC 262 through the town of Pilot Mountain until it junctions with NC 66, 25 miles east of Pilot Mountain.

Follow NC 66 until it junctions with Moore's Springs Road (State Road 1001) and follow signs to the entrance to Hanging Rock State Park. You can also reach the park by following NC 8/89 northwest of Danbury and then taking Hanging Rock Road (State Road 1001 also–this road and Moore's Springs Road are the two extremes of the same road) to the park entrance.

Once inside the park follow signs until you reach the lower or park river access parking area. Here there are rest rooms and picnic tables as well as the beginning of the first suggested hike: the trail to the top of Hanging Rock.

Signs at the trailhead state that the hike is one mile; however, park brochures list the hike at 1.2 miles, one way. The trail starts at the south side of the picnic parking area, and you will follow a wide, paved road for 300 feet. Once you cross a pair of small streams, both with vehicle bridges over them, the pavement ends and you begin a long, wind-

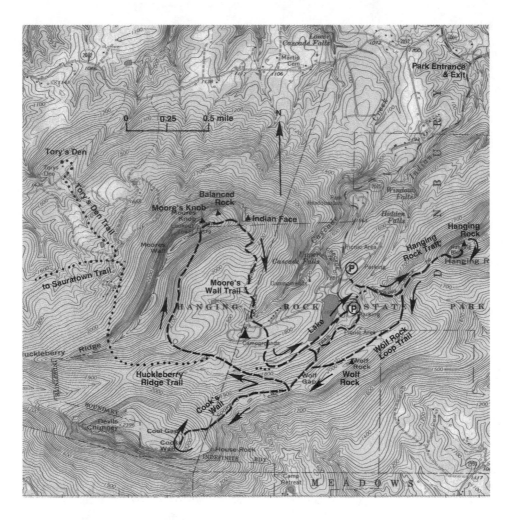

ing road up to the base of the peak for which the park is named.

The footing is good on this road, and there are benches every 300 feet for those who need a breather. While easy to walk, this road is a relentless uphill hike that never varies from its steep ascent until you reach the base of the peak itself. The final several hundred feet of the hike are so steep that it is sometimes necessary to pull yourself up by using small trees for leverage.

The hike begins in a heavily forested area made up of huge poplars, oaks, hickories, pines, and isolated locust trees. You will also see an occasional fire cherry, dogwood, and serviceberry tree.

The forest changes as you hike to the base of the peak. In warmer weather you may encounter yellow jackets and an occasional snake (several varieties inhabit the area, including copperhead and rattler, but these are rare). The bird population includes blue jays, mockingbirds, wrens, slate-colored juncos, hawks, vultures, a few ravens, crows in large numbers, screech owls, barred owls, and whippoorwills, among others.

"The Mountains Away from the Mountains"

Larger animals in the area include white-tailed deer, raccoon, gray fox, opossums, and a rare bobcat. Bats are numerous at dusk and shortly afterward.

Wildflowers include laurel, rhododendron, azalea, galax, pink lady's slipper, turkey-beard, bird-foot violet, fire pink, and ox-eye daisy.

When you reach the end of the climb, at mile 1.1, the trail suddenly levels and leads to the base of the mountain, which, like the other peaks in the area, is a series of monadnocks, or erosion-resistant stone outcroppings.

Geologically, the mountain formation is known as the Sauratown Mountains anticlinorium. An anticlinorium is an area in which the rocks arch upward into dramatic shapes and formations. The monadnocks in the Hanging Rock area jut sharply upward to 1,550 feet above the valleys below.

At the base of the peak, the trail is often very difficult to follow. Many rocks are barely clinging to the steep hillside and they must be crossed carefully.

The final 200 feet of the trail will wind to the east and then abruptly northward as you emerge onto a huge rock outcrop. Here again caution is necessary, because there are no protective rails or other safety devices, and a fall could prove fatal.

By staying well back from the ledges, you can walk around the top of the mountain and enjoy magnificent views of the Dan River and Yadkin River valleys. When you are ready to backtrack down the trail, you will see the trail markers denoting the Wolf Rock Loop Trail (1.9 miles). You passed the marker on the way up the mountain, and as you approach it on the way down, you can take the trail and enjoy a hike to Wolf Rock. It is 0.9 mile from the top of Hanging Rock to the start of Wolf Rock Trail.

As you leave the Hanging Rock Trail, you will pass down a slight incline and through a dense forest of hardwood trees. At the base of Hanging Rock you were in a small forest of Carolina hemlock and Canadian hemlock growing side by side. This is one of the few places where such growth occurs.

As you leave the hemlock area, you will see fewer and fewer of the evergreen trees while you also begin to see more hardwoods that grow to enormous heights and to very impressive thicknesses. Along the woodland trail will be many lizards that scurry over and around the fallen logs and rocks lining the trail.

After about 0.4 mile on the Wolf Rock Trail, the terrain changes dramatically as more and more immense rocks are in evidence. You will see an abundance of rock cliffs where, in good weather, there are often rock climbers scaling the heights.

The rock cliffs are favorite nesting places for ravens and two species of vultures. At 0.5 mile from where you started Wolf Rock Trail, you reach the huge rock for which the trail was named. At this point you have another of the marvelous panoramic views of the valley to the south of the Hanging Rock area.

Continuing along the Wolf Rock Trail, after about 0.5 mile you will circle around the slope of the mountain and reach the junction of the Cook's Wall Trail. You may continue to hike toward Cook's Wall, which offers more magnificent views, or you can turn right and hike up the other side of the Wolf Rock Loop trail to the lower, or second, parking lot near the swimming area, cabins, and campgrounds. From here it is less than 0.5 mile to where you parked your car in the first, or upper, parking area.

The 1.1-mile (one way) hike to Cook's Wall offers superb scenery, majestic peaks and cliffs of rocks that have resisted centuries of erosion and show the scarring effects of weather and man's invasion of the terrain.

You can lengthen your hike even further

Hanging Rock views from Moores Spring Road

by exploring Moore's Wall Loop Trail when you return from the backtrack trail to Cook's Wall. At mile 2.0 you will see a side trail on the left that connects with the Huckleberry Ridge Trail and Tory's Den Trail. Follow the connecting trail approximately 0.9 mile until you see another side trail clearly marked Moore's Wall Loop Trail. This 4.2-mile loop will lead you over some of the highest terrain in the park and in a complete circle around the swimming and boating area.

Major points of interest are Moore's Wall Trail itself, which has stretches of strenuous hiking, Moore's Knob, at about 2.6 miles, Balanced Rock at about 3.1 miles, and Indian Face, at about 3.2 miles.

The ascent is often steep on the Moore's Wall Trail, and in warmer months the heat can add to the challenge. You are urged to take a supply of fresh drinking water (available at several points in the park) and any quick-energy snacks you might need on a hike of this length.

When you reach the top of the rocky trail and start the descent, you will find the shade of the trees to be most welcome if the weather is hot. Be alert for snakes in the isolated parts of the park. You will find that the trails described here, with the exception of the Hanging Rock Trail, are never crowded. It is very probable that you can hike on any weekday, even in the best of weather, and never see more than two or three hikers, at the most.

After descending around three very wide switchbacks, you will arrive at mile 3.7 into the area of the park lake. The trail leads through the hardwood forest surrounding the lake and emerges from the deeper woods along the south shore of the lake where it will then curve into the woods and ascend moderately to join, at mile 4.2, the lower, or second, parking area.

Hike across the lake parking area and then around the paved road to reach the first, or upper, parking area.

11

Hanging Rock State Park: Indian Creek Trail

Total distance (backtrack): 7.4 miles

Hiking time: 4 hours

Vertical rise: 4,040 feet

Rating: Moderate to strenuous

Map: USGS 7.5' Hanging Rock

Some Hanging Rock State Park trails are described in the previous chapter, but other trails also have a great deal to offer the hiker. You might wish to drive to the park, select a campsite, and devote a major part of the first day to hiking. Then, after overnighting in the park, hike the remaining trails, or a portion of them, the following day or days. You may wish to combine three or four short trails or use them separately as warm-ups before starting a longer trail. The trails here are interesting, well-maintained, and varied enough to accommodate nearly any level of difficulty desired.

To reach the park, leave I-77 at Exit 85 (CCC Camp Road) and follow the road east until it intersects with NC 262. Follow NC 262 through the town of Pilot Mountain until it junctions with NC 66, 25 miles east of Pilot Mountain. Follow NC 66 until it junctions with Moore's Springs Road (State Road 1001) and follow signs to the entrance to Hanging Rock State Park. You can also reach the park by following NC 8/89 northwest of Danbury and then taking Hanging Rock Road (State Road 1001) to the park entrance. (Hanging Rock Road and Moore's Springs Road are actually the same road on the state road system, but the name changes at the entrance to the state park.)

As you enter the park, you will see from time to time a stream running almost parallel to the road. This stream is Indian Creek, and the Indian Creek Trail follows the basic path of the creek.

About 1.8 miles from the park entrance, you will arrive at the first picnic area. This is

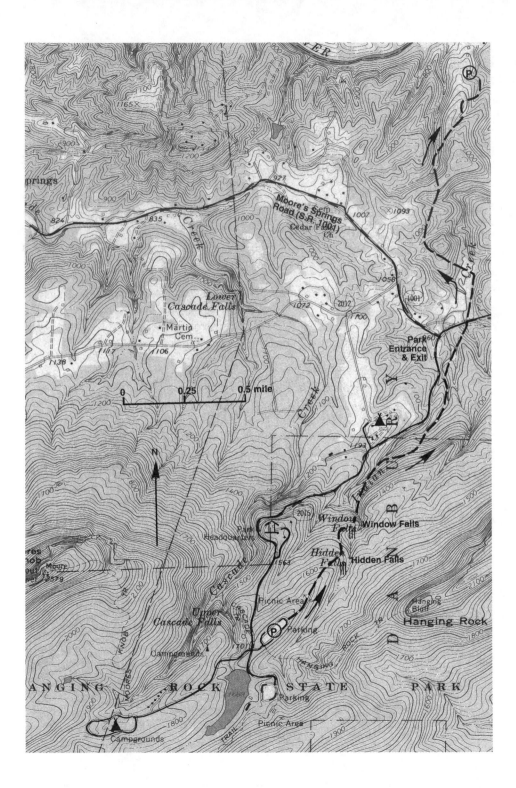

the same parking area where the trailhead to the Hanging Rock Trail is found (see chapter 10). If you prefer not to backtrack, you may use two vehicles by leaving one at the first picnic area and the other at the Dan River parking area. To reach the Dan River parking area by car, follow Hanging Rock Road to the right, as you leave the park, until it intersects with Piedmont Springs Road (State Road 1489) 0.7 mile from the park entrance. Within 0.5 mile the road will intersect with NC 8/89. Take the left, drive for 0.5 mile, and then turn left onto State Road 1482, which will lead you, after 0.8 mile, to the Dan River parking area.

To hike Indian Creek Trail, park at the end of the parking lot near the picnic area. The first part of the hike will lead past picnic tables and rest rooms. The Indian Creek Trail will junction with the Mountains-to-Sea Trail at 0.2 mile.

The combined trails will lead down a steep and rocky slope and at 0.3 mile you will reach a T-intersection of the trail. The trail spur to the right will lead to Hidden Falls. This spur is very short; in less than 0.1 mile you will reach the small waterfall.

Return to the intersection after you have viewed the falls and start toward Window Falls. As you stand facing the signs, the trail to Window Falls will be on your left.

Descend a short flight of steps cut into the embankment and hike downward to the valley. The trail steepens very sharply, and at times the rocky trail surface will give way to dirt banks that have eroded and may be very slippery after heavy rains.

At 1.0 mile you will arrive at a large rock outcropping that overlooks Indian Creek. To reach Window Falls, cross the rock outcropping to your right (or toward the southeast). You will see from the rock ledge a huge rock cliff with a three-foot hole in the

left-center of the cliff. This is the "window" which gave Window Falls its name.

You will have to climb down a short rock cliff and make your way across the rocky gap until you are at the base of the huge rock cliff. You can now approach the window and view Window Falls.

For a closer look at the falls, climb farther down the base of the rocky cliff and make your way—carefully!—around the end of the cliff. You may need to use the stepping-stones in the creek in order to work your way around the end of the cliff.

When you have descended to the creek, you can move up the creek by way of the stepping-stones (or by wading, if you won't mind wet feet) until you are within 20 feet of the falls, which are completely invisible from the edge of the rock cliff.

Return to the rock outcropping and cross it to the northeast side. From this point you can see, in the shallow ravine, another waterfall. This one is 40 feet from the top of the rock outcropping.

On the north side of the rock, you will see a trail that leads from the bottom of the rock shelf and into the forest. You will need to climb down a six-foot drop-off to continue on the trail, which leads through a dense hardwood forest and continues to parallel Indian Creek.

The hike crosses Indian Creek—which is clear and very shallow, and the crossing is always easy—five times.

The hike leads within a few feet of the entrance to Hanging Rock State Park, crosses Hanging Rock Road (State Road 1001) near the park entrance, and continues through the hardwood forest until it terminates at a parking lot on the Dan River, a popular canoeing stream.

Backtrack to the picnic area, for a total round-trip distance of 7.4 miles.

12

Stone Mountain Trail

Total distance (loop): 3.8 miles

Hiking time: 2.5 hours

Vertical rise: 1,200 feet

Rating: Moderate

Map: USGS 7.5' Glade Valley

When you first see Stone Mountain, you might think of some volcano that in eons past shoved the earth apart and forced immense domes of granite into astonishing prominence. The glistening gray monadnock is visible for scores of miles before you are within the general vicinity of the mountain.

The mountain itself is four miles in circumference and rises 2,305 feet above sea level. Two other giant rocks, Wolf and Cedar Rocks, combine with Stone Mountain to form a 25-square-mile pluton of biotite granite, formed 300 million years ago when volcanic action forced molten lava upon the original bedrock.

You can reach Stone Mountain by driving on US 21 between Elkin and Sparta until it intersects with State Road 1002, four miles past the tiny town of Roaring Gap. As you drive into the Stone Mountain area, you might want to detour along State Road 1739, which also leads to Stone Mountain, to get a glimpse of the picturesque Widow's Creek Falls.

The name "Widow" wasn't chosen casually. The Stone Mountain area has been the scene of several fatal accidents, and hikers are cautioned to stay on the trails and above all not to step into the waters of Big Sandy River.

The stream is quite shallow and can be waded—but not safely—at any point. The problem is not one of depth but of precipitous slopes and slippery rocks. Algae and various other growths have for years created a gigantic sliding rock out of the granite that is often moist even past the water's edge.

This is not to say that the trail itself is per-

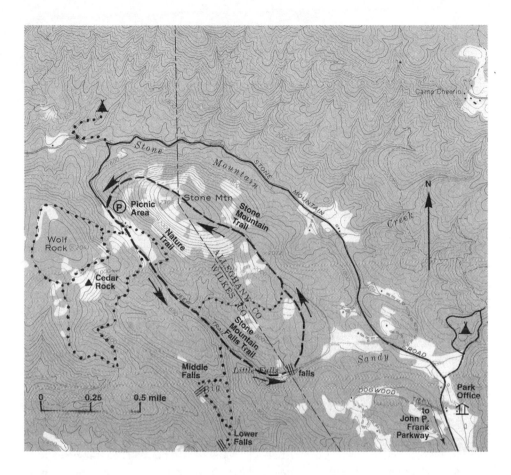

ilous; it isn't. It is, in fact, one of the finest and most fascinating trails in all of North Carolina. But, as with nearly all trails, caution is the key word when you are in potentially dangerous territory.

When you arrive at Stone Mountain, drive past the park office on Stone Mountain Road off the John P. Frank Parkway. Follow the Stone Mountain Road for about four miles through the park, until you see signs directing you to the picnic area and nature trail.

From the picnic area you will walk south, down a huge meadow filled throughout the warm months with high grass and an array of wildflowers. From the meadow you can see the huge gray rock surface of Stone Moun-

tain and, in good weather, what appear to be insects clinging desperately to the unnervingly slick surface.

These "insects" are rock climbers who claim that Stone Mountain is one of the most delightful, challenging, and rewarding climbs east of the Mississippi. There are 13 routes up the face of the monadnock, and some climbers return year after year until they have conquered all of the climbs.

As you leave the meadow, the trail leads into a dense clump of scrub trees and rhododendron bushes. And just as suddenly as you were plunged into darkness, you emerge at the foot of the 200-foot-high Stone Mountain Falls. The entire cascade appears to be somewhat higher than 200 feet, but the height is a reference to the sharpest drop of the Stone Mountain Falls.

At various points in the area's history, the waterfall has been named Deer Falls, Twin Falls, Sandy Creek Cascades, and Beauty Falls. The original name came because of a tradition among local mountaineer families who had agreed to take turns at checking the falls every morning. Their search was to determine whether during the night a deer had waded too far into the waters of Big Sandy River and had fallen over the cascade to its death. The deer's body would be in the huge pool at the base of the falls, and the family that found the deer was entitled to keep the meat.

There are no records to indicate that a significant number of unfortunate beasts died at the falls; perhaps there was only the one isolated incident. Whatever the number, it was enough to keep residents alert for a windfall from the waterfall.

Stone Mountain State Park contains 13,378 acres of rocks, streams, and wilderness. The streams are well populated with brown, rainbow, and brook trout, and the forests teem with deer, beaver, mink, otter, bobcat, and smaller animals. The skies above the rock are seldom without at least one hawk or raven soaring above the granite dome.

You will climb up the switchback trail that leads to the top of the waterfall and to the crest of the rock itself. Part of the trail is steps—289 of them—alongside the waterfall, which is more a cascade than a true waterfall. There are also minor trail departures so that you can shun the steps for the most part and walk on a carpet of pine needles rather than rock treads.

You cannot keep from noticing how impeccably clean the trail is. There is ample reason and precedent for the pristine cleanliness of the entire area.

Decades earlier, R. Philip Hanes, of the Hanes hosiery manufacturing conglomerate, was at the waterfall one day and witnessed a visitor throw trash into the stream. Deeply upset because of this and other acts of thoughtlessness and danger to the environment, Hanes did what many Americans of similar persuasion have desired to do: he bought the waterfall.

He in fact purchased more than a thousand acres that surrounded the rock and the waterfall and the trout streams. He eventually donated 1,100 acres to the state of North Carolina, a gift that has been evaluated at more than $1.75 million.

As you climb the trail, you will keep the cascades of the Big Sandy on your right and close enough to enjoy the roar of the water and the occasional spray when the waterfall crashes onto the huge rock ledges and boulders in its path.

When you reach the top, the trail will lead you across the very top of the monadnock and provide you with an unparalleled view of the mountains to the north, east, and west and the green fields of the Piedmont to the south.

The rock is not bald, as it appears to be from the meadow below. Rather, there are abundant oaks, tulip poplars, pines, and hemlocks that thickly populate the crest.

Before you reach the crest of the dome, you will see trail signs that inform you of side hikes leading to other waterfalls, among them Middle Falls and Lower Falls, the latter a 25-foot sheer drop into a beautiful pool below. These trails are the subject of another trail description in this book (see chapter 13).

You may actually see people dancing at the waterfalls, though such a sight is unlikely. The dimly honored tradition began when Canadian choreographer and dancer Norbert Vesak decided to orchestrate and choreograph a ballet incorporating the attitudes and values of the early mountain people, called *The Gray Goose of Silence.* The sound of the waterfall was included in the musical score for the ballet.

If hiking is more to your liking than dancing, continue along the trail until you have crossed the entire monadnock. You will find that the air is crisp on almost any day of the summer if you are atop Stone Mountain, and it is paradoxically warm there on all but the coldest and windiest days. The scenery is spectacular every month of the year and the hiking is superb on all but a total of two or three weeks out of the year.

As you follow the trail northward, you will be able to see the Blue Ridge Parkway in the distance. A short drive north up I-77 would take you to Mount Airy, the much-visited television home of the beloved Mayberry characters who populated "The Andy Griffith Show" in the early years of situation comedy.

At the other end of the rock the trail descends rather gently into the meadow once again. You will have time to hike several of Stone Mountain's trails in one day, if you get an early start and maintain a respectable pace.

But hurrying is alien to everything that Stone Mountain represents to the state of North Carolina and to the topography of the United States. Anything that required 300 million years to achieve its present status should not be visited hurriedly. Take plenty of time, particularly at the waterfalls and along the crest. Savor the fresh air, the brilliant blue of the sky, the rare butterfly bushes that are covered with specimens of lepidoptera during the warm months.

Enjoy and photograph the fascinating wildflowers that somehow manage to find a roothold in the crevices of the rocks. Take short forays into the groves of pines at the crest. When you descend, if time permits, you can take an unhurried hike along the trout streams and through the forests surrounding the gray magnificence that is Stone Mountain, which is now included among the listing of national natural landmarks. As with all hiking trails in North Carolina that are on public lands, the dictum holds: take nothing but photos and imperishable memories; leave nothing but footprints and your gratitude that there is such a place as Stone Mountain in such a state as North Carolina.

Stone Mountain as seen from the meadow below

13

Stone Mountain Middle and Lower Falls Trail

Total distance (backtrack): 4 miles

Hiking time: 2 hours

Vertical rise: 1,920 feet

Rating: Easy

Map: USGS 7.5' Glade Valley

Two trails at Stone Mountain State Park are described in this book. The first is the Stone Mountain Trail, which crosses the entire rocky top of the mountain and provides a superb view of the surrounding countryside (see chapter 12).

The Middle and Lower Falls Trail is the exact opposite. It has no scenic vistas: when you enter the forest for the first time, you do not emerge from the huge trees until the hike is ended, and the total of your visual experience is limited to the trailside and a short distance into the forest. The enjoyment of this trail, however, derives from the opportunity to see an abundance of lovely forest scenery and woodland items of interest.

Start the trail where the Stone Mountain Trail had its origin: at the parking area just off the Stone Mountain Road. To reach the trailhead, leave US 21 north of Elkin on State Road 1002. Follow State Road 1002 for a little more than a mile to the point where it junctions with the John P. Frank Parkway. Follow the John P. Frank Parkway to the park entrance and on through the park, where the parkway becomes Stone Mountain Road.

If you approach Stone Mountain from the north, exit US 21 at State Road 1100 near Roaring Gap and follow the highway for five miles until it intersects with the John P. Frank Parkway and then proceed to the park entrance.

Follow the parkway (Stone Mountain Road) through the park for approximately four miles until you reach the sign directing you to the picnic area at the handicapped-

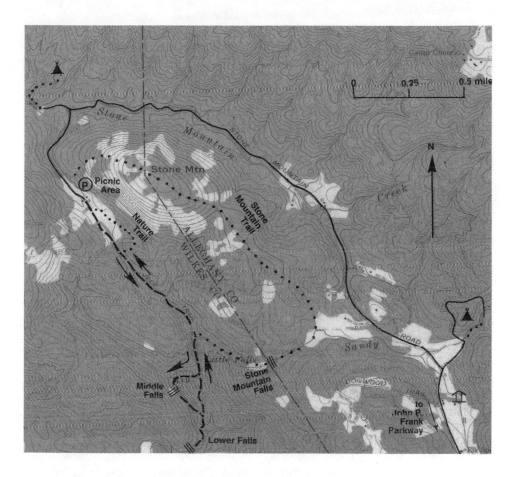

access trail to the view of Stone Mountain. Park at the end of the road and follow the wide, easy trail south up a short set of steps and through a growth of small trees and shrubs into an open meadow from which Stone Mountain can be seen in all its splendor.

A wide, equally easy gravel trail leads across an open meadow and past a bench and information point. Across from the bench you will see a narrow trail through the high grass. This is the self-guiding Nature Trail. The Middle and Lower Falls Trail goes to the right and follows the Stone Mountain Trail.

After you enter the forest of hardwood mixed with pines, you will hike southeast along a wide trail that follows Big Sandy Creek. The creek is wide, clear, and shallow, and the forest in this area is inhabited by deer, bobcats, squirrels, foxes, several species of snakes (including rattlesnakes, although these are rare, and the more common copperhead), and nearly every species of songbird indigenous to both the higher elevations and the flat Piedmont area.

The climate of Stone Mountain is such that plant and animal life common to both extremes—the higher mountains and the Piedmont—can exist easily here. Hardwood trees such as oak, poplar, hickory, and maple flourish, and pines are abundant

Ferns on the Falls Trail

both on the lower trails and on the mountaintop trail.

After approximately 1.3 miles the Stone Mountain Trail will continue straight ahead and the trail to Lower and Middle Falls will veer to the right and descend along a gentle slope as it follows the creek toward the bottom of the mountain. After 0.3 mile the trail becomes increasingly narrow but is well defined.

You will cross the creek a total of four times. In two instances your only crossing is by wading, so this trail should be hiked in warm weather or by removing boots and socks in order to make the crossing. The water is shallow (a foot deep at the most where the crossings are made) and the footing is sound.

Follow the creek and trail, which continue side by side much of the time, until you reach a wide rock where the creek slides over it into a deep pool at the bottom. Here there are several smaller cascades, and you will find Middle Falls near the first large cascade.

Many other smaller falls or short cascades can be glimpsed from along the trail. For a closer view you must follow fishermen's or nature lovers' side trails into the rhododendron and laurel. The footing is very uncertain here, and you will need to hike carefully.

From Middle Falls continue the descent until you reach Lower Falls, which is a more beautiful waterfall from many standpoints. You can follow a spur trail down to the upper part of the waterfall, or you can go below the falls and wend your way through the rhododendron and to the creek itself.

By rock-hopping you can make your way to the middle of the channel and stand on a huge rock and sandbar where you will have a direct, head-on view of the Lower Falls. This is your best photo opportunity of Lower Falls.

From Lower Falls the trail continues down the mountain, and you can follow it, if you wish to lengthen the hike, farther down the slope. Backtrack to the beginning of the trail, or hike to the right when you reach the junction of the Stone Mountain Trail, for a visit to Stone Mountain Falls (described in chapter 12).

III

Blue Ridge Area

Jim Hargan

14

Basin Creek Trail

Total distance (backtrack): 10.9 miles

Hiking time: 7 hours

Vertical rise: 1,560 feet

Rating: Moderate

Map: USGS 7.5' Whitehead

Doughton Park, located at Milepost 238–244 on the Blue Ridge Parkway, is a 6,000-acre area that is primarily wilderness and uninterrupted ridges separated only by trout streams and small creeks and rills. It is an impressive area in many respects, offering some of the finest hiking trails in the state, superb opportunities to enjoy wildlife in many forms, and some of the best scenic views in the South.

Doughton Park, named after Congressman Robert Lee Doughton (1911–1953), has about 36 miles of hiking trails that lead through dense forests, through open pastures, over rolling hills, and up severely steep ridges. The major trails in the park are (with round-trip distances) Bluff Mountain Trail (15 miles), Cedar Ridge Trail (8.8 miles), Grassy Gap Fire Road Trail (13 miles), Basin Creek Trail (10.9 miles), Bluff Ridge Primitive Trail (5.6 miles), Flat Rock Ridge Trail (10 miles), Fodder Stack Trail (4 miles), and Little Glade Millpond Trail (0.4 mile). A series of shorter walks lead to scenic views.

All distances given include backtrack hiking, because some of the trails are such that second-vehicle pickups are impossible. Some of the trails are easy, while others are among the most strenuous trails to be found.

One of the most interesting and enjoyable of the Doughton Park trails is the Basin Creek Trail, which is listed on maps as 3.3 miles. However, no car shuttle is possible, so the backtrack hike makes the trail 6.6 miles long. To this distance, hikers must add 1.5 miles up the Grassy Gap Fire Road and return, which makes the hike 9.6 miles.

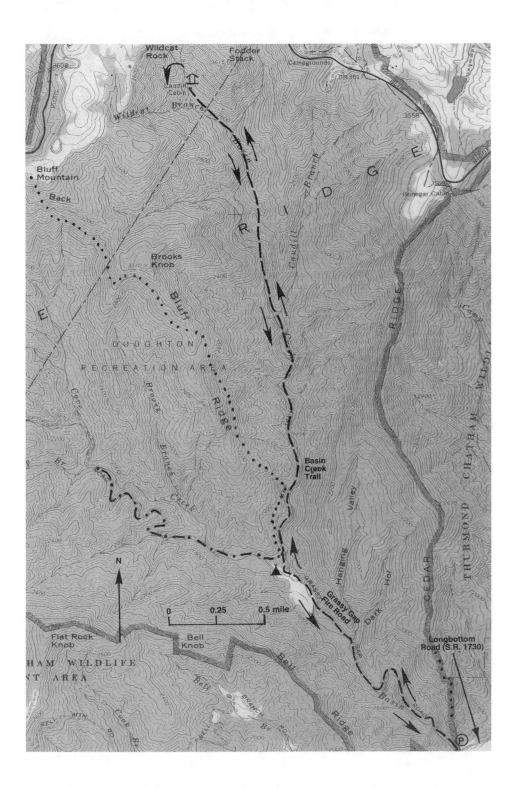

If you hike around the Caudill Cabin and take short side trips to waterfalls and trout pools, the total hiking distance is slightly longer than the map distance, which shows only the shortest route possible.

To get to the trailhead of the Basin Creek Trail, drive south on the parkway out of Doughton Park to the exit for Highway 18 south to North Wilkesboro. Follow NC 18 for 6.2 miles to Long-bottom Road (State Road 1728). Take Longbottom Road left for 4.0 miles until it intersects with State Road 1730. Follow State Road 1730 for 3.0 miles to a bridge over a trout stream. Park on the right side of the road, and begin the trail across the road, where you will find a closed gate to the Grassy Gap Fire Road.

As you enter the fire road and start northwest, you will reach a small dam at 0.2 mile. The road, which is also used as a bridle trail, is wide enough to accommodate park vehicles, and three or four can hike abreast. This 1.5-mile road is a very easy walk (although it may be slightly longer than the map shows: our pedometer measurement indicated the road to be 1.7 rather than 1.5 miles).

At 0.6 mile you will reach a rock wall to the left of the road and along the creek channel, and out from the wall is a beautiful, wide, and deep trout pool. If you care to spend a few minutes in motionless silence, you can see large trout as they move about in the clear water.

The roadway is bounded on the right or north side by steep slopes and on the left by the creek. On the slope and on the other side of the creek are huge poplars, oaks, and maples, with an occasional hickory tree and smaller fire cherries and even smaller dogwoods. The inevitable laurel and rhododendron are present along the creek channel.

At 1.1 miles you will cross a wooden bridge over a small stream that flows into Basin Creek. As you began the hike the creek was only 12 feet below the roadbed, but as the hike progresses the creek soon drops away until it is at the bottom of a steep slope where pines and other evergreens appear among the hardwoods. A thick carpeting of mixed ground-cover greenery adds to the beauty of the terrain. These woodlands are thickly populated with deer and other wildlife, and if you listen carefully for the sounds of the deer moving through the undergrowth you will be rewarded by the sight of two, three, or even more of the graceful animals making their way through the forest.

At mile 1.5 the creek is a jumble of ripples and small cascades as it flows through a rock-studded channel. This is one of the most beautiful sights along the Grassy Gap Fire Road. At mile 1.7 you will cross Basin Creek by rock-hopping or wading. The creek is not deep or wide, and you can wade safely and easily if the water is too high for the stepping-stones to be of value.

If you wish to camp along the trails in the park, you will find a superb primitive campsite just past the Basin Creek crossing and on the left. For the first time now the creek will be on your right as you hike. The primitive campsite is not often crowded but you will need to have a camping permit, which is available from the District Ranger Office, Route 1, Box 263, Laurel Springs, NC 28644. Or you can call (919) 372-8568.

As you pass between the primitive campsites and Basin Creek, you will reach a signpost (at mile 1.8) that directs you to the Basin Creek Trail and to the Caudill Cabin, 3.3 miles away. The trail is marked with a blue blaze.

After you cross the creek the first time, you will have only 13 more crossings to make. The trail winds through the forest and crisscrosses the creek several times within two miles. Along the way you will see evidence of the community that once flourished within this isolated cove. There are chimneys left standing where cabins once stood.

At mile 4.3 you will see the second chimney; the first was at mile 3.8. These chimneys mark the remains of cabins that were washed away in the devastating flood of August 1916. This storm was so fierce and the rainfall so heavy that a grindstone was washed down the stream (at mile 2.5 you can see the stone, still lying in the creek) and, incredible as it may sound, soil was washed away from wells so that one windlass was left 25 feet above the ground and the cylindrical walls of the well were left exposed. It was actually a well above ground!

In the Piedmont below, the water levels around rivers reached the crossbars on utility poles on the town's main street. One heavily traveled bridge washed away with more than two dozen people on it, and several of the workers drowned. Scores of houses were washed away, as were all the houses in the community on Basin Creek, except for the Caudill Cabin.

The trail narrows significantly once you have crossed the creek twice. It becomes a single-file trail with very little room on the creek side between you and the water; at other times the creek is far below you and you are treading a narrow trail only inches from the embankment.

The final stretch of forest land begins at mile 4.9, after you cross the creek for the fourteenth time. The trail leads through a hardwood area filled with oaks, hickories, ash, and the occasional poplar that often dominates the woodlands.

At mile 5.4 you emerge into a tiny clearing on very steep terrain. The Caudill Cabin is located in the center of the clearing. You will note as you cross the clearing that there are only narrow trails that could easily be mistaken for animal trails. One of these leads to the front door of the cabin and another to the back door.

You will also notice that the door frames are built very low. The top of the door will strike a six-foot man at about his shoulder. There were several reasons for such small doorways.

First, shortage of lumber meant that waste was simply not permissible. Second, the family was apparently very short in stature. Third, larger openings admitted more cold air on bitter and frigid winter nights. Fourth, in the event an enemy attempted to enter the cabin, he would need to bend over and expose his vulnerable head to the defenders of the isolated cabin.

As you walk around and through the cabin, keep in mind that in warmer weather there may be snakes in the coolness of the cabin or under it. Spiders also have invaded the cabin.

Another caution: no overnight camping is permitted in the cabin area, and no fires are allowed. Rangers work very hard to protect such relics from the past, and they are not tolerant of those who break rules and regulations.

Backtrack to the parking area when you have toured the tiny cabin to your satisfaction. Be certain to allow plenty of time for the return trip. Being caught by darkness would be a genuine ordeal on such a twisting and uncertain trail.

15

Bluff Mountain Trail

Total distance (one way): 7.5 miles

Hiking time: 5 hours

Vertical rise: 2,160 feet

Rating: Moderate

Map: USGS 7.5' Whitehead

While most of the Bluff Mountain Trail is relatively flat and easy, there are some extremely rugged portions that require stamina and surefootedness. This trail, if hiked from north to south, is easy; if hiked in the reverse direction, it is at times moderate to strenuous.

Our preference is to hike south to north because of the culmination of the trail at the Brinegar Cabin, one of the many picturesque and ancient attractions along the trails of the Doughton Park area. The cabin is in essence an operating farmstead, with old-fashioned weaving and other pioneer activities practiced by staff members.

To get to the trail, drive to Milepost 244.5 on the Blue Ridge Parkway and park at the Basin Cove Overlook. You will need a second car to use for the shuttle trip back to the parking area—or you will need to backtrack 7.5 miles, making the total hike 15 miles.

Because the trail has several accesses to the Blue Ridge Parkway, hikers can lengthen or shorten the hike. If the weather is uncertain, it should be remembered that in this part of the state late-season snowstorms can be devastating. In late May of 1991 a surprise snowstorm dumped more than six feet of snow onto portions of the Blue Ridge Parkway, all within a matter of several hours.

By the same token, summer thunderstorms can be fierce in this area, particularly if you are crossing a series of bare rock ridges and are exposed to lightning. When such storms occur, leave the higher and exposed elevations at once and return to shelter.

When you start north on the Bluff Ridge Trail, you will descend sharply down a hill-

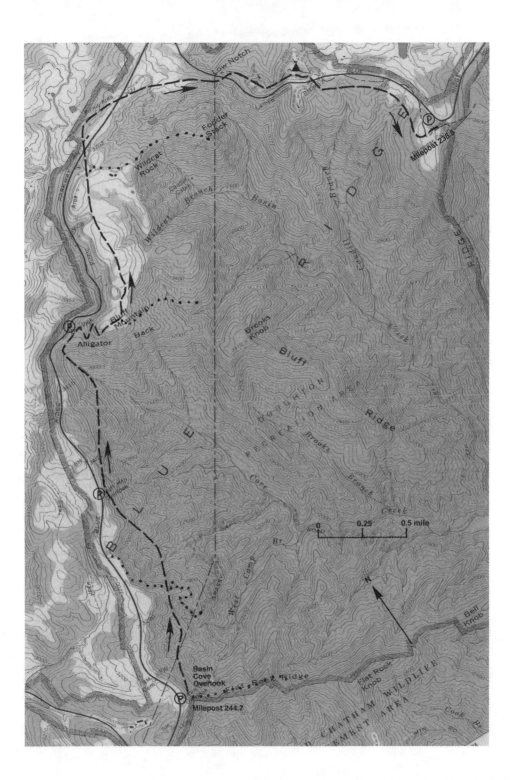

side segment of the trail, and at once the world seems to change. One moment you are on the parkway with the open beauty of the area, and within 100 feet you are in a deep forest where you can see nothing but trees and immediate slopes.

As you continue northward, the trail levels and you will find yourself on a series of very gentle slopes. The trail is bordered on the right by a steep slope descending into thick foliage. You cannot see the bottom of it. On the left the slope ascends sharply toward the parkway to the northwest, but the terrain is so steep and rough that it would not be advisable to attempt to leave the trail in the event you need to reach the parkway quickly.

At 800 feet into the hike you can catch a glimpse through the openings in the trees of a huge rock outcropping to the northeast. This is Stone Mountain, the 600-foot monadnock rising from a flat plain. Stone Mountain, not to be confused with the one by the same name in Georgia, is one of the most picturesque sights in this part of the state.

Incidentally, according to parkway staff members, the openings in the trees were caused by Hurricane Hugo, which devastated a full mile's width of mountain territory after the storm abruptly changed course off the South Carolina coast and moved into the Piedmont and then into the mountains, where it uprooted hundreds of trees and closed portions of several trails until the damage could be corrected.

At 0.2 mile you will enter a dark forest of hardwood trees, including oak, hickory, chestnut oak, poplar, and small dogwoods. As soon as you emerge from this dense growth you will see many uprooted and rotting evergreens, mostly hemlock, that serve as grim reminders of the whims of Nature that can defy all predictions.

At 0.4 mile you can see a split-rail fence at the top of the slope to your left. This fence borders the parkway, and at this point if you need to leave the trail you could, in an emergency situation, do so.

Wildflowers are plentiful along the trail from early April, if the weather is unseasonably warm, through late October. Ferns cover the ground totally in several areas.

When you are 0.5 mile into the trail, you will emerge into a large clearing that offers a spectacular view of Stone Mountain straight ahead of you. To your right you will have a superior view of the Yadkin River valley and Piedmont farms some 3,000 feet below.

Within the next mile you will cross a drainage area from the parkway. A split-rail fence surrounds the upper side of the area. You will have at 0.9 mile a wonderful view of Bluff Mountain through the trees. At 1 mile you will pass a series of wooden pasture posts on the right and enter a thick growth of laurel and rhododendron.

You will intersect with an old service road at mile 1.1, and at 1.3 you will reach trail sign markers pointing to Grassy Gap Trail and Basin Creek Trail, 5 miles long, and to Absher Road, 6.5 miles away. Note the yellow blaze mark on the Siamese-twin tree at 1.4 miles. Two trees apparently sprouted where one had been cut and at six or seven feet the two trees grew together and created an interesting result.

There is a gate (to keep horseback riders from using the trail) at mile 1.6. You have nearly completed the first leg of the hike when you reach this gate—and within 0.1 mile you can find a stairway that leads up to the parkway.

At this point you are within 6 miles of Brinegar Cabin, and the next trail segment ends at Bluff Mountain, 2 miles away. You will start the next trail segment in a dense slick of rhododendron and laurel. There are no large trees nearby, and the trail has been

Brinegar Cabin at dusk

sliced through the tangle growth. Within 0.3 mile you will reach even thicker laurel, a small stream, and a wild apple tree. Because of the thick foliage that prevents the sun from ripening the fruit too quickly, you can often still find apples around this tree in September and October that can be retrieved from the ferns and eaten.

The only climb on this segment of the trail starts 0.4 mile from the beginning of this leg and about 2 miles into the total trail. The climb, while not arduous, continues for more than 1,000 feet. When you reach the 2.6-mile mark you will have your best view yet of Bluff Mountain. You will also start another climb that will culminate, 900 feet later, at Alligator Back Overlook.

As you emerge from the forest there is a huge rock outcropping on the right. You can leave the trail and climb onto the rocks, only 30 feet away, for one of the finest views of the mountain valley but also a

terrific view of Bluff Mountain. You will soon be climbing this mountain, so this is the time to enjoy it in all its beauty. The toughest segment of the trail is only a few feet from you at this point.

Leave the trail and emerge onto the parkway right-of-way, pause if you wish to read the information signs, and plunge into the forest behind the signs. The climb starts instantly, and you will round a series of very steep switchbacks where the trail footing is almost constantly loose rocks. The climb is 0.2 mile but seems much longer.

At the top of the climb you will emerge onto a huge, nearly flat, rock surface, where there is no sign of the trail. Do not walk to the edge of the rock outcropping because there is great danger of an accident, particularly if the rocks are wet.

Go to the northeast corner of the rock expanse and you will find the trail leading into some pines and other evergreens. Follow the trail 0.3 mile to where you emerge into a beautiful open pasture and rolling hills. Halfway across the top of the pasture area you will see a trail leading downhill, toward a gate. This is the Bluff Mountain Trail. If you continue straight ahead, you will reach a shelter.

Take the trail downhill; follow the meadow and climb a sharp but easy grassy ridge as you bypass the picnic-area loop that will be on your left 0.8 mile from the start of this leg of the hike. The access road to the picnic area will remain on your left, though sometimes out of sight, as you ascend the ridge, traverse it, and descend on the north side to the Blue Ridge Parkway.

You will cross the parkway just south of the service station and restaurant and enter the forest behind the service station. For 0.3 mile you will stay on the north side of the parkway as you skirt the edge of the Doughton Park family tent campground.

As you emerge from the forest and cross the parkway a second time, you will be near Wildcat Rock, which will be to your right. Climb a hill and cross a maintenance road, then you will descend and again cross the parkway. The trail continues for 0.6 mile on the north side of the parkway, then crosses again to the south and you will enter the trailer and RV campground area.

The trail may be difficult to find as you cross the campground. You can pick up the final leg of the trail if you walk to the entrance to the campground; where the vehicle loop starts and ends you will find the trail just to the left of the garbage bins.

The remainder of the Bluff Mountain Trail is simply a walk through the woods. Within 1 mile you will emerge at the Brinegar Cabin at the end of the trail. The only caution is that when you emerge from the forest and enter the second clearing, the trail is somewhat obscure.

To locate the trail, note that the trail nears a road and gate. Do not follow the roadway southeast. Instead, near the gate look carefully and you will see the trail as it enters the final section of forest. From this point it is easy to follow until it emerges at the parking area for the Brinegar Cabin.

Along the way the most notable form of wildlife you are likely to see is that of white-tailed deer. The Doughton Park area is densely populated with the deer, and it is not unusual to see as many as 8 to 10 deer within a mile or two of hiking.

If you desire to camp, there are campgrounds for tents and recreational vehicles nearby, and there is a service station and a restaurant on the parkway at Milepost 241.

16

Boone Fork Loop Trail

Total distance (loop): 4.9 miles

Hiking time: 3 hours

Vertical rise: 2,920 feet

Rating: Moderate

Maps: USGS 7.5' Valle Crucis and USGS 7.5' Boone

It would be difficult to locate a trail in North Carolina that offers more than does the Boone Fork Trail, a 4.9-mile loop that leads from the campground at Price Lake on the Blue Ridge Parkway through forests, meadows, and along a series of beautiful streams, and returns in a loop to the starting point.

The best place to start is at the amphitheater parking lot on the lower extent of Price Lake. To reach the parking area, drive along the Blue Ridge Parkway to Milepost 297.1. If you are approaching from the south, there will be a campground on your left and the amphitheater parking area is directly across the road from the campground. Turn right on the first paved road into the Price Lake area.

If you arrive from the north, you will pass a picnic area on your right at Milepost 296.6. Cross a bridge over the Price Lake spillway and take the second left past the campground office and park at the lake front. You will see a large information board that depicts the lake shoreline as well as three hiking trails. One of the trails is the Price Lake Loop Trail (described in chapter 17) and the Green Knob Trail (described in chapter 22).

The other trail is the Boone Fork Loop Trail, which starts at the information board. Study the Boone Fork Trail to see how it winds through forests and meadows and drops into the denser woods to Bee Tree Creek and then to Boone Fork Creek.

When you are familiar with the trail map, start the actual hike by walking to your left (as you are facing the information board) along the paved parking area until you see a paved walk that leads through a small

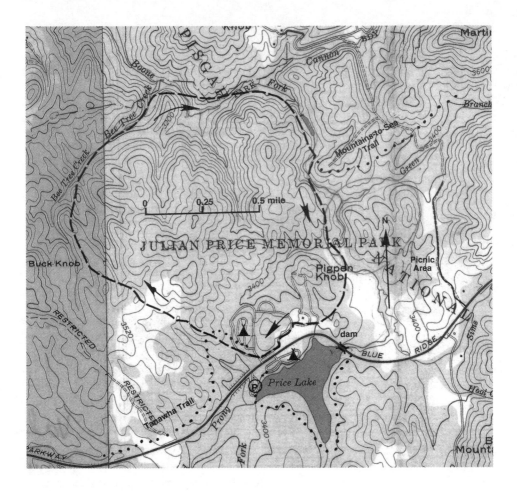

laurel and rhododendron thicket into the forest along the lake.

Inside the forest you will see the amphitheater 30 feet ahead of you. The trail leads along the back of the amphitheater and toward the parkway. You will see trail markers depicting the Boone Fork and Tanawha trails.

Follow the trail to the parkway, then walk across the parkway and enter the southern edge of the campground on the opposite side. A very narrow trail leads through a tangle of ground cover and to the edge of a hardwood forest. Within 75 feet the trail will bend sharply to your left and you will

follow it into a heavy growth of pines that are thick enough to block out the sunlight. A heavy pad of pine needles is underfoot, and the trail descends in a gentle slope toward an open meadow. (You will be hiking a portion of the Tanawha Trail (described in chapter 24), along with the Boone Fork Trail, for about 1 mile before the Tanawha Trail continues to the left and the Boone Fork Trail veers to the right. At this point your trail merges with the Mountains-to-Sea Trail and the two trails overlap for the majority of the remainder of the hike. When you have covered 3.5 miles of the trail, the Mountains-to-Sea Trail will veer left and cross the stream, and the Boone Fork Trail continues straight ahead.)

When you leave the pine growth the trail opens into a wide and beautiful area of meadow and incredibly green rolling hills. The hike is very easy along this stretch and remains so until you cross two hills and descend sharply into a forest. You will arrive at a stile that permits hikers free access in and out of the pasture land but prevents cattle from leaving the pasture.

At the 1-mile point (actual distance will vary considerably, depending upon whether you began measuring the trail at Price Lake or from the campground side of the parkway), veer right at the signpost to follow the Mountains-to-Sea Trail and Boone Fork Trail.

From this point the trail becomes rougher and far steeper, but it is easily hiked if you slow your pace and watch your footing. The trail continues to descend into the forest and quickly the sound of any distant traffic is gone. You start to pick up, from the valley, the low roar of cascading water.

At 1.2 miles you will notice a trickle of a stream. This is the beginning of Bee Tree Creek, which crosses the trail several times and grows with pleasant regularity as it is joined by springs and runoff from the mountainside.

The creek never leaves the trail for more than a few paces. You will step across it easily at first, then cross by using stepping-stones, and finally by using a series of footbridges.

Heavy rains often swell the stream so that crossing is not as easy as it is in dry weather. High winds have also toppled some immense trees and some of these have fallen across the creek and across the trail. You may have to duck under some of the trees or clamber over them until the maintenance staff has had an opportunity to cut away the trail obstructions.

As the creek grows in size and volume, sometimes the current damages bridges or washes them away. You can cross the stream easily via stepping stones or by wading if bridges are damaged. The stream is shallow and the footing is good. At 2.1 miles (again, depending upon where you started counting) you will cross Bee Tree Creek on a series of high rocks. In the stream below you can perhaps see the remnants of past bridges that did not survive the occasional high waters.

The trail continues through a dense and moist woodland, with laurel and rhododendron flanking the trail on both sides and huge hardwood trees on the upper slopes. Hemlock, spruce, and fir are mixed in with the poplars, hickories, and birch.

If you are hiking in the colder months, the branches of the laurel and rhododendron that trail near or into the water will be coated with ice. Spray from the stream freezes two to three feet above the waterline and creates a spectacle worth the cold trip.

Because of the density of the thickets, the sun's rays do not penetrate the area except in thinned growth areas, and the trail remains moist most of the year. In cold weather there may be frozen ground under your feet and patches of ice along the trail. These icy spots remain for several days after the temperatures along the parkway have warmed considerably past the thaw point.

At 2.4 miles you can hear a loud roar to your left. Bee Tree Creek has left the trail temporarily and out of your vision there is a large cascade. Almost immediately you will reach the Boone Fork Creek, which deserves to be called a river at this point.

The trail climbs along up the slope (but not to the ridge) and stays from 10 to 150 feet from the creek. As you hike along the higher slopes you often get a striking view of one of the many waterfalls along the creek.

The waterfalls, in fact, are among the most spectacular sights along the trail. At times huge cascades roar down slanted rocks and crash into the pools below, or the swift current of the stream strikes enormous boulders and sends spray flying into the air.

Follow the creek, which is clear, clean, and scenic at all times, as it follows the valley down from the Price Lake spillway. At times the trail descends so that you can stand at the edge of the water and watch the current swirling past.

At the 3.5-mile point you will arrive at a series of huge flat rocks spaced two feet or so apart across the width of the Boone Fork Creek. The Mountains-to-Sea Trail leaves the Boone Fork Trail at this point and veers left across the stream by way of the huge stepping-stones. The Boone Fork Trail continues up the side of the stream and leads to, at mile 4.5, an open meadow that was for centuries a favorite gathering place for Indians who lived in these mountains.

At the end of the meadow you will see a bridge that crosses the stream and leads into a picnic area. Do not cross the bridge; instead, follow the trail as it veers to the right and enters the forest again. The trail from this point leads into the north side of the campground from which you started.

You can emerge near the campground registration office that you passed as you drove to the entrance to the Price Lake parking area. Follow the pavement to the parkway, cross the highway, and then rejoin the trail that leads to the amphitheater and to the parking lot where you started the hike, which features some of the greatest variety of landscapes and scenic points of interest in the state.

17

Price Lake Loop Trail

Total distance (loop): 2.5 miles

Hiking time: 1.5 hours

Vertical rise: 200 feet

Rating: Easy

Map: USGS 7.5' Boone

Julian Price Memorial Park is located at Milepost 297.1 on the Blue Ridge Parkway and is among the busiest tourist areas during the summer. Closest towns to the lake and hiking trail are the resort town of Blowing Rock and the university town of Boone, both in northern North Carolina. The park has facilities for camping, trout streams, a trout lake, picnic areas, and easy walks, as well as campfire talks, lectures, and slide presentations.

If you arrive too late to make any of the several hikes, you can rent a boat and paddle around the large man made lake; try your hand at trout fishing in either the lake or the streams leading into and out of the lake (state fishing regulations apply and a special trout license required; special one-day or longer permits can be purchased at nearby Blowing Rock); or set up camp in any of the available sites, many of which are situated within a few feet of the water. The lake itself is picturesque and calm virtually all of the time, except in the roughest weather.

The park occupies more than 4,000 acres of beautiful rolling hills and streams. At the park there are 134 tent campsites and 60 trailer sites. The only facilities are rest rooms, water fountains, and campfire circles and grill areas. There is no electricity or hot water provided in the campground.

A short distance away, at Milepost 296.6, there is a splendid picnic ground with tables, rest rooms, and grill facilities. Two superb streams flow through the picnic area, and there are huge fields open for various forms of outdoor recreation.

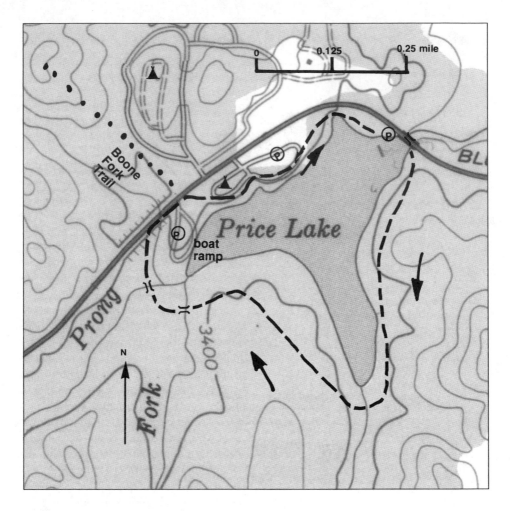

The Julian Price Memorial Park was originally purchased by Jefferson Standard Life Insurance Company. When Julian Price, one of the key figures and organizers of the company, died in 1946, the property was donated to the National Park Service for public enjoyment.

Historically, the area enjoys the reputation of having the celebrated frontiersman Daniel Boone as one of the early white men to explore the territory before he moved westward into Tennessee and Kentucky.

It is a matter of preference whether to start the hike around the lake by beginning at the dam or at the boat ramp. The authors of this book have, for no good reason, preferred to start at the parking area at the Price Lake dam and to proceed clockwise around the body of water.

If you start at the dam parking lot you can hike 38 yards to the dam itself and follow the paved pedestrian crossing along the highway bridge. On the north side of the bridge you can cross the Parkway and climb down to the spillway on the opposite side for a close-up view of the Boone Fork Creek as it leaves Price Lake. Return to the parkway, cross the pavement, and descend into a shallow hollow at the edge of the lake.

The trail follows the shoreline of the lake entirely around the impoundment, except for a short jaunt through the forest at 0.9 mile from the dam parking area. The trail is uniformly easy in its entire length, and the hike can be made in less than an hour of steady walking. The extra time given in the hike statistics assumes you want to stop to enjoy special points of interest.

You will encounter several wet spots along the trail where spring-fed rills or wet-weather springs feed the lake. Along the eastern shoreline you will likely encounter trout fishermen. You can pass these sportsmen without disturbing their angling simply by staying on the trail. The fishermen will be several feet below you at most points.

The forest land you pass through is composed of immense spruce and firs, gigantic poplars, hickories, oaks, and occasional birch or beech. Beavers have been reintroduced into the area in recent years, and you will notice a number of trees that have been felled and debarked by these creatures.

As the trail rises slightly above the lake level, you can catch glimpses of huge trout lying in the deeper waters. The park is also home for a large number of deer, which can often be seen coming to the lake for a drink of water. Best bets for spotting deer are on the western shoreline in the densely wooded area where three streams feed into the lake.

There are also numerous songbirds, game birds, and birds of prey within the park boundaries. Quail, rare grouse, pileated woodpeckers, hawks, owls, and vultures are among the more notable birds. The lake and feeder streams are also homes for muskrats, otters, and trout, including native.

Bobcats and other nocturnal animals may be heard at night, and rather often raccoons make nighttime raids into the campgrounds and picnic areas. Foxes are, while seldom seen, also residents of the park.

At 0.6 mile you will reach a boggy section of the lake, and often the trail is soft and sometimes wet in these areas. At 0.7 mile you veer slightly away from the lake and make your way around the cove of shallow water and rare algae.

As you begin the back half of the loop you will cross three feeder streams, all of which have excellent and picturesque footbridges crossing them. The first stream is Laurel Creek, at mile 0.9, followed by Boone Fork Creek (mile point 1.6), and Cold Prong Creek at mile 1.8.

In the area of the three bridges you will see great evidence of the presence of beavers. Small trees, often with still-green foliage, lie near the trail, while a few feet from the trail you can see the telltale rounded stumps or trunks of the modest-sized trees. Around the stumps of trees you can find slivers of wood that bear the distinctive marks of the teeth of the beavers.

You will remain in the hardwood forest, with the exception of a stretch of 0.2 mile, the remainder of the hike around the Price Lake Loop Trail. At the remaining bridges there are beaver signs, and you can see tracks of raccoon and opossums in the soft white sand along the banks of feeder streams.

As you pass over the final of the three bridges on the southwestern side of the lake you will enter a thicket of laurel and rhododendron, which will be in full bloom from about June 12 through July 15 in this area. In the area of the small coves of the lake on the northwest side, at mile 1.9, you will see far more signs of beaver activity.

Smaller feeder streams with correspondingly small footbridges, which are often only treated timbers laid across the

Price Lake from the Boone Fork overlook

streams, flow through the laurel and rhododendron thickets as you round the final cove to emerge at the boat ramp. In good weather the ramp area is almost always occupied by trout fishermen.

As you pass the boat dock (no motor-propelled boats are permitted on the lake; you can rent a boat or launch your own canoe at this point) you will see an information sign (at mile 2.0) with information about Price Lake and other trails in the vicinity. From the information sign and map you can quickly find your way onto the Boone Fork Trail, the Mountains-to-Sea Trail, and the fantastic Tanawha Trail. More detailed information about these trails is provided elsewhere in this book.

To continue the Price Lake trail, cross the boat-ramp parking area to where a trail leads into the rhododendron thicket. The trail passes around the back of the amphitheater and continues along the edge of the lake, or you can take the auto road through the campground. The trail around the shoreline will lead you back to the parking area at the dam.

The final 0.3 mile of the trail is through dense laurel and rhododendron, with immense spruce and hardwood trees along the fringe of the thickets.

The Price Lake Loop Trail is easy but enjoyable hiking in almost every month (with the exception of snow days when the parkway is closed). The elevation here is less than 3,000 feet and the weather is unusually mild for the Blue Ridge Parkway in North Carolina.

If you plan to camp at Price Lake, you can get an early start on one of the other trails the following day. Some of the finest hiking trails in the state are located in this park area.

18

Richland Balsam Trail

Total distance: 1.5 miles (loop)

Hiking time: 1 hour

Vertical rise: 540 feet

Rating: Moderate

Map: USGS 7.5' Sam Knob

The Richland Balsam Trail is not simply a mountain hike; it is an educational experience that should be of interest to everyone who treasures the beauties of nature. The lesson starts long before you park the car and look up at the mountain, which is one of the highest peaks in North Carolina and also one of the highest in the East.

Standing 6,410 feet in elevation, Richland Balsam is only 274 feet lower than the peak of Mount Mitchell (6,684), and both peaks have a great deal in common. The comparison, however, is not all good. Both mountains, like so much of the Southern Highlands and the mountains of North Carolina in general have not fared well in the fight against pollution, acid rain, and a tiny but incredibly destructive insect known as the balsam woolly adelgid.

As you approach Richland Balsam, you can see the ghosts of dead trees dotting the landscape. Some have deteriorated and fallen to the forest floor, while others are slowly dying as they stand. For many years the deaths of the Fraser firs were blamed on the air pollution, as exhaust from factories, automobiles, and even households banked up against the mountain and slowly suffocated the trees. The blame was then fixed on acid rain, also a product of air pollution. In more recent years the woolly adelgid was recognized as the real killer.

The adelgid, like the blight that killed the chestnut and elm trees, was introduced into this country by accident around 1900; however, it did not make its way to the Southern Highlands and the Great Balsams until about 1970. At that point the trees began to die slowly, and at first no one

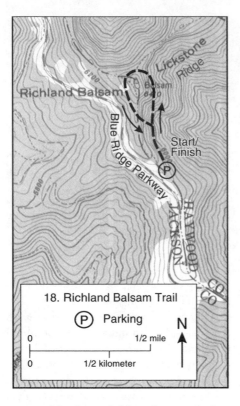

18. Richland Balsam Trail

Ⓟ Parking   **N**

0 ———————————— 1/2 mile

0 ———————————— 1/2 kilometer

Ridge Parkway just south of Mount Pisgah. Drive south on the Parkway past Devil's Courthouse and Graveyard Fields to Milepost 431. Richland Balsam is on the right side of the Parkway.

Begin this loop hike by taking the right fork in the trail. You can hike in either direction, of course, and if you elect to hike the trail in reverse, you will begin by taking the left fork in the trail. The ascent in reverse order is slightly more difficult than the traditional way, but you will also have a much smoother hike on the descent.

The trail is marked by 23 numbered posts that provide mileage and information on the trail. Number 2, for example, identifies and explains witherod viburnum, or the shonny haw growth. The bark of this tree was used by Shawnee Indians and early settlers to help reduce fevers caused by various infections. This tree has dark berries in the summer called wild raisins.

At the third stop you can read about the effects of the woolly adelgid. The insect feeds off the tree and at the same time injects a deadly substance into the tree. A rough comparison would be a cancer-causing mosquito. When the toxin, for want of a better term, is left in the tree, it causes an abnormal growth that chokes off the nutrients so that the tree dies of starvation.

But don't be too depressed by this desolate scene. Instead, look at the young trees sprouting from the ruins of the older ones. As the mature trees die, the young ones quickly take their place in the forest. This is not to say that the picture is rosy, only that the battle is far from lost.

As you climb toward the summit, you will see lush green hardwoods, but it is the firs that will attract your attention. At stop number 12, for instance, you will see trees that appear to have white lint on them. This "lint" is actually the adelgid in great numbers.

was unduly alarmed. After all, trees die for a wide variety of reasons. Then more and more trees began to turn brown and die, and a full-scale investigation was launched.

The mortality rate is horrendously high. Most firs die upon infection, and you can see the results of the tragedy as you stand in the parking lot and look at the mountain, and you can see it up close and personal as you hike the Richland Balsam Trail.

To get to Richland Balsam from the Great Smoky Mountains National Park, drive north on the Blue Ridge Parkway to Milepost 431. The mountain is on the left side of the road.

From Asheville, follow the Parkway south to Milepost 431. The trailhead is on the righthand side of the road.

From South Carolina take I-85 to the US 276 exit in Greenville. Follow US 276 through the Brevard area and intersect with the Blue

Two generations of Williamses at the summit of Richland Balsam.

Once the adelgids are so numerous as to be visible to the naked eye, as they are here, the tree is doomed.

At the summit, a marker indicates that you are 6,410 feet above sea level. Just before the summit, if you are hiking in summertime, you will see blackberry briars six feet tall or higher. The blackberries are one of the intermediate plants that appear as soon as a tree falls. The briars will last until the new sprouts shade them out.

As you start back down the trail, the footing is rocky and rough. The trail, which started out wide, is now so narrow that only single-file hiking is comfortable.

One final consideration: you are at the tenth-highest peak in the South and in the East. (Mount Washington in New Hampshire is 6,288 feet above sea level, and Mount Katahdin in Maine is 5,268.) The highest peaks in the East are all in either North Carolina or Tennessee. The highest local peaks are: Mount Mitchell, 6,684; Mount Craig, 6,647; Clingman's Dome, 6,643; Mount Guyot, 6,621, Balsam Cone, 6,611; Mount LeConte, 6,593; Mount Gibbes, 6,571; Potato Hill, 6,475; Mount Chapman, 6,417; and Richland Balsam, 6,410. Also included in this book are hikes to Clingman's Dome and Mount Mitchell. If you hike them, you will have conquered three of the top ten. The other seven are within a fairly short driving distance, and you might want to try them as well.

19

Moses Cone Memorial Park Trails

Total distance (loop): 5.7 miles

Hiking time: 2 hours

Vertical rise: 1,220 feet

Rating: Moderate

Map: USGS 7.5' Boone

The Moses Cone trails are converted carriage roads, holdovers from another age and another way of life far removed from that of the latter part of the 20th century. The trail area, in fact, predates the Roaring Twenties.

In 1897 Moses Cone, the textile magnate whose manufacturing products earned for him the title "Denim King," took his wife to Blowing Rock, North Carolina, for the purpose of designing and building their summer mansion and estate. The results of their efforts were incomparable for the time and area.

The property, along with the entire 3,516 acres of land, was donated to the National Park Service in 1950 for public use.

Cone, whose health was tenuous at best, wanted a home where he could enjoy the bracing air and cool temperatures of the North Carolina mountains. A lover of the outdoors, Cone wanted a place where he could become a part of nature and still remain, when he desired, apart from it as much as possible.

Part of his love of the outdoors was manifested in a gift he made to his wife, Bertha: he "gave" her 25 miles of carriage roads where she could enjoy the scenery and climate of the mountains in summer and yet remain isolated from the world in general.

The Cone mansion was a 20-room manor that was built on top of a hill and overlooked the newly established apple orchard, a bass lake, and seemingly endless peaks and valleys. Today the 25-mile carriage-road system has been converted to bridle trails and hiking trails.

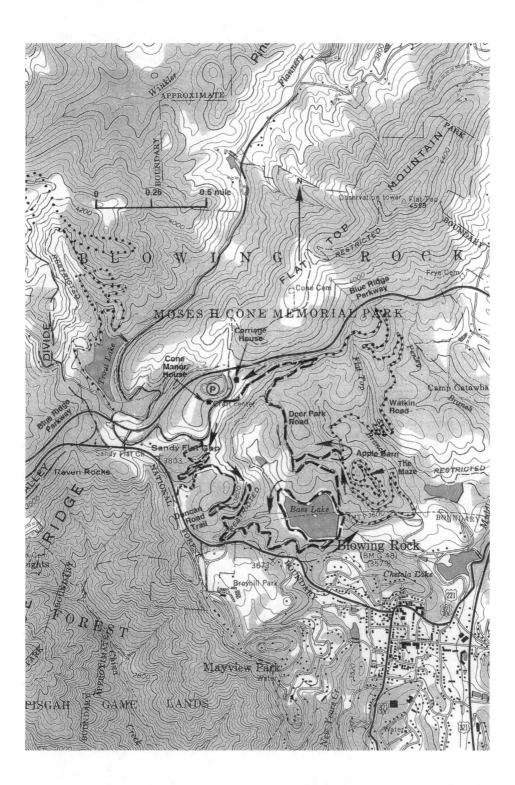

To get to the Cone Park area, follow the Blue Ridge Parkway to Milepost 294. Signs direct you to the Moses Cone Park, which is very near the towns of Blowing Rock and Boone, the latter the home of Appalachian State University.

While all of the trails are enjoyable to hike, the one most likely to acquaint you with the park is that of Duncan Road and Deer Park Road. This trail leads from the manor house and carriage barn west down a paved road for 0.4 mile to where the carriage road curves sharply left into the forest. Follow the carriage road through the mixed hardwood and evergreen forest.

As you curve through the gentle forest slopes, you will find that the trail is wide enough for four people to walk abreast, and the terrain is uniformly even and easy. The only slight inconvenience is that the trail is also used by equestrians and you may occasionally need to share the road with them.

At 0.6 mile you will pass, on your left, the Cone apple orchard, or the major part of it. At one time the orchard consisted of 40,000 apple trees, many of them bearing prize-winning fruit. The apple house, where apples were once packed and then shipped to various parts of the country, is still standing on the property.

On your right as you pass the apple orchard you can see in the forest hemlock trees, white pines, serviceberry or Juneberry trees, and even sugar maples. The latter tree is unusual in this part of the country, and its presence is due to the fact that Moses Cone had the sugar maples shipped from New England to the North Carolina mountains.

When you reach 1.6 miles you will see more and more mountain laurel, rhododendron (including purple or Catawba rhododendron, rosebay rhododendron, and mountain laurel), and cherry trees. The cherry trees were valued not only for their fruit but for their beautiful wood which was made into handcrafted furniture for the manor house.

Other members of the forest include black oak, red oak, and white oak, as well as hickory, birch, and red maple. At 3.2 miles you will reach the bass lake, which is visible from the front porch or veranda of the house. From the lake there is also a fine view of the manor house.

The bass lake, which includes more than 20 acres of water surface, is open to the public for fishing. Be sure to check with local officials for the types of licenses or permits required.

The trail leads around the bass lake, and the 0.8-mile loop, in a counterclockwise direction, will lead you through a huge forest of hemlock, across an open field or pasture area, and along a shoreline decorated in early summer by the blossoms of the laurel and rhododendron growth.

The next leg of the hike leads 0.5 mile through a huge evergreen forest and up an incline that, while not difficult, may become tiring because of its duration. A 0.2-mile spur trail leads to the old apple house. Return to the original trail and continue the climb for 0.7 mile through the same type of terrain to a point near the crest of the hill.

When you reach the crest you are within sight of the Blue Ridge Parkway. From the time you left the bass lake you have been on the part of the trail known as the Deer Park Road. At the top of the hill, curve severely back to the left and hike another 0.6 mile back to the manor house.

At the manor house you can investigate the carriage barn and stop in the craft shop.

Your hike thus far has been 5.7 miles. If you want to lengthen it without leaving the area, you can add 2.3 miles, thus making

Moses Cone Manor House

the trail 8 miles in length, by hiking the Maze, which is a trail consisting of five severe switchbacks that will bring you almost in contact with the parts of the trail just hiked.

At the end of the Maze you can turn back to the left and hit the apple-barn spur and rejoin the Deer Park Road. If you want still more hiking, you can take the Black Bottom Road 0.5 mile to where it intersects with the Watkin Road; the Watkin Road climbs the mountain and in 2.3 more miles intersects with the Deer Park Road and the main hiking trail or carriage trail.

This latter addition will bring the total mileage of the hike to 10.8. You can, by continuing to hike the connecting roads and trails, make the hike a 25-mile challenge.

20

Crabtree Falls Loop Trail

Total distance (loop): 2.5 miles

Hiking time: 1.75 hours

Vertical rise: 1,920 feet

Rating: Moderate to strenuous

Map: USGS 7.5' Celo

Located at Milepost 339.5 of the Blue Ridge Parkway is the Crabtree Falls Loop Trail (altitude 3,735 feet). The falls, which plummet for 60 feet, offer their spectacular beauty to the hiker at 1.0 mile into the trail.

The trailhead is designated at an information sign in the campground parking area of Crabtree Meadows, a delightful campground that can accommodate tents or camping trailers. At the campground you can purchase gas, enjoy a meal in the restaurant, have a picnic in the nearby picnic area, set up camp, or shop in the gift shop.

Crabtree Meadows is a 250-acre recreation area that borders part of the Pisgah National Forest. Years ago the flowering crabtree flourished in the forest along Crabtree Creek in Yancey County. Now most of the trees are gone, but in late spring the delightful blossoms of red, pink, or carmine punctuate the hillsides, and in mid- to late summer the tiny, tart, and wonderfully flavored apples are nearing their peak of ripeness. The major use of the apples is for jelly making or pickling: they are too tart to enjoy as eating apples.

But the major attraction of the recreation area is the waterfall at the bottom of a precipitous trail that starts from the parking area near the campground and goes to the footbridge over Crabtree Creek.

The trail is a loop, and you have the choice of completing the loop, once you reach the falls, or backtracking to the starting point. Either trip is great exercise and the forest alongside the trail is healthy and beautiful at all times of the year.

The trail starts through a hardwood for-

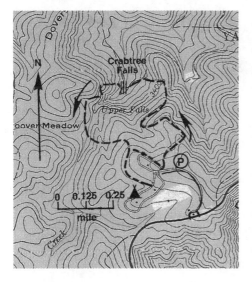

est composed mostly of white oak, shag-bark hickory, black locust, plus occasional maples and a variety of evergreens. The hike leads along a rocky trail that is some-times damp but seldom wet. The walking is good and very easy on the way down and rather strenuous on the way back up.

After hiking 800 feet on the trail to Crabtree Falls, you will find an intersecting trail from the campground area. At 0.4 mile, you can hear the water's rush from the falls, although they are not yet in sight. Continu-ing your descent, you encounter at the 0.5-mile point 27 stone steps with a small log handrail. After completing a series of switchbacks along the trail you will cross, at the 0.6-mile point, a footbridge which is two boards wide. Nearby are two-tier stone steps with 22 steps in the first series fol-lowed by 24 steps in the second section. From the bottom of the steps until you reach the waterfalls you will be hiking on a rocky trail.

When you reach the waterfalls, you will find the viewing opportunities are numer-ous, although from the bottom of the falls only. Photo opportunities are also great.

The distance to the waterfall is 0.9 mile. The return trip, if you complete the loop, is slightly longer (a total hike of 2.5 miles) but easier than the backtrack trail.

Along the return half of the loop you will pass, in season, through growths of wild orchids, trillium, great laurel, mountain lau-rel, and a wide range of ferns.

The return of the loop involves climbing many stone steps; these are set in soil and are well maintained. As soon as you cross the viewing bridge at the falls, you find the path leads to 22 rock steps followed by an acute turn and 9 steps more. Another 0.4 mile from the falls will bring you to 11 stone steps with a handrail. The trail continues at this point with a rock wall along the edge of the path before reaching another series of 12 stone steps.

Continuing the upward hike you will cross, via a rustic footbridge, Crabtree Creek and a series of smaller rills that feed the creek. The creek is 0.6 mile from the falls; wildflowers are 0.8 mile from the falls.

Complete your hike by emerging at the lower side of the campground and either crossing the campground or following the paved road back to the parking area.

The campground is a fee campground. There is no daily opening or closing time as such, and no admission is charged. You should allow one and three-quarters hours for an easy hike plus photographing of the waterfall. There is no fee for using the facili-ties, except for the campsites. Comfort sta-tions and fresh drinking water are also available.

This trail is one of the few described in this book that may be crowded, particularly on weekends. Partly because of the prox-imity of the campground to the hiking trail (the return half of the loop actually leads through part of the camping area) and

Crabtree Falls

Robert L. Williams

partly because of the popularity of the Blue Ridge Parkway in nearly all times of the year, there are often two dozen or more hikers on the trail.

If you want a calmer time, hike to the falls during the week, rather than on a weekend. Try hiking in the morning rather than in the afternoon. On a seasonal basis, spring is less crowded than the summer and fall months. Late autumn is also a good time to be on the trail.

For the best photos, carry along a wide-angle lens. Because it is difficult to stay back far enough to capture the entire height of the falls, you will need extra width so that you can stand on the wooden bridge across Crabtree Creek (the bridge you cross in order to continue the loop).

21

Craggy Gardens Trails

Total distance: 4.9 miles (4.3-mile loop; 0.6-mile backtrack)

Hiking time: 2.5 hours

Vertical rise: 3,640 feet

Rating: Moderate

Maps: USGS 7.5' Craggy Pinnacle and USGS 7.5' Montreat

The Craggy Gardens area consists of about 700 acres of hiking trails, scenic views, and some of the most beautiful displays of flowering shrubs anywhere in the mountains of North Carolina. The single greatest attraction to the recreational area is the annual blooming of the rhododendron.

In mid-June to late June, depending upon the weather in any particular year, the entire mountainside seems to be one giant flower garden. Each year thousands of people drive to the area to hike, enjoy the flowers, picnic, and delight in the scenery, which includes not only the rhododendron but scores of other wildflowers and exceptional views of the mountains and valleys of the area.

The hiking trails here are relatively short, but there is so much beauty along the trails that the tendency of the typical hiker is to stretch the trip into twice the time needed. The elevation of the flower displays is 5,220 feet. Atop Craggy Pinnacle the elevation is 5,892 feet.

To get to Craggy Gardens, leave the Blue Ridge Parkway at Milepost 364.5 and park at the visitor center. Here you can pick up information, including hiking trail maps, to enable you to make the best use of your time.

You can start the Craggy Gardens Trail, the first leg of the hike, at the south end of the parking lot at the visitor center. A somewhat hard-to-spot trail leads off the very end of the parking area and drops into a thicket of rhododendron. In early summer this thicket is ablaze with blossoms, and in most months the soil is wet or damp because sunlight rarely filters through the thick foliage.

Along the trail you will see information or

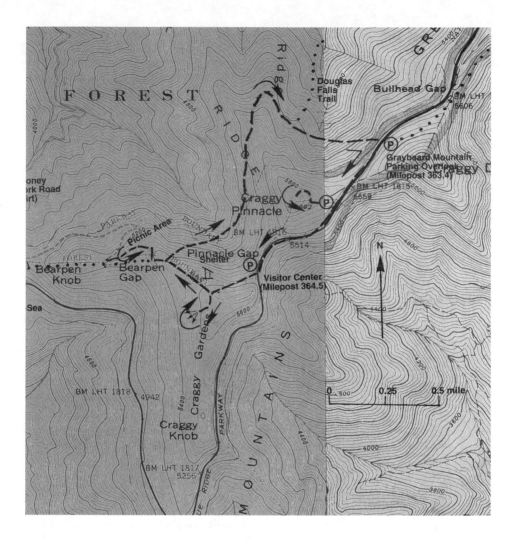

identification markers to help you to appreciate what you are seeing. Follow the trail and its steady climb, after a short descent, to a picnic shelter in an open area surrounded by rhododendron shrubs.

The picnic shelter was constructed decades ago from chestnut logs (back when the chestnut tree dominated the forests of the Southern highlands and very nearly dominated the economy of some parts of the South). Now, years after most wood would have deteriorated as a result of constant exposure to dampness, wind, and sunlight, the huge chestnut timbers appear to be as sound as they were when the picnic shelter was built.

The picnic shelter is 0.4 mile into the trail. From the shelter hike south up a knoll, also covered with rhododendron, to the end of the spur trail (which is 0.3 mile long) to a barrier that affords an overlook to the valleys south toward Asheville.

Backtrack to the shelter and continue the hike, which resumes on the west side of

A view over Catawba rhododendron toward Asheville

the shelter (you approached from the east). The trail continues, according to the trail map, to a large picnic area on the other side of the mountain. The trail map indicates that the round- trip to the picnic area is 0.8 mile, but expect to hike considerably longer than 0.4 mile in order to reach the picnic area.

On your backtrack hike, 0.3 mile after leaving the picnic area (which has water, comfort stations, and tables), you will intersect with the Mountains-to-Sea Trail. Turn left and follow the Mountains-to-Sea Trail for 1.5 miles until it joins the Douglas Falls Trail.

Along the Mountains-to-Sea Trail you will find generally easy hiking as far as footing is concerned and superb vistas awaiting at many points along the way.

The Mountains-to-Sea Trail swings northeast for 0.7 mile and then curves gently back north for 0.3 mile before swinging abruptly to the southeast for 0.5 mile. At the union of the Mountains-to-Sea Trail and the Douglas Falls Trail you will be one mile from the parkway.

At about Milepost 363.6, you will emerge from the trail. From this point you may hike a little less than 1 mile along the parkway back to your car or, if you have a second vehicle, arrange to leave the second vehicle at Milepost 363.4, which is the overlook for Gray-beard Mountain.

Between the visitor center and Graybeard Mountain you will find another parking area at Craggy Pinnacle. For a short but spectacular hike, take the 0.3-mile trail from the parking lot to the peak of Craggy Pinnacle.

The trail to the top of Craggy Pinnacle is wide and easy, but steep. You climb among the rhododendron shrubs for the entire hike. When you arrive at the top, you will have a splendid view in 360 degrees. You can see all of the major peaks in the entire area.

22

Green Knob Trail

Total distance (loop): 2.4 miles

Hiking time: 2.5 hours

Vertical rise: 2,040 feet

Rating: Moderate

Map: USGS 7.5' Boone

This trail makes available the best characteristics of the Appalachian Mountains generally and the Blue Ridge Mountains in particular. It is ideally suited for the times when you don't have enough daylight left for a long hike but you're still looking for a good workout.

You can stretch the hike comfortably into a three-hour jaunt, or longer, or you can compress it, for a real physical workout, into two hours. Whatever the time, you will get to see several different types of terrain and vegetation during a short period of time.

Start the hike at the Sims Pond overlook just north of the bridge at Price Lake (at Blue Ridge Parkway Milepost 297) by descending the rock stairway from the parking area down to the spillway from Sims Pond. A wooden footbridge spans the spillway, and you will hike across the earthen dam that forms the impoundment at Sims Pond. From the parking area to the opposite side of the pond you will hike 0.1 mile, or slightly more.

In all seasons you will likely see some form of aquatic life at the pond. On winter days wild ducks are frequent visitors; these birds are so accustomed to human beings that you can approach very near to them and observe them at your leisure.

From the hillside above the pond you can often see large trout swimming or feeding near the banks. For those who wish to fish at the pond, there are several restrictions. You must use artificial lures with single hooks only. Treble-hook lures are decidedly illegal. Creel limit is five trout, and

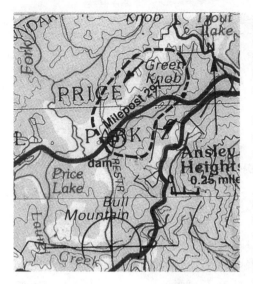

the size limit is seven inches. Any type of natural bait in your possession is illegal.

On the far side of the pond you will veer northward through a dense thicket of laurel and rhododendron. As you hike you will follow (and cross several times) feeder streams flowing into the pond. At several points the streams are very narrow, and when they are too wide to step across you will find stepping-stones that make crossing easy and dry.

Ten minutes into the hike (0.4 mile) you will reach a small spillway on one of the feeder streams (Sims Creek), a remnant of some dam used decades ago and now fallen into disuse but remaining just off the trail, no more than 15 feet from the clearly marked path.

Hovering above the laurel thickets are huge poplar, hickory, fir, and occasional oak trees. Alongside the trail at 0.5 mile stands an immense fir tree so large that two grown men would not be able to reach around it. The tree overshadows all of the other growth along the trail.

At 0.6 mile there is a bench beside the trail, but the hike is easy enough that most well-conditioned hikers would not need to

rest at this point. The trail descends and borders the creek so closely that you must walk along a sloping bank and hold to overhanging tree limbs in order to keep from getting wet feet.

You will hear highway traffic (from the Blue Ridge Parkway) as you emerge from the hardwood forest, and within 300 yards of the huge fir tree you will see the outline of the parkway through the trees.

Your route takes you directly under the parkway, and you may find it startling to realize how high the parkway is from the streambed. Almost half a mile of the belly of the parkway is visible as you leave one hardwood forest and enter another, both within 50 yards of each other. You will realize that in fact you did not leave a forest but simply entered the cutaway zone for clearing under the highway.

As you pass under the parkway you will cross the feeder stream several times and then begin a gradual climb through a dense hardwood forest. The trail winds in several directions before you emerge into a pasture with a carpet of thick grass. At the very edge of the clearing (at mile 0.8) you will see a chimney in the woods to your left, just past a barbed-wire fence. Here you will see the remnants of an old farmstead house, with the fireplace and chimney still intact. The house has passed into history.

From the barbed-wire fence that is the boundary between the forest and the pasture, you will see a small tree with a bench under it in the middle of the pasture. While you rest under the thorn tree you can enjoy the beauty of this green knob, which is the highest point on the trail, and the pasture, which is a picture-postcard scene.

This point is one of the best photo spots along the trail, if you wish to take photos of a serene mountain pasture. As you leave the tree and bench, you will join a pasture

Rhododendron and mountain laurel are at their peak in June

Robert L. Williams

road. You are at mile 1.5 when you join the road. The hike is easy along the road, and as you move through the hardwood forest you will begin to descend toward the parkway once again.

The road is rather steep, but the footing is good in all but extremely wet weather, and you can hike comfortably as you move downward and enter another pasture. Move at a leisurely pace along the descent road, because from your altitude you have a magnificent view of Price Lake to the west.

On hot August days the haze may thwart your chance of getting the maximum beauty of the view, but in fall, mid-winter, and spring the view is clear and highly rewarding.

The trail descends into the pasture of a working farm (at mile 1.8) where on any given day you may see farmers and their equipment as they cut and bale hay, work with cattle, or perform other necessary chores. It is startling to see such industry after having spent the past hour or more deep in the forests or on a hillside of a secluded pasture knob.

Between you and the farm work, the pasture slopes sharply, and on the hillside you can see the remnants of a foundation wall. The wall is in good condition, but there is nothing to suggest what sort of structure may have existed there earlier.

Go sharply left at the bottom of the hill and pass through the barbed-wire barricade that separates the pasture from the forest. The remainder of the hike is slightly uphill but very easy.

At mile 2.2 you will notice that the rhododendron and laurel growth begins to thicken, and you can again hear the sound of traffic on the parkway. Almost without warning you will pass through a small thicket of laurel and you will see the parkway in front of you. Your vehicle will be parked on the other side of the parkway (the south side) and slightly to your north.

The loop trail has offered you in rapid succession a nice pond, a hike alongside Sims Creek, a close encounter with some stepping-stones and at times a wet trail, the underside of the parkway, a delightful green knob (for which the trail was named), pastures, hardwood forests, and farmland.

The variety along the trail is one of its strongest points. At this elevation the blossoms of the laurel and rhododendron will be at their peak in mid-June. Wildflowers of many varieties will be in bloom from late April through October. The denseness of the laurel slicks prevents frost from killing blooms, and there is a prolonged autumn season in this part of North Carolina.

If your time and energy permit, you can hike three very fine trails without having to drive more than a mile, once you have reached Price Lake. In addition to the Green Knob Trail loop, there is the Price Lake Loop, a very easy trail of 2.5 miles that can be hiked without difficulty (see chapter 17), and the Boone Fork Trail, also a loop, of 4.9 miles (see chapter 16).

The total hiking in this area is slightly less than 10 miles and involves a hiking time of 5 to 6 hours. Travel time between trailheads is less than five minutes. If you decide to hike all three trails in one day, start with the Boone Fork Trail, follow it with the Green Knob Trail, and conclude with the Price Lake Loop Trail, which is by far the easiest of the trio and takes less time.

23

E. B. Jeffress Park Trails

Total distance: 2.2 miles (1.2-mile loop; 1-mile backtrack)

Hiking time: 1.5 hours

Vertical rise: 600 feet

Rating: Easy

Map: USGS 7.5' Maple Springs

To hike two delightful and very easy trails, drive to Blue Ridge Parkway Milepost 272 and enter E. B. Jeffress Park. Here there are picnic tables, rest rooms, water, and two nice hikes that can be made on a day when your major desire is to enjoy a relaxing walk, see some spectacular scenery, make a leisurely trip into the past to rub elbows with some American mountain heritage, and in general enjoy being outdoors.

The first trail leads in a loop to the seemingly endless waterfall known as the Cascades. The Cascades are formed as Falls Creek begins to slide gently down the rocky face of the mountain and then descend sharply, and finally drop precipitously for several hundred feet.

Falls Creek begins as a spring and a series of tiny and clear tributaries near the top of the mountain, and as it flows down the slope it is joined by a series of other rills until it is a fairly large creek.

As the streams become Falls Creek, so begins a journey that takes the stream to the valley below, where it joins the Yadkin River, which in turn flows into the Pee Dee River and finally into the Atlantic Ocean at Winyah Bay, South Carolina.

Along the Cascades Trail, you can see a wide range of wildflowers and forest growth. One of the most interesting growths is dog hobble, an attractive evergreen matting of leaves and branches that grow in a twining fashion. The tangled growth is named, according to older residents of the area, because a bear hound, loping along with its nose to the ground and paying attention to little other than the

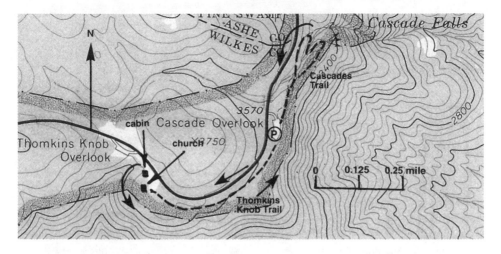

bear's scent, would plunge into the thicket or low growth and become hopelessly entangled or "hobbled" by the foliage and thus become helpless prey to the angered bear.

Other prominent vegetation along the trail includes the tulip poplar or yellow poplar, which in rare instances can reach a height of 200 feet but averages 100 feet in height and has a trunk diameter of up to 12 feet but averages 4 feet. This majestic tree, which is often arrow-straight and limbless until near the top, yields exceptionally good logs of up to 60 or 70 feet that will produce 8-by-10 timbers that are free of knots and defects along their entire lengths.

The wood of the green tulip poplar is soft, easily cut, and extremely heavy until cured, at which time it is light and still easy to cut. Eventually it cures into a very hard wood suitable for all types of building projects. Log cabins made of these giant trees have lasted for more than 200 years in the South—as long as the cured wood is kept dry. Prolonged dampness causes decay.

This tree is sometimes called catface poplar because, when the log is cut straight across, the heartwood often has a dark shape that closely resembles the head and ears of a cat. The tree lives as long as 300 years, and in warm weather it produces beautiful flowers resembling tulips. These "tulips" range in color from light green to orange and are two inches high.

The tulip poplar, which is one of the most common trees along the Cascades Trail, keeps company with hickory, black cherry, white pine, chestnut, black walnut, basswood, butternut, and serviceberry trees; however, it is intolerant of oaks and is rarely found growing in oak groves.

Another common tree along the trail is the black locust, which demonstrates two highly interesting qualities. First, its roots act as hosts to nitrogen-fixing bacteria, so the tree actually enriches rather than depletes the soil. Second, the tree is so decay-resistant that it is often used for fence posts, railroad ties, and telephone-pole arms. It has numerous uses on Southern farms.

Seeds of the black locust, like those of the tulip poplar, are commonly eaten by quail, deer, and rabbits. The roots, leaves, and bark are poisonous to man, however, and should not be ingested or chewed.

Two varieties of hickory trees that are common to the trail are pignut, or broom hickory, and shagbark, or shellbark, hickory. Two of the most majestic trees in the Cas-

---

cades Trail area are the scarlet oak and black oak, both of which are hardy, durable, and virtually free of insect problems.

Red maples and less-common sugar maples may be found along the trail, or they may be seen in the distant forests above the trail as you hike toward the Cascades. Even though the red maple is often found in low-lying areas and swamps, it is found as high as 4,000-foot elevations in northern North Carolina and Virginia.

Witch hazel is another tree common to the trail. The witch hazel, which reaches a maximum height of 25 feet, is noted for its traditional use in making camp brooms and toothbrushes (for campers of earlier ages) as well as for its highly distinctive odor. The leaves and twigs of the shrub or small tree are used as additives to rubbing alcohol, and small twigs on a campfire produce the familiar fragrance of the witch hazel. One interesting quality of the tree is its resistance to wilting. So able is the tree to retain its vigor, even when cut, that it was for years recommended by the United States Army for use in camouflage.

Rosebay rhododendron appears frequently along the trail. This low-growing tree or shrub grows so thick, and the branches tend to crisscross each other in such a dense fashion as it matures, that the impenetrable thickets are called rhododendron hells.

You will strike the trail beside the rest rooms and water fountain. The pathway, an easy, wide trail, will divide within 0.2 mile. Because the trail is a modified loop, you may take either direction. The left, or north, direction will lead you along a gentle slope and beside a small stream that, like so many mountain streams, seems to grow slightly larger every few feet.

You will cross rustic and unique footbridges as you hike into the dark woods where the laurel and rhododendron block out the sun, and almost as soon as you cross the bridges you will hear the roar of the cascades. When you reach the patch of dog hobble on the left, or northeast, side of the trail, at the 0.6-mile point, you are almost at the top of the waterfall.

The trail then curves sharply and you will descend a long series of steps to a point where the trail divides. The right spur will lead you to an overlook so close to the water that you will be sprayed by mist on a windy day. You can see the overlook, which is only 40 feet from the trail division. You will stop along a high wall that is designed to keep sight-seers from becoming too adventurous and falling over the rocky cliffs. Please stay on established trails.

When you return to the trail dividing point, the left-hand trail will take you to an even lower overlook that is only 100 feet or so beyond the first. Here you will get another delightful view of the waterfall. You can see the falls above and below you, and in either direction is a rewarding spectacle.

To return to the parking area, take the left-hand trail at the fork 30 feet from the first bridge. This trail completes the loop and brings you out of the forest near the point where you started.

At the far end of the parking lot you will find the Thomkins Knob Trail, a 0.5-mile, very easy trail that leads through a deeply forested section of woodland to a grassy opening where stand the ancient Cool Spring Baptist Church and the Jesse Brown settler's cabin.

In the early years of this century, circuit-riding preachers Willie Lee or Bill Church held meetings at the site. Farmers and families from miles around would ride to the spot and listen to the old-time religion as it was expounded by the itinerant ministers, who often spent the nights in the Jesse Brown cabin 100 yards to the northwest.

The lower falls at Fall Creek Cascades

Robert L. Williams

At the meadow you can enjoy the shade of the church shelter, which was intended as a relief from bad weather, and you can walk around the cabin, which is not open to the public.

You can hike back the same way you arrived. At this point, you are very near Doughton Park, also on the Blue Ridge Parkway, where you will find an abundance of hiking trails for your enjoyment.

24

Tanawha Trail

Total distance (one way): 13.5 miles

Hiking time: 5 hours

Vertical rise: 6,920 feet

Rating: Moderate to strenuous

Maps: USGS 7.5' Grandfather Mountain, USGS 7.5' Valle Crucis, and USGS 7.5' Boone

One of the newest hiking trails along the Blue Ridge Parkway, the Tanawha Trail offers an amazing variety of mountain experiences and scenic delights: waterfalls, overlooks that provide fine views of distant peaks and nearby valleys, a fragile and antique ecosystem, tunnels of laurel and rhododendron, glades filled with an array of wildflowers, and an unusual variety of wildlife.

Completed in September 1987, the Tanawha (the name is the Cherokee Indian word for "fabulous hawk or eagle") Trail starts at the Beacon Heights parking area (Blue Ridge Parkway Milepost 305.5) at the juncture with Beacon Heights Trail. From that point it proceeds north and parallels the parkway roughly around the south border of Grandfather Mountain. It ends at the juncture of the Boone Fork Trail near Price Lake, one of the most beautiful bodies of water along the entire Blue Ridge Parkway.

Weather is unpredictable in this part of the state, and you may encounter sunshine, rain, snow, and wind, all on the same day as you hike. Carry along rain gear and proper all-weather clothing.

Two unique characteristics set the trail apart from nearly all other hiking trails in the nation. The first is that the trail starts under the world-famous Linn Cove Viaduct, the marvel of engineering that completed the Blue Ridge Parkway in 1987. The parkway previously had ended in the Linn Cove area, as for years the federal government sought to find a way to complete the parkway without damaging the fragile environmental status of the area.

The Linn Cove viaduct as seen from the eastern slope of Grandfather Mountain

When engineers completed plans for the viaduct, which seems to cling to the side of the mountain without becoming an actual part of it, the land was donated so that the parkway could be completed without man's encroachment on the world of nature that had been preserved for so many years on the huge stone formation that is said to resemble an aged man as he sleeps.

The second delight of the trail is that you can start or stop at a number of locations so that you do not have to worry about two cars or an inordinately long trek. If you have two cars, you can park one at the north end of the trail and then drive the other to the Beacon Heights Parking area.

If you have access to only one vehicle, you can hike the trail in segments and return to move the car farther north so that you never find yourself a discouraging distance from your vehicle.

Starting from Beacon Heights, you will encounter the roughest terrain by far almost as soon as you pass under the viaduct. You will encounter immense boulders with the trail winding upward and among the boulders for the first 15 minutes to half an hour of hiking. These boulders provide narrow tunnel-like passageways; you will find yourself in deep recesses that are almost caves at one moment and a few steps later you will be moving across the tops of adjacent boulders.

Within 0.6 mile the trail levels out and you move easily through a deep cove of birch and beech trees. The trail is wide and almost level until you reach Wilson Creek with its impressive cascades, a distance of 2.7 miles north.

You can leave the trail and return to the parkway at Stack Rock, 0.8 mile from the start of the trail, if you prefer. If you continue north past Wilson Creek, the trail crosses a huge rock formation featuring large flat

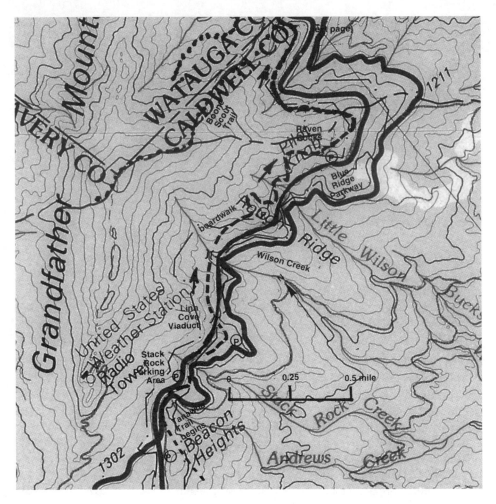

rocks and extremely easy walking. After you cross the rock field, you will begin to climb sharply again until you reach Rough Ridge (another departure point from the trail) and its 200-foot-long boardwalk, which provides a superb overlook view of the Linn Cove Viaduct, South Mountain, Hawksbill Mountain, and Table Rock Mountain.

You are now 4.8 miles from Beacon Heights, and as you cross the vast flat stone surface you will enter almost immediately a thick forest of poplar, yellow birch, and oak trees that provide welcome shade in warm months and exciting color in autumn.

Raven Rocks is the next major point along the trail. You will emerge from the hardwood forest and into another vast expanse of flat-topped boulders and a natural rock garden that features ferns in profusion growing from the crevices in the rocks and cascading down like a small green stream. A wide variety of wildflowers in bloom may be seen from early spring until the first killing frost in autumn, usually in early October.

Three miles from Raven Rocks you enter a thicket of laurel and rhododendron that extends for almost a mile. The shrubs are in

---

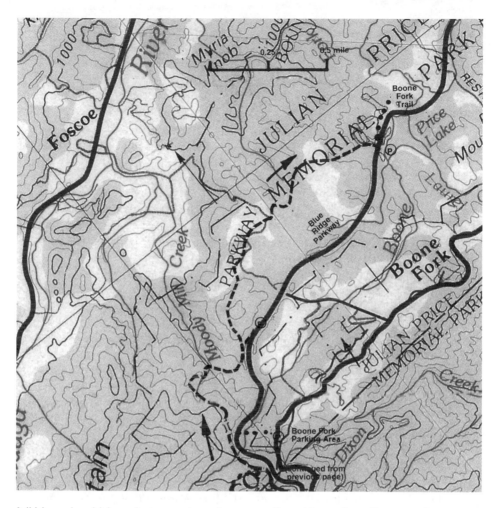

full bloom in mid-June, but as early as June 1 and as late as July 10 you can find a rewarding number of blooms.

As delectable as the flowers are to the eye, do not forget that both laurel and rhododendron contain a highly toxic sap that can be fatal if ingested in significant amounts. Chewing on a twig can be sufficient to cause instant and severe illness. The Native Americans who inhabited areas thickly overgrown with these two shrubs used the poisonous sap to "treat" their arrows, and one tribe is said to have used it as a suicide potion.

Do not leave the trail at any point, except to take a departure trail to the parkway. While the Tanawha Trail is very easy once you pass the first half-hour's walk, the terrain is treacherous if you leave the trail. In warm months there are copperheads and rattlers active in the area, and there is always the danger of falling on the slippery rocks in the off-trail areas.

Though rare, wildcats, skunks, and other animals are occasionally spotted in the region, and bears are still present in this part of the North Carolina mountains. Groundhogs, rabbits, foxes, squirrels, and several other smaller animals are abundant.

Yellow jackets and hornets can be a problem if you leave the trail. These insects are content to endure the presence of hikers along the trail but they deeply resent intrusions into their terrain.

The greatest danger by far is not what will happen to you but what you will do to the ecology if you leave the trail. Fragile plants, root systems, and precarious rocks can be dislodged to the detriment of the entire section of the trail.

The Tanawha Trail is joined by the Daniel Boone Scout Trail and the Grandfather Trail 2.9 miles north of Raven Rocks. You must purchase a hiking permit to travel on either of these trails. There is no fee at any time on the Tanawha Trail, but do not leave it to make brief excursions along other trails.

For detailed information on hiking fees and locations where the permits may be secured, see chapter 25; you may also contact the backcountry manager at Grandfather Mountain at the address given in the "Introduction" of this book in the section entitled "Information Sources."

After you reach the Boone Fork portion of the trail (3.8 miles north of Raven Rocks), you will suddenly emerge from the deeper thickets and woods and into an open field. Several waterfalls are visible from the trail and there are open fields of wildflowers along this part of the trail.

In rapid succession you will reach an old logging road, then a hardwood forest, and the open fields where you will cross the Holloway Mountain Road, apple orchards, an old graveyard, and open pastureland.

The trail joins the Boone Fork Trail, which leads into the Price Lake Campground, where the Tanawha Trail ends.

You have seven parking areas where you may leave the trail if you wish. You can start at Price Lake, if you prefer, and work your way south, saving the most difficult part of the trail for last.

You can camp at Price Lake if you wish. The area is part of the National Park Service territory and you must pay a fee if you camp in the warm months. There is also hiking, trout fishing, and canoeing at the lake.

North Carolina is one of the most beautiful states in the Union and is rightly proud of its scenery and cleanliness. You are urged to leave all flowers for others and to refrain from cutting or breaking tree limbs or saplings.

If you see any indications of fires or emergency situations as you travel the Tanawha Trail area you are urged to call 1-800-PARKWAY. If you need general parkway information you can call (704) 259-0701.

25

Grandfather Trail and Daniel Boone Scout Trail

Total distance (one way): 6.7 miles

Hiking time: 8 hours, or overnight

Vertical rise: 3,720 feet

Rating: Strenuous

Map: USGS 7.5' Grandfather Mountain

At Grandfather Mountain you can take advantage of not only a mountain with hiking trails but an entire outdoor recreation facility, including overlooks, a nature museum, picnic area, visitor center, wildlife habitats, and a mile-high swinging bridge.

The wildlife habitats include such animals as black bears (and their cubs), cougars or mountain lions, deer, eagles, and groundhogs. The museum holds displays showing the history and the present conditions at Grandfather Mountain, which is the highest peak in the Blue Ridge Mountains.

The hiking-trail system includes at least eight trails that are among the most difficult in the South. Of these trails, two of the most fascinating and challenging are the Grandfather Trail and the Daniel Boone Scout Trail. These, combined, offer 9.9 miles of hiking adventure and spectacular scenery. You can also enjoy overnight camping if you do not plan to attempt to hike the entire two-trail distance in one day.

Fees are charged at the entrance gate for auto access to Grandfather Mountain and for the hiking trail system. It is possible to buy a hiking permit without paying the gate fee, which is $9 per adult (at this writing) and $5 for children from 4 to 12 years of age. Hiking permits cost $4.50 per day for adults and $2.50 for children age 4 to 12. You can also buy a season pass for the hiking trails or the gate permit.

The trails here are extremely interesting and well kept, and there are special considerations that must be observed. Before you begin to hike, be certain to obtain a trail map and read the regulations carefully.

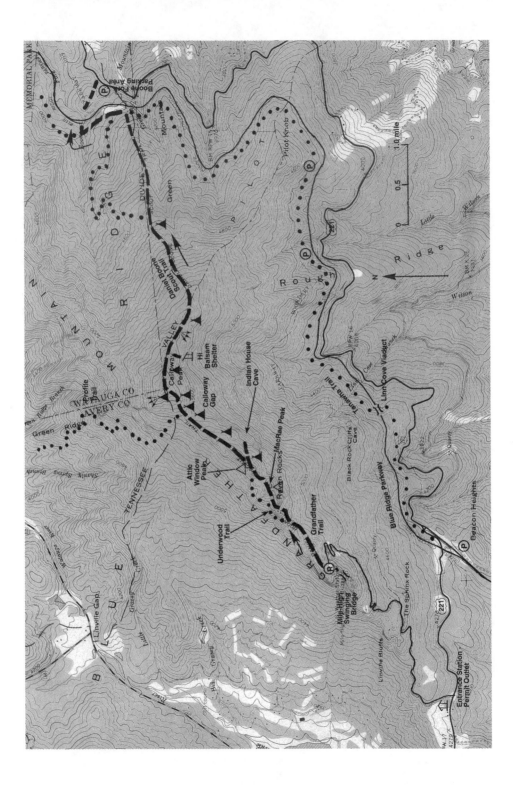

Fishing, for instance, is not allowed anywhere on the mountain, despite the fact that there are streams with native trout in them.

In other areas, fires are not permitted for camping purposes. Where fires are permitted, you must use only existing fire rings. You cannot build new ones. Fires may be fueled only by deadfall; you may not cut any standing tree or part of one.

If all of this seems unduly strict, you must realize that the mountain is a fragile piece of history and biology, and there are areas where unauthorized hiking may damage the ecology severely, and fire-hazard areas where one thoughtless act may eradicate untold amounts of timber, animals, and very rare plants.

To reach the entrance gate to Grandfather Mountain, leave the Blue Ridge Parkway at Milepost 305 and head north on US 221. In 1 mile you will enter at the gate and drive to the top of the mountain. To hike the Grandfather Trail and the Daniel Boone Scout Trail, you will start across the parking lot from the Mile-High Swinging Bridge.

Hikers are warned that if you drive to the Swinging Bridge parking area to hike and you are not back by the time the park closes, a search party will be sent to look for you. So when you start the trail at the top, at the Swinging Bridge, you should make arrangements either to return by the closing time posted on signs, usually 7 p.m. in summer, 4 p.m. in winter, or to have someone drop you off and then drive the car to an outside pickup site like the Boone Fork parking area at Milepost 298 on the Blue Ridge Parkway.

At the start of the trail there is a huge sign showing all of the trails on the mountain and a very stern warning: "Are you ready to climb ladders up sheer cliffs? If not, turn back now. This trail is not for first-time hikers. It is steep, very rocky, strenuous, and subject to lightning strikes. Please take this warning seriously. This is one of the South's most difficult trails."

Hikers are also warned that they will need one to two liters of water, snacks, and rain gear. All experienced hikers realize that proper shoes or boots are a necessity on any real mountain trail, but on this trail the admonition to dress properly has a very strong meaning.

Winds up to 100 miles per hour have been recorded on the mountain; and in winter, deep snows, freezing rain, and below-zero temperatures are not unusual. The warning stands at all times of the year that if bad weather strikes, you are to get off the mountain immediately.

When you start Grandfather Trail, it is rugged and rather strenuous from the outset. The footing is rocky and uncertain. The trail weaves, dips, and climbs. Within 0.2 mile you will find the first of hiker's aids—this one in the form of a rope stretched from top to bottom of a climb to assist hikers in making their way up or down the incline.

You will hike through rhododendron and later through evergreen forests, and within 0.5 mile a trail spur or alternate route called the Underwood Trail forks left. You have the option of taking this trail, which is far easier, or hiking the regular Grandfather Trail.

Grandfather Trail leads to MacRae Peak (elevation 5,939) and to Attic Window Peak (elevation 5,949). At MacRae Peak you will reach the ladders that are needed to ascend and descend the sheer cliffs.

The first campsite is at mile 1.2. At 1.3 miles a spur trail leads to Indian House Cave, and at mile 1.5 you will reach the second campsite. No fires are permitted at this site.

At 2.2 miles you will reach a fork in the trail where Calloway Trail leads to the left. The trail to the right now becomes the Daniel Boone Scout Trail. There are two campsites at the fork in the trail and a third

The Mile-High Swinging Bridge

and fourth are located at the 0.1- and 0.2-mile points on the new trail.

Along the way you will pass Calloway Gap (elevation 5,600) on your right, and at 0.3 mile you will reach Calloway Peak (elevation 5,964). At 0.4 of the Daniel Boone Scout Trail you will reach an overlook above the Linn Cove Viaduct, one of the most unusual engineering feats along the Blue Ridge Parkway.

You now have 1.8 miles (approximately) left on the Daniel Boone Scout Trail. At 0.1 mile from the overlook you will find another overnight area. You will be descending at a comfortable rate for the remainder of the hike, which leads through hardwood forests.

At 2.5 miles you will intersect with the Tanawha Trail, which parallels the Blue Ridge Parkway. Hike 1.5 miles north on the Tanawha Trail until you intersect with the 0.5-mile trail to the Boone Fork parking area.

Graveyard Fields Waterfalls Trail

Total distance (loop): 3.2 miles

Hiking time: 1.5 hours

Vertical rise: 1,920 feet

Rating: Moderate

Map: USGS 7.5' Shining Rock

It isn't often that graveyards are associated with paradise, but the Graveyard Fields area of western North Carolina comes as close to being an Eden as any place in the state. In a nutshell, the area is a narrow mountain valley that opens with a waterfall at the extreme western end and closes with a waterfall at the other end. Between the two waterfalls, there is virtually anything that the hiker could want or expect.

The hiking trail is easy, well marked, and beautiful. The two waterfalls are unusually impressive for a stream as small as the Yellowstone Prong, and at the lower falls there is a natural and nearly perfect swimming pool where the water is icy and clear.

Between the two waterfalls, the Yellowstone Prong has carved the bedrock of the valley into wonderfully ornate designs, and the layered rocks reveal unusual coloring as well as erosion artwork.

Alongside the river there are literally thousands of wild blueberry bushes, interspersed with gooseberries, blackberries, dewberries, and other delectables. The gentle slope leading away from the river is also covered with the berry bushes, and in the evenings small herds of deer emerge from the forest covering and feast in season on the berries.

Overnight camping is permitted, and many hikers like to carry in their sleeping bag, camp by the river, and perhaps enjoy the added bonus of a fresh trout for supper. All state fish and game laws apply to fishermen and hunters.

To reach this graveyard paradise, drive down the Blue Ridge Parkway to Milepost

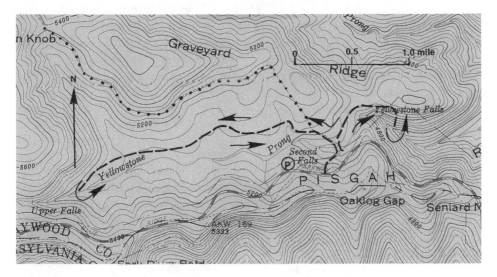

418.8. The area is near both the Cherokee Indian Reservation and the Great Smoky Mountain National Park to the south, and Mount Pisgah, Asheville, and Mount Mitchell to the north.

The name "Graveyard Fields" was applied to the area, once rich in chestnut trees and other prime timbers, when more than 25,000 acres of forest were burned by arsonists in 1925.

The forest fires broke out at the beginning of what had promised to be the best trout season in years. More than 200 anglers, young and old, had entered the Pisgah National Forest to take part in the opening day of trout season when the first columns of smoke were noticed, and before the fires were extinguished, many people had to take refuge in the icy waters of the trout streams.

Survivors reported that they waded into the stream, ducked their heads under water, and stayed submerged as long as they could before they had to face the searing heat anew. Some removed part of their clothing and wrapped their heads in the soaked garments.

One fisherman reported seeing leaves that floated in the stream suddenly ignite from the intense heat.

After the fire, the area was dotted with charred stumps of trees that looked, from a distance, like ancient tombstones. The name "Graveyard Fields" has stuck ever since.

In late April of 1942 another forest fire raged through the Pisgah National Forest and destroyed 12,000 acres of timber and forest lands. Within three weeks, 25,000 more acres of forest land were burned, apparently as a result of arsonists. Because it was in the midst of World War II, many local persons believed that the fires were set as part of an Axis espionage and terrorist effort. Patriotic feelings ran so high that some parents in the area named their children after General Douglas MacArthur.

When you approach the parking area alongside the Blue Ridge Parkway, you will be able to see the waterfalls, from either direction, at Milepost 418 before you reach the overlook. From the north you can see the lower falls, and there is a pull-off where you can park and enjoy the view before you begin the hike.

From the south you must look to the left shortly after leaving the Devil's Courthouse area. The waterfall is visible briefly as you make your approach.

When you park, you will see a map and other information displayed near a set of steps that will lead you into the valley. Study the map before entering to get a good overview of the land below you.

You will descend the steps into a thicket of rhododendron and laurel, both of which grow virtually everywhere in the area, and the soil beneath them is composed of four to six inches of peat underlain by a gray podzolic surface horizon.

As you hike deeper you will enter a forest composed of red spruce, Fraser fir, yellow birch, mountain ash, wood sorrel, poplars, and a scattering of oaks, pines, cedars, and dogwoods. The purple laurel is easily recognized by its brilliant blossoms in May and June in the area.

The predominant ground covers are *Aster acuminatus*, *Aster diveracatus*, *Athyrium asplenoides*, and *Eupatorium rugosum*. The laurel shrubland, often called laurel slicks or heath balds, includes mountain laurel, fetterbush, and highbush blueberry.

In addition there are many samplings of hay-scented fern, galax, and ground pine. Growing alongside trails are common blackberry, angelica, and dodder. At least 32 varieties of herbs may be found on or near the trail.

The open land above the trail includes growths of oat grass, hair grass, and timothy. On the upper part of the trail you will see serviceberry—with its profusion of delicate white blossoms that bloom in early April in the lower elevations and as late as May in higher elevations—mountain holly, and fire cherry.

Bush honeysuckle, bluets, and running club moss may be found growing among the deciduous plants, with nodding sedge and manna grass less plentiful.

The trail to the bottom of the slope descends gently 250 feet to a wooden footbridge 0.2 mile from the parking area. The trail is paved until you are within 50 feet of the river.

Stop at the river and enjoy the fantastic designs carved into the stone by the stream. The river flows over huge expanses of rock that reflect a wide range of colors, from darkest grays to light reds and faint orange.

When you cross the footbridge, turn right and follow the trail (which remains wet much of the year because of the abundant rainfall in the area) and follow it 0.2 mile to where it curves sharply to the right and descends 20 feet to the base of the lower falls.

Backtrack to the bridge, when you have enjoyed the lower falls to your satisfaction, and follow the trail, which is almost level, as it winds upstream, following the river.

Hike upstream 1.2 miles to view Upper Falls. Along the way you will pass through blackberry and blueberry bushes (with ripe fruit, respectively, in late June and July to early August and in very late August and early September). Labor Day is the traditional day for hundreds of people to descend upon Graveyard Fields for the berry-picking delights. At night viewed from the parking area, their campfires twinkle like so many stars in the dark valley.

At mile 0.6 as you hike from the footbridge you will meet a trail that returns to the south end of the parking overlook. You began the hike from the north end of the parking area and the return loop trail will bring you back to the parking area via the south part of the loop.

The elevation at the parking area is 5,200 feet; at the footbridge the elevation is approximately 5,000 feet. By the time you reach the lower falls you have descended nearly 50 feet, and at Upper Falls

The top of Yellowstone Falls in autumn.

you have regained most of the descent from the footbridge.

While the lower waterfall is a wide cascade, the Upper Falls are both higher and steeper in the descent. Do not attempt to climb the rocks alongside the falls. The footing is slippery from the falls.

As you return from the falls, you can cross the river and follow the return loop trail back to the parking lot. If you start the hike early in the morning or conclude it late in the evening, your chances of seeing several deer are much better.

The best times of the year to hike the Graveyard Fields trail are May through October. The best time of day, to avoid the frequent rainstorms, is either early morning or after three o'clock in the afternoon.

27

Mount Jefferson and New River Trails

Total distance (loops): 1.7 miles and 1.0 mile

Hiking time: 1.5 hours and 0.5 hour

Vertical rise: 960 feet and 400 feet

Rating: Easy

Map: USGS 7.5'Jefferson

In the northwest corner of North Carolina flows the New River, America's oldest river and the second oldest in the world. Nearby Mount Jefferson (elevation 4,900 feet) was carved from the early waters of the New River and other erosive streams. Both landmarks contain trails that can be hiked in one day at a casual pace, allowing the hiker to enjoy the natural beauty as well as to absorb the history of the area.

The hiking trails in Mount Jefferson State Park include a main trail, which climbs to a North Carolina Forest Service lookout tower, a trail along the ridge to Luther's Rock Overlook, and the Rhododendron Trail which is a self-guiding nature trail. The trails intersect and have a combined distance of 1.7 miles, with a total time for hiking at a moderate pace of one hour and 30 minutes.

The park, officially named Mount Jefferson State Park in 1955 in honor of the Jefferson family, covers 541 acres. Peter Jefferson, the father of Thomas Jefferson, was one of the surveyors of the North Carolina–Virginia state line and also owned land in the immediate area.

The park is located in Ashe County midway between the towns of Jefferson and West Jefferson. The mountain itself rises extravagantly for 1,600 feet above the surrounding territory and can be viewed for miles around. Researchers claim that the underlying rocks forming Mount Jefferson resisted the erosive forces cutting through a once-high, broad plateau. The mountains in this area of the state are the remains of the weathering effects from past geologi-

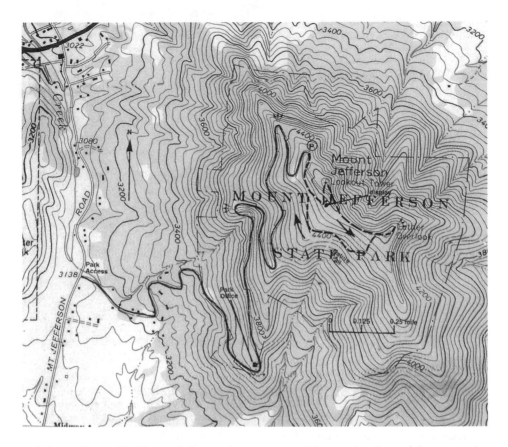

cal times. Pointedly, Mount Jefferson is a formation of the North Fork and South Fork New River drainage divide. When he completed his hike of Mount Jefferson in 1827, Dr. Elisha Mitchell, for whom Mount Mitchell is named, described the area as "an ocean of mountains."

To reach the park, watch for a sign and take the Mount Jefferson Road off US 221. The three-mile access road leads to the park office and information center, then farther to a parking and picnic area at the summit. In a well-maintained wooded area are picnic tables, outdoor cooking pits with grills, available fresh water, and rest rooms.

A naturalist's paradise, the park includes dozens of species of trees, flowering shrubs, and an abundance of wildflowers, all of which vary at different elevations of the mountain. The lower areas contain sugar maple, red maple, black locust, mountain ash, white ash, mountain maple, bigtooth aspen, hickory, poplar, yellow birch, basswood, chestnut oak, white oak, white pine, and many northern red oak varieties. The upper areas contain chestnut oak, purple rhododendron, and mountain laurel. Scattered throughout the mountain are serviceberry, bush honeysuckle, flame azalea, and dogwoods.

In 1975 the National Park Service named Mount Jefferson Park a Natural National Landmark because of its unusual plant varieties. Wildflowers along the trails include wild iris, jack-in-the-pulpit, galax, wood lilacs, white beebalm, false lily of the valley, wild azalea, and dutchman's breeches.

The New River, second oldest in the world

A variety of wildlife inhabits Mount Jefferson. You are likely to see slate-colored juncos, chipmunks, red and gray squirrels, deer, woodchucks, and, on occasion, red and gray foxes.

From the picnic area, begin hiking on the main trail along the summit of the mountain. This trail splits, leading right to Luther's Rock Overlook, or left to the lookout tower.

The tower trail itself is a well-established path, lightly graveled, as it rises openly through a wooded area. On clear days at multiple points along the trail the hiker can view various peaks of other North Carolina mountains as well as into Tennessee and Whitetop Mountain in Virginia.

From the lookout tower, hike 0.2 mile southeast to reach an information display entitled "As Time Goes By." In the display the growth rings of a tree-trunk section are labeled with important events and dates. The time table goes back as far as 1827,

when Dr. Elisha Mitchell climbed to the top of Mount Jefferson and wrote that he had never seen anything more beautiful than the view from the top. Other important dates are the establishment of other state parks including Mount Mitchell, the first in 1915, and the latest date of 1991, the 75th anniversary of the state park system.

Hike another 0.1 mile to Luther's Rock Overlook where you have an excellent view of the New River. When you leave the overlook, you continue left for the Rhododendron Trail which rejoins the main trail near the picnic and parking areas.

On the one-mile Rhododendron Trail, the park service provides booklets that are numbered to matched posts to point out key aspects of the natural surroundings. The booklet also includes some of the history and legends of the area.

In addition to the greenery growing along the trail, you are guided to observe the slopes of the mountain where, in years past, the American chestnut tree grew until the chestnut blight hit. Now, you see only large trunks of what were once majestic trees. However, many young sprouts have appeared from the old root systems and perhaps will flourish.

Among the unique characteristics of the Mount Jefferson area are the "black rocks." You will readily notice that the soil has a black appearance. Geologists explain that the black rocks at one time were the sediment in a shallow area. Around 300 million years ago, when Africa and the Americas drifted together, soft rocks formed from this sediment and crystallized. The result is the mountain formations of today.

Other points of interest on the Mount Jefferson trails are views of both forks and then their union of the New River below, a panoramic view of the surrounding area from various elevations, Three-Top Mountain in the same Ashe County, plus various animals and plants including an uncut northern red oak forest.

When you leave Mount Jefferson State Park and drive four miles to New River State Park, you have entered what is almost an entirely different world. Rather than huge mountains, you will find a low, quiet valley that has been carved over hundreds of thousands of years by the New River.

When you start toward New River State Park, which is located in Ashe and Alleghany counties, drive north on NC 16 until you reach the intersection of NC 16 and NC 88. Follow NC 88 for 1.2 miles until you intersect with Wagoner Road (State Road 1590). The state park is within two miles of the turnoff onto Wagoner Road.

Inside the park you will find a canoe landing, facilities for canoe camping, picnicking, fishing, and wildlife and nature study. As you enter the park you will pass a

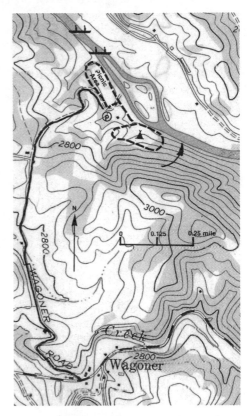

gate and an office building on the left side of the road. This building is not a part of the state park resources. Drive on until you see the park headquarters building. The trailhead is almost directly across the road from the park headquarters building.

This is a loop trail that can be hiked easily in half an hour, but you may wish to prolong the trip and devote extra time to studying the plant life along the trail.

As you hike you will pass, at 0.1 mile, an old spring, complete with spout. Do not drink the water. As the trail curves up a gentle incline, you will pass a tiny creek (0.2 mile) and a growth of silky dogwood, through rhododendron or laurel slicks, sometimes known as laurel hells. This very dense thicket-like growth provides food for deer and gives them shelter for sleeping, giving birth, and escaping from predators.

Two common trees you will pass are white pine and shagbark hickory. At 0.4 mile you will reach an interesting growth called walking fern, which puts down roots and "walks" across rocks and other barren areas.

At various points along the trail you will see stumps of what were once majestic chestnut trees, and along the river itself you can see evidence of beavers that once again inhabit the mountain streams of North Carolina.

At 0.7 mile you will emerge from the forest trail and walk along the banks of the river. The remainder of the trail follows the river until you reach the end of the loop, at which point you cross a grassy meadow and rejoin the trail at the starting point.

28

Ivestor Gap Trail

Total distance (backtrack): 8.9 miles

Hiking time: 4.5 hours

Vertical rise: 1,360 feet

Rating: Moderate

Map: USFS Shining Rock Wilderness

The Shining Rock Wilderness area of Haywood County is among the most popular hiking terrain in western North Carolina. The trails through the wilderness offer camping, nature study, a wide range of spectacular views of the surrounding mountains and valleys from ridges and balds, and many peaks between 5,000 and 6,000 feet.

Shining Rock Wilderness was designated as a Wild Area on May 7, 1964. With the signing of the Wilderness Act of 1964, the 13,600 acres became part of the original National Wilderness System. In 1984 the area was increased in size to 18,500 acres by the North Carolina Wilderness Act.

Because there is little shade, the best time to hike the Ivestor Gap trail is early fall through late spring. In summer it is often hot along the trail. Peak seasons for wildflowers are from mid-April through early October.

The old logging road, which forms the basis of the trail from the trailhead to the boundary of the Shining Rock Wilderness at Ivestor Gap, is rocky from the beginning of the trail all the way to Ivestor Gap. And from Ivestor Gap to Shining Rock, the trail is very rocky for long stretches. But although tricky at times because of the wet and rocky footing, the trail is never difficult and is almost invariably rewarding in terms of scenery, wildlife, and primitive condition.

To get to the trail, follow the Blue Ridge Parkway to Milepost 420, then turn north off the parkway onto Forest Service Road 816. Stay on Forest Service Road 816 for 0.7 mile. At 0.6 mile you will pass a small parking area, but you should continue to the end of the road where there is a larger parking area, rest-

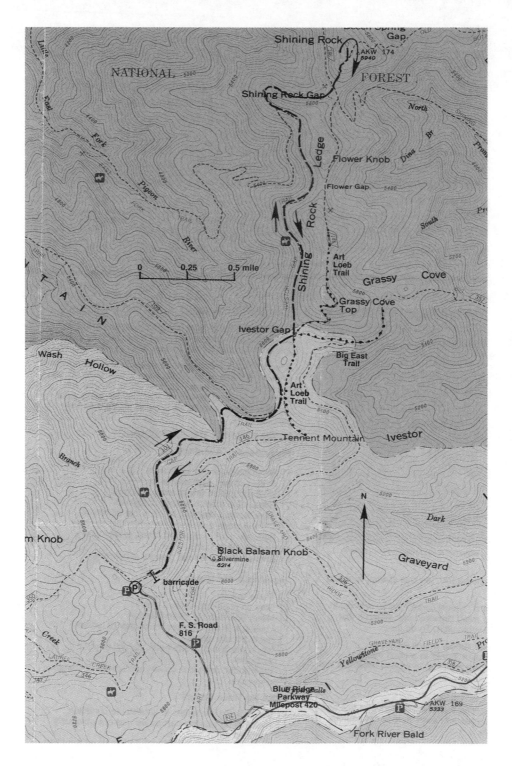

room facilities in the form of portable toilets, and an information board.

From the parking area walk east to a barricade across the old logging road. This is the beginning of the Ivestor Gap Trail that leads to Shining Rock. You can pass around the barricade on either end of it and start the hike down the gentle slope that follows the contour of the mountain nearly all the way to Ivestor Gap.

Along the trail there are numerous places to camp, but no designated camping areas. Hikers and campers are urged to avoid the more crowded areas and to make efforts to lessen the impact on the wilderness area by staying at one location a very brief time. If you are overnighting, follow wilderness area recommendations and stop for the evening meal and then continue your hike until you are ready to set up camp for the night. In the morning, to follow the recommendations, you should rise and begin the hike, delaying breakfast until you are well away from the campsite.

You will find that the rocky roadbed trail is often very wet, sometimes for distances of 200 to 300 feet. Springs flow into the roadbed and trickle among the rocks until the entire surface of the road is wet. You can step from rock to rock and avoid wet feet in these sections, and the water is seldom if ever more than a few inches deep.

At 2.5 miles you will reach Ivestor Gap. Here you will find a Shining Rock Wilderness boundary sign and the convergence of two other trails. The Art Loeb Trail crosses the gap in a north-south direction, and the Big East Trail enters from the east.

There are no trail markers at any point along the hike, and you should carry a map of the trails in the area to avoid possible confusion. The Ivestor Gap Trail continues directly behind the Shining Rock Wilderness sign.

Between the trailhead and Ivestor Gap you will be able to enjoy striking vistas at almost every point. Prominent peaks and mountains within clear view are Sam Knob to the west and Black Balsam Knob to the east.

When you pass Ivestor Gap and hike the next section of the trail, you will continue the gentle ascent up a trail that is not as wide as the trail to Ivestor Gap but that is equally rocky and wet. Again, the footing is almost entirely rocks of various sizes, and many springs empty into the road.

The vegetation to this point has been dominated by the laurel and rhododendron flats and thickets, with occasional spruce and balsam pines. You will pass thick and tall blackberry growths and blueberry bushes at sporadic intervals.

For 0.6 mile from Ivestor Gap the trail rises steadily but gently, and the grassy knobs give way to heavily forested ridges, with spruce and balsam again dominating. If you look and listen carefully as you hike you may see and hear deer among the underbrush that grows along the slopes among the taller trees.

Other animal life along the forested ridge are squirrels, hawks, owls, crows, opossums, a rare bobcat, an occasional bear, and a variety of songbirds.

As you continue to hike, you will pass through a dense forest, with steep inclines on either side of the trail, and follow the trail until it narrows suddenly and becomes only a footpath through a hardwood forest. You will find poplar, a few oaks, fire cherry, dogwood, maple, and occasional hickory trees as you follow the contour of the ridge. Through the trees you will catch glimpses, and as you reach the 3.8-mile mark, the first view of Shining Rock itself.

You can actually see the rock before you reach Ivestor Gap, but at that distance the

The view east from Grassy Cove Top

rock appears to be only a white blotch through the tree limbs; however, upon a closer view, you will see that the rock actually appears to glisten as sunlight hits it.

From the time when you first see the rock across the narrow valley, you will need to follow the footpath, which doubles as a horse trail, as it leads to a large grassy clearing. Inside the clearing you will note that trails lead in several directions out of the circle. Many of these trails are not mapped. They were made by campers and hikers who wished to explore the area near the base of Shining Rock.

The trail you need to follow is almost directly across the clearing from the point where you entered. Make a careful note of the trail from which you entered, because when you are ready to return you will find that there are other paths that may prove to be confusing.

When you cross the clearing, you will enter a dense tangle of laurel and rhododendron, as well as more spruce and a few hardwood trees. Erosion and hiker use have worn the trail deep into the soil of the mountain, and you will walk among head-high growth until you reenter the spruce forest and begin to climb a more severe incline.

The trail leads 500 feet, from the clearing to the base of Shining Rock. Dim trails wander about the base of the rock. As you explore these rather indistinct paths, do not lose sight of the trail that led you to the rock. You will need to follow this trail back to the clearing when you are ready to leave.

Backtrack to the clearing and from there go back down the trail to Ivestor Gap. From Ivestor Gap continue your backtrack hike to the parking area and your vehicle.

The Blue Ridge Area

29

Devil's Courthouse Trail

Total distance (one way): 0.8 mile

Hiking time: 1.5 hours

Vertical rise: 1,400 feet

Rating: Strenuous

Map: USGS 7.5' Sam Knob

From the parking lot at the head of the Devil's Courthouse Trail, the distance to the top of the peak is only 0.8 mile. However, allow about one and one-half hours for a leisurely hike to the top and ample time to enjoy some of the most rewarding vistas possible in the North Carolina mountains.

To get to Devil's Courthouse the best highway is the Blue Ridge Parkway. If it seems that this spectacular highway is the link to many North Carolina trails, it is because this parkway stretches across the entire mountain region of North Carolina. Leave the parkway at Milepost 422.4 and park in the lot slightly west of the peak called Devil's Courthouse. From the parking lot you can see the peak clearly. The grimly beautiful mountain was considered by the Cherokee Indians to be the headquarters of Judacullah, a god who sat in judgment of their courage and morality.

At the east edge of the parking space, you can read a sign placed by the Department of Interior, which informs travelers: "The Balsam Range is rich in legendary superstitions and to the Indians these mountains assumed mysterious shapes and forms. Here at Devil's Courthouse his Satanic majesty was believed to have sat in judgment of all who were lacking in courage or had strayed from a strict code of virtue. Cherokee superstitions coupled many natural phenomena with the mysterious spirits that peopled the area."

Start the trail by hiking up the right side of the parkway (heading north). Before you reach the tunnel you will see a trail leading up the mountain. The walk to the trail is

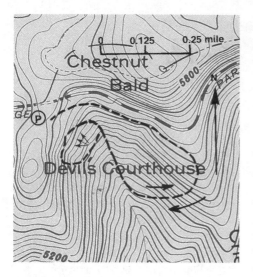

rocks is a very real one, and you are encouraged to leave the peak if you see a thunderstorm approaching.

The best months of the year to hike up Devil's Courthouse are late April, May, October, and early November; best time of day is early morning. If you plan to hike in late afternoon, be certain to allow enough time to descend from the peak while there is still adequate light.

When you near the top you will find that the terrain begins to flatten slightly, and at the peak itself you will walk on level land for 300 feet. Hike through a narrow passageway between the rocks and then you will emerge onto the peak itself. There you will find a protective wall to prevent spectators from coming too close to the ledge, and around the wall you will find plaques that help you to identify the peaks seen in the distance.

You will have virtually a 360-degree panoramic view of the entire area, and you can see into South Carolina, Georgia, and Tennessee. You can also climb onto the rocks for varying views of the mountains and valleys before you, but you should keep in mind at all times that you should exert the greatest care toward your own safety. Some of the rocks are in safe terrain, and the footing is good. Stay well back of the ledges.

If you want an even better look at the ridges and valleys than that afforded from the overlook, you can climb the rocks on the east side of the peak and gain an added 30 feet. In this way, particularly if you are photographing the scene, you can take in the overlook as well as the rest of the scene.

You will find that the clearest views are found in the cooler months, and you can climb Devil's Courthouse virtually any time that the Blue Ridge Parkway is open to traffic. However, it is far better to avoid extremes in climate, whether winter or summer, and in winter the wind-chill factor can greatly interfere with the joys of the climb.

paved, and where the pavement ends the trail proper starts.

For the next 0.7-mile trek, the terrain is all uphill, until you reach the very peak of the mountain. The climb is steep and unrelenting, although there are benches to permit hikers to catch their breath.

The trail is wide enough for two or three people to walk side by side, for the first third of the climb. As the trail climbs toward the top, the pathway narrows slightly until by the time you reach the peak it is a single-file trail.

The woodland on both sides of the trail is home to deer, bobcats, rabbits, squirrels, chipmunks, hawks, owls, crows, and other creatures common to the higher peaks. There are several types of snakes, but these reptiles are not common and do not constitute a threat to the hiker.

There are hardwood trees scattered throughout the balsam range, and the woodland floor is alive with wildflowers from early spring into midautumn. Like so many mountain peaks, Devil's Courthouse seems to change with each change in the atmosphere, and the changes are plentiful.

In summer months a mid-afternoon thunderstorm is highly predictable. The danger of lightning while you are exposed on the

The Devil's Courthouse in autumn

30

Erwins View and Dugger's Creek Loop Trails

Total distance (combined backtrack and loop): 1.5 mile

Hiking time: 1.5 hours

Vertical rise: 960 feet

Rating: Moderate, handicapped accessible

Map: USGS 7.5' Linville Falls

These two short trails in the Linville Gorge Recreation Area can be hiked as one trail in a very short time. Start with the Erwins View Trail and finish the jaunts with the Dugger's Creek Loop Trail.

To get to the Linville Gorge Recreation area, the easiest route is to follow the Blue Ridge Parkway to Milepost 316.3. Follow the spur road marked Linville Gorge Recreation Area off the parkway to the south for two miles until you reach the parking area and the headquarters building.

The Erwins View Trail, like the other trails starting at the ranger station at the Linville Gorge Recreation Area, leads to a view of the popular Linville Falls. (Other hiking possibilities in the Linville Gorge area are described in chapters 31 and 32.)

The trail starts at the ranger offices and leads across a wide bridge. The trail itself, except for the spur trails that lead to the best views of the waterfalls available on the west side of the Linville River, consists of a wide and smooth maintenance road. The trail is easy enough that, while not a common sight, you can see handicapped and elderly persons making the hike without difficulty.

If time demands, you can bypass some of the spur trails and shorten the hike considerably. There are three overlooks that offer wonderful views of the falls from interesting perspectives. From the ranger offices to the bridge over the Linville River is a distance of only 65 feet. A short spur trail which veers off to the left of the stream offers a close look at the rocky riverbed.

When you reach the 0.1-mile point, you

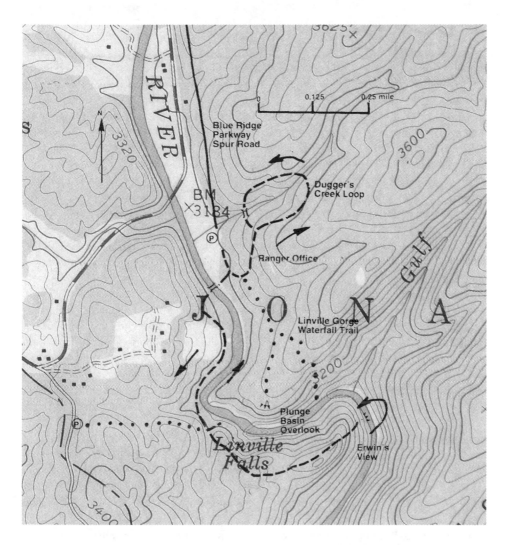

will see a series of signs pointing to the access points easily reached from the spot. One short trail leads to the right and to the gravel parking lot that serves as overflow parking for the Linville Falls Recreation Area.

A second short spur trail leads to the left. It will take you along a wide, clear trail that is lined with hardwood trees and some striking specimens of hemlock, fir, locust, and the comparatively rare Carolina hemlock.

Upon reaching the first overlook, you will find a superb view of the Upper Falls, which are really one waterfall divided by the boulders in the stream. These falls are 12 feet high and are impressively beautiful, though less so than the Lower Falls.

When you walk to the end of the overlook you can see the sluice rock formation through which the Linville River roars in the first of three abrupt turns as the water plunges through the rocks and exits the other side (not visible from the first overlook) into the majestic Lower Falls.

A plaque near the rock wall provides information about the falls, the river, and the formation of the gorge as it exists today. Return to the major trail by backtracking 500 feet.

The elevation at the Upper Falls is 3,000 feet, about the same altitude as that of the ranger offices. From this point on the elevation increases gradually but steadily.

The trail climbs through the same type of terrain for 430 more feet until you reach the spur trail to the second overlook. You are slightly past the 0.3-mile point here.

You will find that the spur trail to the Chimney View Overlook narrows now, and you will proceed single file to a set of stone steps, complete with handrail, that curves around laurel and rhododendron and emerges into a wide overlook with a protective rock wall surrounding it.

You are now approximately 1,500 feet above the river. To your left, as you enter the overlook, you have a superior view of both the Upper Falls and Lower Falls. To the right you have a splendid view of the Linville River and the Linville Gorge as they stretch 12 miles to the south before terminating at Lake James.

The trees, constantly nourished by the frequent rains and the rich soil of the gorge area, soar to impressive heights. One white pine in the gorge has been calculated to be nearly 150 feet tall. Directly in front of you, and straight down as you look over the wall, is the chimney-rock structure that gives the overlook its name.

In this section of the gorge you may see three distinct varieties of rhododendron growing side by side: the rosebay, Catawba, and Carolina. Pink azalea is common in the area. This shrub grows to about six feet in height and is relatively frequent in sour soils and in swamps and bogs.

This azalea is recognizable by the leaves, which are four inches long and demonstrate hairy margins when the plants are very young, and by the pink and white flowers, which are two inches in width and are two-lipped. These shrubs bloom profusely in late April and through May, perhaps into June, at the 3,000-foot elevation level. Cherokee Indians and Catawba Indians reportedly ate the juicy gall that is found on twigs and leaves by the end of May.

The largest of the rhododendron family, the great laurel, grows to 40 feet in height in this area, with trunk diameters reaching one foot. The white, purple, or rose-colored flowers are in full bloom in June and July.

The wood of the great laurel is extremely dense and similarly very strong. Green parts of the plant contain the highly poisonous *andromedotoxin,* which can be fatal if ingested. Honey made from the blossoms of this plant can also be poisonous. Leaves of the great laurel are up to 7 inches in length and 2.5 inches in width. There are about 100 species very similar to this particular tree.

Another highly common small tree found along the banks of the Linville River is the mountain laurel, which occasionally grows to 40 feet in height but is more commonly limited to a 20-foot shrub growth. This tree can be distinguished from its close relative, the great laurel, by the much thinner leaves of the mountain laurel. The laurel leaves are typically 1.5 inches wide and 5 inches long. Flowers are pink or white and three-quarters of an inch across. Like the great laurel, the green parts of the mountain laurel contain the poison *andromedotoxin.* This small tree is often called spoonwood, broad-leafed kalmia, ivy bush, big-leafed ivy, poison laurel, calico bush, and American laurel.

When you leave the chimney overlook, return to the main trail and hike to the third

The Linville River above Upper Falls

vantage point, Erwins View. When you enter this final overlook, you cannot see the falls unless you take the spur trail to your left just as you enter the overlook. From the spur trail (150 feet) you will have a super view of the waterfalls.

A trail marker inside the overlook informs visitors of the two ridges that enclose your view from this point. "The valley between them has been cut by the Linville River," the information states. "When the river had eroded a wide valley down to almost this level, earth movements must have pushed the mountains higher. The river flowed faster and cut the inner gorge. This valley will continue to change. The river cuts deeper as it drops 1700 feet in 12 miles, from the foot of the falls to the mouth of the gorge."

Retrace your steps back along the main trail to hike the Dugger's Creek Loop Trail.

This is a very short but enjoyable trail that leads from the trailhead at the northeast corner of the headquarters building through a thick evergreen-and-hardwood mixed forest and back to the parking lot. Total length is 0.3 mile.

The trail includes several crossings of small streams via rustic and interesting bridges. A small waterfall is one of the special attractions you will reach within 0.1 mile into the trail.

Along the trail you will also see signposts containing ecological and philosophical messages from such thinkers as Henry David Thoreau, John Muir, and Edwin Way Teal. At 0.2 mile you will reach the Edwin Way Teal marker, which reads: "Our minds, as well as our bodies, have need of the out-of-doors. Our spirits, too, need simple things, elemental things, the sun and the wind and the rain, moonlight and starlight, sunrise and mist and mossy forest trails, the perfumes of dawn and smell of fresh-turned earth and the ancient music of wind among the trees."

Five hundred feet later you will reach the John Muir marker with the following message: ". . . Every raincloud, however fleeting, leaves its mark, not only on trees and flowers whose pulses are quickened, and on the replenished streams and lakes, but also on the rocks are its marks engraved whether we can see them or not. . . ."

At this point you are virtually at the end of the trail, and within five minutes you will be back at the parking lot.

31

Linville Gorge Waterfall Trail and Plunge Basin Overlook Trail

Total distance (backtracks): 2.4 miles

Hiking time: 1.5 hours

Vertical rise: 880 feet

Rating: Moderate

Map: USGS 7.5' Linville Falls

The Linville Gorge Recreation Area offers four separate trails with a combined length of about four miles. All four can be hiked easily in one afternoon. In this chapter the Linville Gorge Waterfall Trail and the Plunge Basin Overlook Trail are described as one hike, while the Dugger's Creek Loop Trail and Erwins View Trail are described as a single hike in chapter 30. The longer, completely separate Linville Gorge Wilderness Trail descends into the gorge from a different trailhead (see chapter 32).

To get to the Linville Gorge Recreation area, the easiest route is to follow the Blue Ridge Parkway to Milepost 316.3. Follow the spur road marked Linville Gorge Recreation Area off the parkway to the south for two miles until you reach the parking area and the headquarters building.

The Linville River was called by the Cherokees "Eeseeoh," meaning "a river of many cliffs." The description is an accurate one. The river flows over a rock bed that has been in a state of constant but imperceptible change for millions of years, during which time the eroding power of the river cut through the immense mass of quartz particles and created the gorge and the awesome rock cliffs bordering the river.

Scholars are of the opinion that half a billion years ago the area known today as Linville Gorge lay at the bottom of a sea. The sand grains, buried deep under layers of several types of rocks, were cemented into sandstone.

As centuries passed, the rock beds were pushed up and "folded," and the sandstone recrystallized into denser rock,

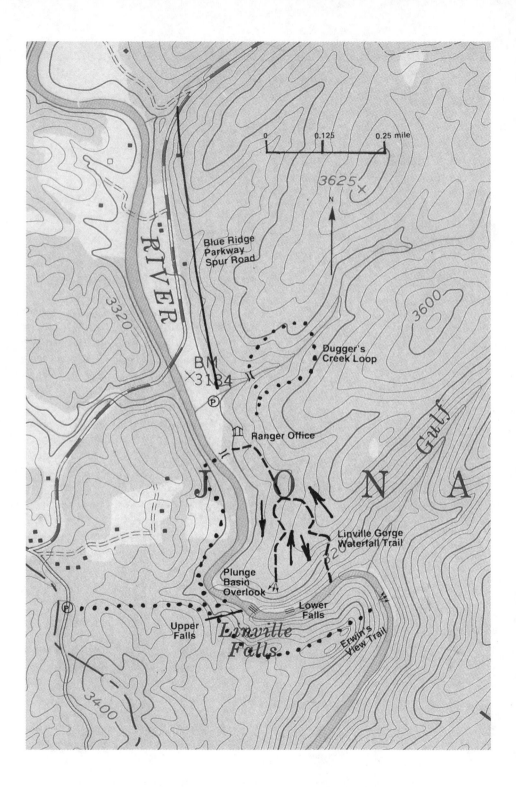

0   0.125   0.25 mile

3625 ×

N

3320

3600

RIVER

Blue Ridge
Parkway
Spur Road

Dugger's
Creek Loop

BM
× 3184

Ⓟ

Ranger Office

J   O   N   A

Gulf

Linville Gorge
Waterfall Trail

Plunge
Basin
Overlook

Lower
Falls

Ⓟ

Upper
Falls

*Linville
Falls*

Erwin's
View Trail

3400

which is called today Erwin quartzite. The name comes from Erwin, Tennessee, where the formation was described scientifically many years ago.

At Linville Falls one of the immense rock "folds" tipped so far that it broke and pushed older rock beds on top of the quartzite. Erosion then cut through the older rocks, leaving what is referred to as "windows" through which the quartzite is exposed. Quartzite itself is seen as sandstone that has simply been converted into solid quartz rocks but, unlike sandstone, is free from pores and fractures with smoothness, not the ragged edge that is associated with sandstone.

Quartzite as a scientific term suggests a high degree of induration or welding and also a high content of quartz. Most quartzite contains from 90 percent up to 99 percent of quartz itself and constitutes the largest and purest concentrations of silica in the earth's crust.

Many of the most prominent ridges in the Appalachian chain of mountains are highly resistant tilted beds of Paleozoic quartzite. The rock masses along the Linville River bear eloquent testimony to the power of erosions by the wind and rain and the river; the remaining cliffs, left after the river cut its way through the softer rock beds, have been significant protectors of the pristine nature of the gorge.

The river was given its English name after Cherokee warriors in 1766 surprised and massacred William Linville and his son, who, along with John W. Williams, had explored the area. The three men were asleep in their camp alongside the river when the Cherokees attacked. Williams, wounded but able to flee, managed to escape the marauders.

William Linville himself, according to local lore, was a relative of the wife of Daniel Boone. The gorge area was visited in 1752 by Bishop Spangenberg, and by 1818 white settlers had begun to enter the deep forests.

Few remained, however, because, as one of them put it, "You can't farm a waterfall." Nevertheless, a series of hardy pioneers did in fact settle in the area, and during the Civil War a forge located on the Linville River manufactured rifles for the Confederate Army.

After World War I the Rockefeller Foundation purchased the 1,200-acre tract for $92,000. During World War II the cliffs became a survival-skills training ground for American soldiers. After the war the Rockefeller Foundation donated the land to the National Park Service on the condition that the forest and stream be protected and allowed to exist in thier natural state.

The Linville Gorge Trail, 1.4 miles in length, is an excursion from the mountains above the gorge to the river itself. The trail ends 0.1 mile downstream from the Lower Falls, the highest waterfall on the Linville River. The Plunge Basin Overlook Trail is 1.0 mile in length.

To get to the trailheads for the Plunge Basin Overlook Trail and the Linville Gorge Waterfall Trail, walk to the east, past the headquarters building, and ascend the short flight of stairs. After you hike a slight incline, you will follow the trail into forest. Immediately you will reach signs directing you to the trails in the area, all of which start with a common trailhead.

Take the right-hand trail and follow it for 0.3 mile to a second set of signs. At this point the trail forks. The Plunge Basin Overlook Trail leads straight ahead, while the Linville Gorge Waterfall Trail turns sharply to the left and follows the rise of the mountain upward for a short distance.

Continue straight ahead for 0.6 mile to reach the Plunge Basin Overlook. The trail is well traveled and easily followed. At the overlook itself, you will have a superb view of the top of the Lower Falls as the water plunges into the basin below and then continues its rush down the river.

Retrace your steps back to the signpost and follow the left fork to complete the second trail, the Linville Gorge Waterfall Trail. The trail continues for 0.4 mile down the opposite side of the ridge and to the bottom of the gorge.

Start down the slope to the river. Within 200 feet you will reach a wooden barricade that serves as a warning not to proceed past the barrier. The trail leads to the left of the barrier, at which point you will begin a sharp descent.

At 160 feet past the barricade you will reach a wooden fence composed of two-by-four timbers and posts. Do not leave the trail from this point until you reach the river.

From vantage points along the trail, as along other trails in the area, you can view cliffs that rise dramatically 2,000 feet from the river level to the tops of the ridges.

You can also see "islands" of rocks that have crashed from the cliffs and landed in the middle of the river where they will remain until erosive forces wear them down during the coming centuries.

Three hundred feet down the sharp descent there is an immense uprooted tree that had somehow managed to grow on the rock bed. The root ball that rose when the tree fell exposed the rock and permits the very narrow trail to pass between the exposed roots and the steep hillside to your left.

The trail drops severely for the next 85 feet, and you will find wooden steps, along with a handrail, to make the descent safer and easier. Through a series of switchbacks the trail winds gently from the steps to an awesome rock cliff 0.2 mile later.

The cliff, which is several hundred feet long and so sheer that it appears almost to be a wall, is well over 100 feet high. It is, in fact, higher than the huge trees that grow alongside it.

The trail continues to descend sharply, and 200 feet later you will reach a portion of the trail that is almost completely rock surface. You will step from rock to rock as you continue downward, and at the start of the rock trail you can catch glimpses of the Linville River through the trees.

The final stretch of rocky trail lasts for 800 feet, at which time you will be at the bottom of the gorge and within a few feet of the river. You can leave the trail and walk to the river at the point where the trail turns sharply to the right.

Do not mistake the river as the end of the trail. If you wish you can step out upon the huge rocks in the river and watch for some of the many birds and animals that populate the area. When you leave the short trail spur you can follow the original trail, which will now be on your left, through dense underbrush and alongside a lichen-covered rock cliff as you head toward the end of the trail.

Within 400 more feet you will reach the trail's end. At this point you will see in the river to your left a huge squared boulder that is perched precariously upon another rock in the middle of the stream.

Directly ahead of you there is a superb stream-level view of the Lower Falls, better known simply as Linville Falls. At this level you are exposed to the loud roar of the falls, and you can see the spray and mist clearly as it rises from the plunge basin.

As late as 1876 the Upper and Lower Falls were about the same height: 35 feet high. Between 1876 and 1902 a series of floods eroded the rock bed so severely that the ledge of the Upper Falls gave way and crashed to the riverbed below. The loss of

Linville Falls as seen from the overlook

Robert L. Williams

the ledge shortened the Upper Falls to 20 feet and lengthened the Lower Falls.

Backtrack to reach the signpost at the trail fork. From this point it is 0.3 mile back to the ranger office and parking areas.

As you study the forest, you will note three trees that are considered rare in the mountains: butternut, sycamore, and iron-wood. On both sides of the trail you will see giant hemlock, pine, and hardwood trees. The Carolina hemlock exists only in a stretch 20 miles wide and 150 miles long along the gorge. It is said that the hemlocks in the gorge represent the largest virgin forest of this species known to exist on earth today.

Linville Gorge Waterfall Trail and Plunge Basin Overlook Trail

32

Linville Gorge Trails

Total distance (one way): 12–15.9 miles

Hiking time: 8–10 hours, or overnight

Vertical rise: 7,960 feet

Rating: Strenuous

Map: USFS 7.5' Linville Gorge Wilderness

One of the great beauties of the Linville Gorge Wilderness Trail (not to be confused with other Linville Gorge trails described in chapters 30 and 31) is that hikers have a choice of eight access trails into and out of the gorge.

For those who wish to make a two-day hike of the entire length of the gorge, the first step is to secure the necessary permits. This gorge is said to be the most rugged wilderness east of the Mississippi River, and no one is allowed to camp in the gorge on weekends and holidays without a permit.

To secure a permit, write to: District Ranger, P.O. Box 519, Marion, NC 28752, or call (704) 652-4841.

You should also be familiar with the National Forest Service advisory that the Linville Gorge Wilderness Area is "a private environment where you will be faced with the challenge of being entirely self-sufficient for whatever time you decide to remain there. There will be no shelters, campgrounds, water spigots, restrooms, or detailed trail signs. . . . You will meet and live with nature on its own terms."

The ideal plan is to enter the gorge via the 0.7-mile Pine Gap Trail, follow the Linville Gorge Trail along the stream all the way to the south end of the gorge, 11.5 miles, and then backtrack, 1.9 miles, to climb the Pinch In Trail, 1.8 miles, for a total hike of 15.9 miles. Arrange a shuttle vehicle at the Pinch In Trail access area for an all-day or overnight hike.

To get to the Linville Gorge Wilderness trails, leave the Blue Ridge Parkway on US

221 near the Linville Falls Recreation Area, which is at Milepost 316. Follow the parkway south to the intersection of the two roads and then follow US 221 south through the tiny town of Linville Falls.

Leave Linville Falls via NC 183 and drive south slightly more than one mile until you reach the junction of Kistler Memorial Highway. Take the Kistler Memorial Highway, which is a secondary road rather than the suggested improved highway. Within the first half-mile on the Kistler Memorial Highway you will see the first parking area for the access trails into Linville Gorge.

The handiest access or exit trail is the Pine Gap Trail, which follows the curvature of the mountain rather gently until you reach the Linville River. This trail is generally clear, well-worn, and relatively easy to hike.

The trailhead is visible from the parking space alongside the road. You will enter by passing the Linville Gorge Wilderness Area signs and following a well-worn trail down to the Linville River. This trail passes through a hardwood forest mixed with firs and hemlocks. The trail is bordered by huge rocks and boulders as well as cliffs.

Along this trail there are huge hardwood forest growths and, in season, a wide array of wildflowers, scuppernongs or muscadines growing a few feet from the path, a variety of butterflies that are attracted to the blossoms and moisture along the trail, large numbers of lizards, and an occasional snake.

Rattlesnakes are often seen in the gorge, and you should not hike the trails without having a first-aid kit with you.

You will hike through a series of gentle switchbacks as the trail begins to narrow. Within 0.4 mile you will pass huge rock outcroppings and boulders along the path.

At 0.8 mile you will reach the Linville River which, along this stretch, is a constantly changing ribbon of water that is at one point whitewater rapids, at another a gently flowing shallow mountain stream, and at still others smaller waterfalls with deep plunge pools at the bases.

At times the trail is within inches of the stream, and at other times, depending upon the amount of recent rainfall, it is 15 or more feet from the river.

When you have hiked along the river for approximately one mile, you will pass a boulder field where the trail leads during high-water seasons. This stretch of 200 feet of solid small-to-large boulders makes for treacherous footing at times.

If the water is at a normal level, you can avoid the boulder field and stay near the river. You will junction with others of the access trails as you hike. You may leave the gorge at any time via any of these trails.

The trail leads alongside a natural wall of rock within 1.8 miles after you reach the river. These rocks have trickles of water seeping or trickling through them at almost any time of the year, but you are again cautioned against drinking the water without first boiling it or treating it with iodine in specified amounts.

If you brought along fly rod and flies, you can try your luck at some of the fine trout pools along the river—pools that are seldom fished because of the difficulty in reaching the river via the Linville Gorge Wilderness Trail. Be sure that you have appropriate trout and state fishing permits.

Almost as soon as you reach the river, it will describe a horseshoe and then flow southwest for 0.7 mile. The trail in this area is generally smooth and easy, although very narrow.

Abruptly the river changes direction to the southeast for 0.4 mile, and at this point the trail proceeds straight ahead through the hardwood forest while the river curves

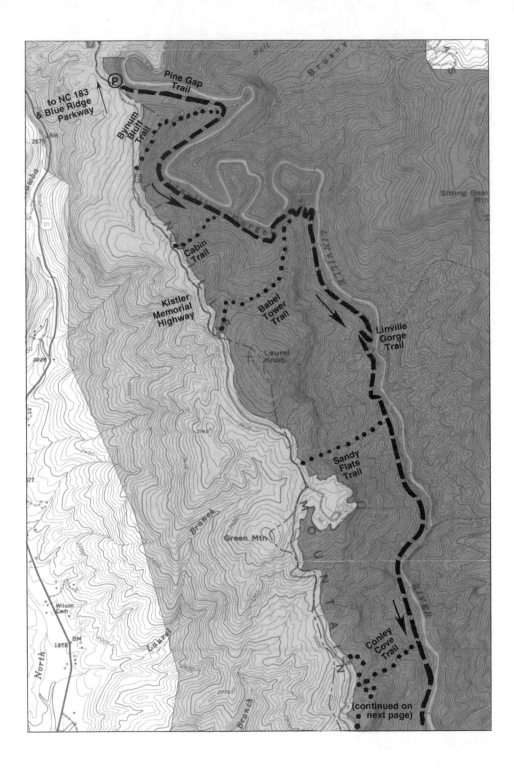

(continued on next page)

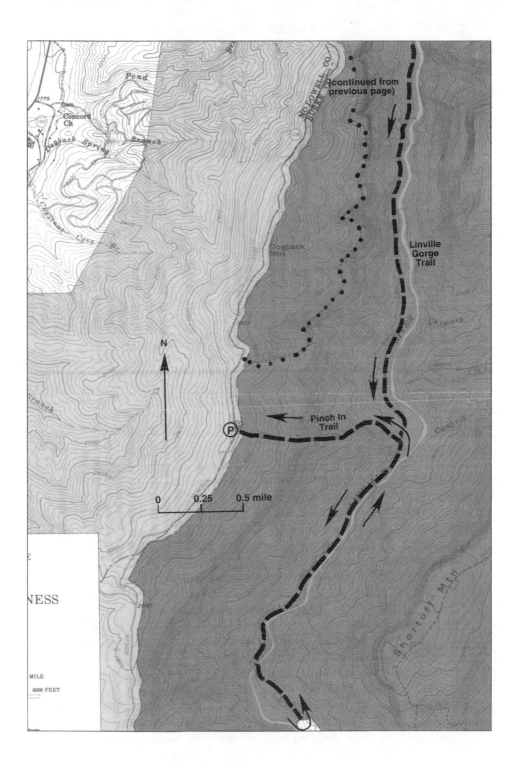

Pond

Cem
Concord
Ch

Dogback Spring

Branch

Chestnut Cove Br

Dogback Mtn

McDOWELL CO.
BURKE CO.

(continued from
previous page)

Linville Gorge Trail

Chimney

N

P

Pinch In Trail

Cambric

0   0.25   0.5 mile

NESS

Shortoff Mtn

MILE

6000 FEET

Boulders along the trail

northward and nearly completes a full circle. The woodland trail is 650 feet from where the river flows north until trail and river join again.

Within 0.5 mile the river again separates from the trail and flows northeast while the trail continues in an easterly direction. When they rejoin, the trail and river continue in the same direction.

From this point to the end of the hike the trail remains essentially easy most of the time, with occasional strenuous but short maneuvers around huge boulders. The terrain is generally flat or leading slightly downhill as it follows the river.

When you have hiked the gorge trail for 9.1 miles, you juncture with the Pinch In Trail, the suggested exit trail. However, if you wish to explore the entire Linville Gorge Trail, continue hiking south along the river.

At 11 miles the trail crosses the river in a shallow area, and in another 0.5 mile you reach the end of the wilderness area, which is posted with boundary signs. Retrace the gorge trail to the Pinch In Trail, a round trip hike of 2.4 miles. Follow the Pinch In Trail to your shuttle vehicle.

If you do not have the time or energy to hike the entire Linville Gorge Trail, you can select the distance you wish to hike and then select an access trail to make the loop closer to the desired length. For example, enter by the Pine Gap Trail and follow the Linville Gorge Trail to the intersection of the Cabin Trail, 1.2 miles distant. Follow the Cabin Trail back to the highway for a 2.7-mile hike.

As you hike the Linville Gorge Trail you will notice that parts of the trail appear little used, while other sections are clear and well-worn. The purpose of the administration of the Gorge is to keep the terrain as close to a perfectly natural state as possible. Consequently there are no facilities at all; there are no firepits, sleeping areas, or first-aid accommodations. When you enter the Gorge, you are on your own.

When the Linville River is high because of heavy rains, the trails will have some very slick spots. At other times you will find that the trail is virtually invisible because of lack of use in some of the more strenuous areas. At times the water covers the trail and you will need to make your own way.

The Linville Gorge terrain is impressive not only in its beauty but in its geographic inclusions. The Gorge includes a total of 10,975 acres, nearly all of which is total primitive wilderness, in addition to the Linville Falls Recreation Area, where the major waterfalls are located.

Linville Gorge itself is composed of Jonas Ridge, elevation 4,120 feet at its highest point, on the east and Linville Mountain, elevation 3,745 feet, on the west. Ginger-cake Mountain, at 4,120 feet, is the highest point along the gorge boundaries.

In Linville Gorge Wilderness, you share in the natural habitat of bears, deer, bobcats, timber rattlers, copperheads, raccoons, opossums, many species of lizards and other reptiles, wild turkey, grouse, quail, turkey vultures, owls, hawks, and a variety of smaller mammals in addition to a wide range of wild birds. The waters of the Linville River are home for brown and rainbow trout.

Primary trees include fir, hemlock, locust, dogwood, pine, maple, oak, hickory, and poplar. Hundreds of wildflowers and scores of massive rock formations add to the visual adventure of Linville Gorge, but the most impressive sight of all is that of the unspoiled wilderness area where the terrain is essentially identical to that explored and used by the first settlers, the Native Americans of North Carolina.

It is the goal of wilderness lovers to keep the Gorge in its primitive status and condition.

33

Upper Creek Trail and Greentown Trail

Total distance (backtrack): 10.4 miles

Hiking time: 6 hours

Vertical rise: 5,120 feet

Rating: Moderate

Map: USGS 7.5' Chestnut Mountain

Upper Creek Trail and Greentown Trail are very similar to the Upper Creek Falls Trail (described in chapter 34). The major points of similarity are the type of terrain, vegetation, animal life, and ground covering. The points of difference are that on these trails you will descend (and thus ascend later) gradually rather than precipitously and that there are several feeder streams that you will cross a number of times.

Reach the Upper Creek and Greentown trails by driving north from I-40 through Morganton and Oak Hill or by driving south from the Blue Ridge Parkway. In either case, you will drive NC 181. If you are driving south on NC 181, pass the Barkhouse Picnic Area on your right and 0.5 mile later you will see a small pull-off parking space on the left. A trail marker points to Upper Creek Trail.

If you are arriving from the Morganton area, follow NC 181 north of Oak Hill until you see the sign designating Upper Creek Trail on the right side of the road. If you miss the sign, turn around at the Barkhouse Picnic Area and return to the parking area.

There is room for only four or five cars in the parking area, so you are assured that the trail will never be crowded. The greatest use of the trail is by trout fishermen during season. But even with the fishermen there is no real overuse of the trail, which is located in the Wilson Creek area of the Pisgah National Forest.

When you leave your car, walk outside the highway railing until you reach a primitive road. Enter the trail at this point. Both

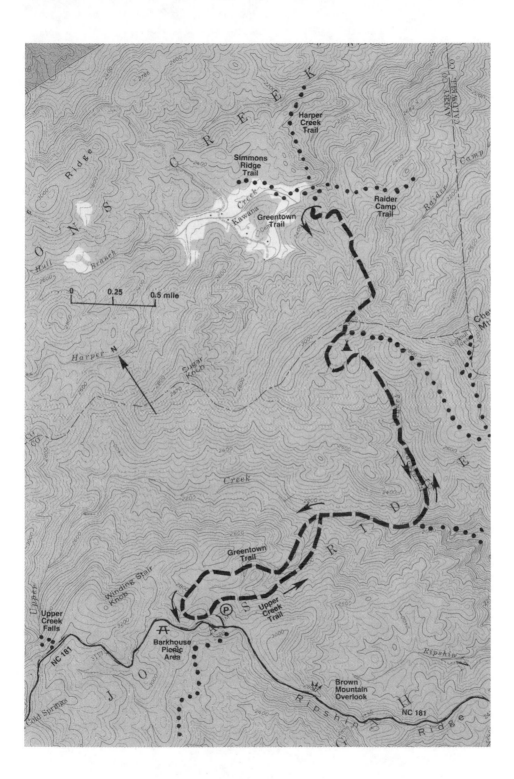

the Upper Creek Trail and the Greentown Trail begin with the same trailhead.

The early stages of the trail are graveled as it follows an old logging road, but within 50 yards you will be on an earthen trail. You will start to descend the ridge gradually. The forest is hardwood here (and will remain so throughout most of the hike), with a scattering of large pines and sourwoods. Smaller dogwoods and occasional serviceberry trees are seen off the trail a short distance.

At 0.2 mile you will see signs directing you either to Greentown, a former logging settlement, or to Upper Creek. The Greentown Trail ends 6.6 miles from the sign and leads to the left, off Upper Creek Trail. On this hike, however, you will take the Upper Creek Trail to its juncture with the Greentown Trail. Then continue on the Greentown Trail (bear right at the fork) until it ends near Harper Creek. Backtrack to reach the parking area.

Three hundred yards after leaving the Greentown–Upper Creek Trail marker you will see signs informing trout fishermen of the restrictions on trout angling. You enter a denser forest growth at this point and will pass many wild cherry trees and holly trees on both sides of the trail.

At 0.1 mile on the Upper Creek Trail there will be a small brook that runs along beside the trail for a considerable distance. You will cross the brook several times and it will continue to grow in width and volume as it is joined by several other smaller rills flowing from springs in the forest.

The trail is blazed by white dots on trees. You will see these blazes every 100 to 150 feet. The trail is so clear and open that you are in no danger of losing it, but the blazes are reassuring.

At 0.2 mile you will cross a small stream that cuts across the trail. Stepping-stones are strategically placed so that you do not need to wade the stream.

Along this portion of the trail in winter the mountain laurel and rhododendron add a pleasant green color to the landscape, and the bare limbs of the hardwood trees stand out in dramatic stark contrast to the skyline.

Shortly after you cross the stream there will be a confluence of two smaller streams that combine to form a strong flow down the steep mountainside. On your left there will remain the hardwood forest, while on your right the laurel thicket is the primary vegetation.

Within 200 yards of the confluence of the streams you arrive at a long cascade where the water plunges noisily down the slope for a drop of approximately 50 feet. An island is formed by the stream (at least after a heavy rain) as it divides and flows on both sides of a huge boulder and some smaller trees.

Immediately past the cascades you will leave the stream for 0.1 mile and hike through the hardwood forest. You are seldom far enough away from the stream that you cannot hear the rush of the water, however, and the trail levels out slightly for the easiest part of the hike. You can walk two abreast along the trail, and in the hot months the thick shade of the trees offers a welcome relief from the sun's rays.

The trail winds gently down toward the stream again and at 0.4 mile you will see another cascade, this one larger and longer than the earlier one. The stream has grown steadily as a result of many feeder rills and branches, and at this point it is a full-fledged creek. The cascade is impressive, although it is difficult to see clearly from the trail.

You can leave the trail and climb down to the stream, but the embankment is very steep and can be dangerous to those not in good physical shape. Photo opportunities are limited because of the thickness of the laurel flats.

When you reach 0.8 mile you will see a rustic sign that directs you back up the trail to NC 181 or right for Greentown Trail. At this point the smaller streams flow into Upper Creek, which you cross to continue the longer hike.

The Greentown Trail will parallel closely the channel of Upper Creek for 0.6 mile and then turn up Burnthouse Branch, which the trail follows for 1.5 miles. At 1.4 miles the trail skirts the edge of a primitive camping area, but instead of entering the campground you will veer sharply to the left and nearly describe a full 180-degree turn.

The trail will continue in a southeasterly direction for 0.3 mile and then will swing back north and then northeast, at which point it passes the primitive campground.

This is a good place to spend the night. If you do not plan to overnight on the trail, continue on the trail (which is marked No. 268 on signs and USFS maps) for 2 miles to the junction with Harper Creek Trail, Raider Camp Trail, and Simmons Ridge Trail. Backtrack to State Road 181 from the junction of the three trails.

34

Upper Creek Falls Trail

Total distance (loop): 1.6 miles

Hiking time: 2.5 hours

Vertical rise: 880 feet

Rating: Moderate

Map: USGS 7.5' Chestnut Mountain

Many years ago, in the latter part of the 19th century, Thomas Alva Edison, unparalleled genius and inventor who helped to revolutionize the lifestyle of Americans and of the world, lived in the Piedmont area of North Carolina. He was searching for a fuel that would prevent an energy shortage that he had somehow foreseen.

While living outside Lincolnton, he became close friends with his host family, and one night he and the head of the household were discussing natural wonders. Edison, always the scientist, remarked that there was nothing in the physical world that did not have a logical explanation.

Weeks later the two saddled horses and rode to the region of Upper Creek Falls. Camped on a mountainside, they waited and watched for the famous Brown Mountain Lights.

Edison, skeptical but willing to investigate, doubted the existence of such lights, but when they appeared, suddenly and mysteriously, in the valley below, the inventor became immensely excited. When the friends were ready to depart for home, the host asked Edison for his explanation of one of the mysteries of the physical world.

"You ought to know," Edison reportedly said good-naturedly, "that there are some things that we must accept without scientific explanation."

And to this day the mystery of the Brown Mountain Lights is as clouded as it was when Edison saw the phenomenon, which has been part of American lore for centuries. Indian mythology mentions the lights

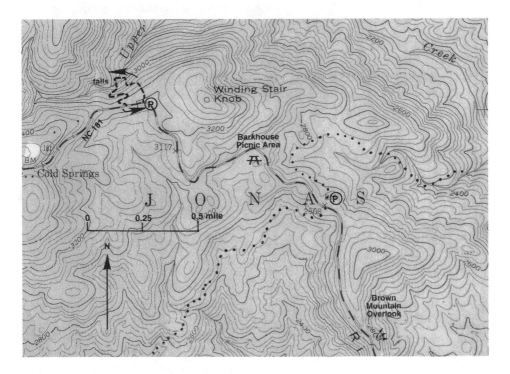

frequently, and Geraud de Brahm, in 1771, witnessed the strange lights.

Popular explanations of the lights include the theories that they are caused by natural swamp gases that escape from underground crevices and ignite when they encounter above-ground air currents. Some insist that the lights are reflections from nearby towns. Some have even suggested that the lights are merely reflected headlights from traffic in the Wilson's Creek area.

The problem with the last two explanations is that the lights were seen by Cherokee Indians before the nearby towns existed and before automobiles and headlights had been invented.

A folktale explanation has been passed down by Lafayette Wiseman, a soldier under General Robert E. Lee during the Civil War. Wiseman heard the story of a planter from the lowland area who traveled to the valley to hunt, and he apparently became lost and died in the wilderness. But a faithful old slave went out night after night to look for his master, and his lantern light could be seen by people traveling along the ridges. Today, decades later, the legend persists that the ghost of the old slave still searches for the ghost of his master.

Whatever the explanation, the Brown Mountain Lights themselves are not folklore. They have been seen by hundreds, perhaps thousands, of people who can attest to their existence. We are among those who have witnessed the lights.

When you choose to hike Upper Creek trails, either the Upper Creek Falls Trail described here or the Greentown and Upper Creek trails, described in chapter 33, you will be in the region of the Brown Mountain Lights, and after the hike is completed, you may wish to drive a short distance down the road to a parking overlook and wait to see the lights.

To get to the Upper Creek territory in the Wilson Creek area, you can leave I-40 at Morganton, take US 18 through downtown to where the highway merges with NC 181. Drive north of Morganton through Oak Hill and toward the Blue Ridge Parkway.

You will pass the Barkhouse Picnic Area on the left as you drive north. Drive 0.9 mile farther until you see a small trail sign on the right. A dirt road leads to a parking area that cannot be seen from the highway.

Enter the drive and proceed 300 feet to a parking lot that is seldom if ever crowded. When you park, you will find the trailhead on the highway side of the parking lot.

What follows is a very wide, clearly visible trail that winds in a seemingly endless series of switchbacks down to Upper Creek, one of the finest trout-fishing streams in the South. The trail is used by fishermen as often as it is by hikers, but it is never crowded.

The first 250 feet of the trail is level, leading through a forest of huge hardwood trees, intermixed with huge pines and occasional poplars and hickories. In all warm months there will be a profusion of wildflowers visible alongside the trail.

Do not leave the trail. A short distance from the trail you will encounter thick rhododendron thickets or flats. These are so thick that it would be difficult for an average-sized man to slip between them.

A very large deer herd thrives in this thickly wooded forest, and in recent years bears have been reintroduced into the area. You may also see a number of squirrels, chipmunks, rabbits, grouse, quail, and, if you are lucky, a wild turkey.

When you are 0.3 mile into the hike you will leave the thick forest and enter a glade or clearing that was apparently once a pasture or orchard. A solitary apple tree grows near the trail.

By the time you are halfway to the stream known only as Upper Creek, the trail on both sides of you is completely enclosed by mountain laurel and rhododendron. The thickets are almost impenetrable.

As you hike around the switchbacks, you will see from time to time shortcuts that descend almost straight down the mountain slope to join the trail below.

You are urged not to use these shortcuts. First, they are dangerous. The cut-offs are not maintained and tend to wash out badly during heavy rains. The moisture seeps out of the ground for days after a rain, and the bare spots are extremely slippery. The trails are far safer than are the cut-offs.

But one of the major reasons for staying on the trails is to protect the environment. The trails have been established for the best protection of the plants and ground cover, and by sticking to the prescribed trails you aid the forest and its protectors.

As you hike deeper into the forest, you will enter a mixture of extremely large hardwood trees, with immense poplars mixed with beech, birch, and oaks, and the forest undergrowth is composed of thickets of laurel and rhododendron.

At 0.7 mile you will hear the crashing of the waterfalls at the bottom of the trail. Within 100 yards you will be able to catch a glimpse of one of the sets of falls wherever there is an opening in the foliage. For best trail views of the falls it is better to hike in spring before full leafing has occurred or in fall after the leaves have fallen.

When you plan fall or winter hikes, remember that the Upper Creek Falls Trail is located within the Pisgah National Forest and that controlled hunting is permitted within the forest boundaries. This fact is another good reason for sticking to trails rather than striking out on your own.

At the bottom of the trail you can look to

your left as you emerge from the woods and see one set of waterfalls 150 yards up the creek. The stream itself is wide, clear, and startlingly beautiful. It is more like a small river than a typical creek.

To your right there will be huge rock formations. You can climb across these rocks and follow the trail to the base of the second waterfall, which is higher and more dramatic than the first set of falls. You are at the 0.9-mile mark when you reach the creek. By the time you have reached the waterfalls and explored the valley for a while, you will have passed the 1.4-mile mark.

Exert extreme caution as you cross the rocks around the waterfall and around the creek generally. Do not climb near the edge of the falls. At the bottom of the trail you can cross the creek via stepping stones or by wading. You are likely to leave the area, in any event, with wet feet.

After you have enjoyed the falls, you can return to the parking lot by backtracking or by hiking southeast along the creek banks for a short distance to a return trail. By joining this lower trail your hike becomes a loop and gives you the opportunity to enjoy more of the terrain.

When you leave the valley area of the falls, you begin the ascent to the parking area by hiking a series of switchbacks that lead through vegetation and forest growth similar to the trail to the falls. Huge hardwood trees are interspersed with thick rhododendron thickets.

The hike down the hill was very easy; the climb back up the mountain slope is considerably more strenuous. It is wise to leave the falls with considerable daylight time left. Your return trip will require more time, and you do not want to complete the hike when visibility is poor.

On the return you will emerge on the opposite side of the parking area. It is 0.7 mile to the creek from this other angle, and by the time you have completed the hike you will have enjoyed 1.6 miles of forest and stream beauty.

35

Lost Cove Trail

Total distance (loop): 6.3 miles

Hiking time: 4 hours

Vertical rise: 2,520 feet

Rating: Moderate

Map: USFS Wilson Creek Area

The Lost Cove Trail is in the Wilson Creek Area, which is part of the Pisgah National Forest near the Blue Ridge Parkway in the Linville vicinity. To get to Lost Cove, exit the Blue Ridge Parkway at Milepost 308 and follow State Road 1511 southeast toward the community of Roseboro (or Roseborough).

Follow State Road 1511 until it intersects with Forest Road 192 near Roseboro, approximately five miles from the parkway. Just past the intersection (0.2 mile) you will see a bridge and two parking areas, one on each side of the bridge. Turn right off State Road 1511 just before you reach the bridge, and within 100 feet you see a small space for parking. You will leave the vehicle within 15 feet of the Gragg Prong Creek.

Reach the trailhead at the west end of the parking area and follow the clear and wide trail into the forest. You will follow the Gragg Prong closely for the next 1.5 miles.

The Wilson Creek Area where you are hiking is bounded on the west by Grandfather Mountain, on the southwest by Linville Gorge, on the east by Brown Mountain, and on the south by a series of low hills and farmland. The elevation range within Wilson Creek Area is from 1,100 feet to 3,700 feet.

The forest land within the Wilson Creek Area of the Pisgah National Forest was once the summer hunting grounds of the Cherokee Indians. White settlers arrived in the latter part of the 18th century and established small communities in the wilderness, the largest of which was Mortimer.

In the early years of the 20th century lumbering was one of the major economic

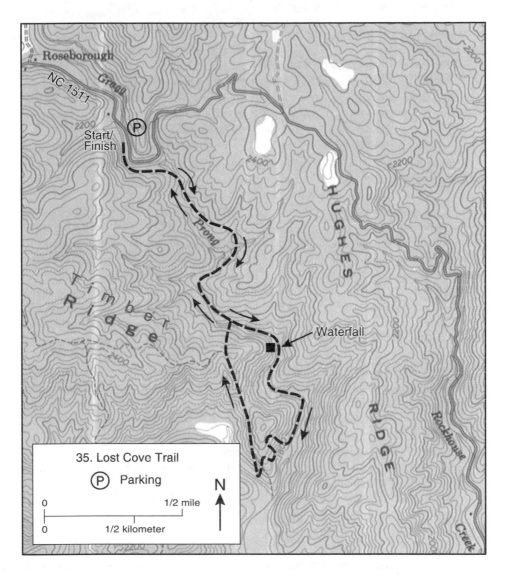

35. Lost Cove Trail

P Parking

N

0   1/2 mile

0   1/2 kilometer

activities in the area. A railroad spur line was constructed into the community and operated until a huge forest fire, followed by a devastating flood, destroyed the railroad and lumber operation. Several later efforts to rebuild the town and industry were met with flooding and more forest fires. In 1940 the sawmill and a textile mill, which jointly employed most of the 800 residents of the community, were again destroyed by floods.

When you start the hike into the Gragg Prong and Lost Cove territory, you will follow Gragg Prong through a forest composed largely of birch, sycamore, oak, hickory, maple, and occasional locust trees. Thickets of laurel and rhododendron are common along the ridges bordering the streams of the forest.

Major wildlife includes bears, deer, grouse, quail, wild turkeys, foxes, and bobcats. The streams of the area are noted for their trophy-sized trout.

For the first 0.6 mile the trail is easy and wide, and the creek is a thing of beauty as it flows across and among rocks. The stream is 20 feet wide, clear, and clean. At the 0.6 mile point you will need to ford the creek. Watch carefully for the double blaze marks that indicate a trail change. If you miss the marks you will continue ahead on a dead-end trail. At the creek ford you can see the trail blazes continue on the other side of the stream.

If the weather is cold you may wish to remove boots and socks and put them on again when you reach the other side. But if the weather is mild you may prefer to wade the creek with boots on. The rocks are slippery and you may need the boot treads for safer walking.

At 0.9 mile you will cross a tiny stream as you leave the creek briefly and hike along a gentle slope that follows the contour of the ridge. At 1.1 miles you will cross another small stream. At 1.2 miles the trail leads along a 100-foot cliff that offers an exceptional view of the stream and the rocky bed below.

Continue hiking in a southeasterly direction. The trail is at times 300 feet from Gragg Prong, but most of the time you are within view of the stream and often within a few feet of it.

At 1.4 miles you will ford the creek again, and just as you reach the opposite bank you will cross a small rill. Look for orange arrows on tree trunks to direct you correctly. Almost immediately you will reach a fork in the trail. Follow the left fork and continue through the forest to the next ford, which is at 1.8 miles.

Watch carefully for the ford. You can find it by looking across the creek to a camping area with fire circles and obvious signs of trail use. If you continue straight ahead, rather than fording the creek, you will follow the bank of the stream so closely that at times you are wading the edge of it. Four hundred feet downstream you will reach a huge rock outcropping above a huge waterfall.

If you reach this point, backtrack until you can spot the trail blazes on the other side of the creek. Do not attempt to continue along the outcropping.

At 2.1 miles you will descend a long hill to a curve just at the edge of a huge flat rock formation. The rock inclines gently to the creek, and you can see a superior series of waterfalls in both directions. You can walk carefully down the rock surface to the edge of the creek, where one of the largest waterfalls on the creek begins its descent.

At 2.3 miles you will reach the largest waterfall on the trail. The waterfall appears well over 100 feet high. A short distance below the falls the creek plunges through a rock formation so narrow that the creek is only three feet wide. Yet immediately afterward the land flattens and the creek spreads to a width of close to 100 feet.

You descend rapidly now through a hardwood forest where the ground underfoot is soft and easy to hike. The impressive rock formations are behind you, and the terrain seems to flatten with each step.

The trail curves sharply several times and you hike in a southwesterly direction. At 3.1 miles you will ford the stream the final time. Then you hike through a very flat area and reach the creek, after having left it for several hundred feet. At mile 3.2, you will turn sharply right and hike back in a northwesterly direction. The creek is posted at this point with "No Fishing" signs, and you will stay on the creek, with the stream on your left, for 300 feet, until you see a trail leading up a sharp incline.

One of several waterfalls seen from Lost Cove Trail

Robert L. Williams

There are no blazes on the trees and no marks of any sort because the trail is a very new one, but it is worn sufficiently for you to follow it without any difficulty. You will continue to climb Timber Ridge until you reach an old signpost at mile 4.1.

A trail leads to the left, but you will continue straight ahead until the trail emerges back on Gragg Prong Creek. The trail is not named on the maps of the Wilson Creek Area, but it leads back to the creek, and you will emerge from the hike within a few feet of State Road 1511, within 100 feet of where you left your vehicle at the start of the hike.

36

Table Rock Summit Trail

Total distance (backtrack): 2.4 miles

Hiking time: 2 hours

Vertical rise: 1,640 feet

Rating: Moderate

Map: USGS 7.5' Linville Falls

Miles before you reach Table Rock, you can see the startling shape of the mountain. If you approach by way of Morganton, you will leave I-40 at the US 18 Exit and drive north. Even south of Morganton you can see the flat top of the table rock standing out like a giant sculpture.

As you drive north, in the center of downtown Morganton you will merge with NC 181. Stay on NC 181 as you drive through the tiny community of Oak Hill and continue heading northward.

On your left you will see, virtually at all times, the top of the rock, and as you round curve after curve, you will note that the rock mountain is constantly changing shapes.

When you first see Table Rock from south of Morganton, the rocky face of the peak appears to be almost totally flat. Before you reach the turnoff to the rock, you will note that the peak seems to sharpen until it finally appears as an inverted ice cream cone. Neither view reveals the total truth. The top of Table Rock is neither flat nor conical. Instead, you will find when you complete the climb, there are immense boulders with large crevices between them, and these huge carved shapes make up the top of the mountain.

Continue driving on NC 181 north for 9 miles from Morganton until you turn left onto State Road 1264, known as the Old Gingercake Road. You can also exit NC 181 to the left at Rose Creek Drive, about 5 miles north of SR 1264, and drive west. This road also intersects with the road leading to Table Rock.

You can also approach Table Rock from

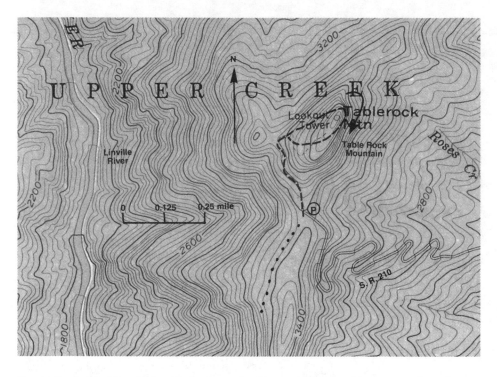

the north via the Blue Ridge Parkway and NC 181 south. You will see Table Rock hovering above the other lower peaks almost as soon as you leave the small community of Jonas Ridge.

If you approach from the parkway, drive south on NC 181 for 3.1 miles until you reach the Old Gingercake Road (State Road 1264). Turn right off NC 181 and follow the state road slowly. At 0.3 mile you will note that the road forks. You need to take the upper, or left, fork and continue slowly through the community called Gingercake Acres. This will be the only turn you will make for several miles.

You are now on State Road 210, and you should drive very slowly and carefully for two reasons: the road is often in poor repair, with huge potholes which can be disconcerting, and you will round a series of blind curves where you may meet vehicles traveling in the opposite direction.

Because the road is narrow, there is very little passing room, and you must hug your side in order to avoid a collision.

Several trailheads are along the road, and you will see parking areas with a number of cars parked in them. Do not stop at these areas. Continue until you see the first road to the right, toward Table Rock, which is the road you will take.

As you near the destination, you will pass the entrance to the Outward Bound facilities, and there are often people walking or jogging along the road. Drive carefully.

At 1.7 miles from the Table Rock parking area you will pass a gate which is kept locked during winter and very early spring. The road is very steep and curving, and it is treacherous in poor weather. You will be forced to hike the remainder of the way if the gate is locked.

A paved road progresses upward in a series of severe switchbacks until it ends at the Table Rock parking area and picnic grounds. The hiking trail begins at the picnic table area.

As you climb the paved road, whether on foot or by vehicle, you will see Table Rock looming through the trees as you round the switchbacks. At the picnic area you can park and walk across the road to the beginning of the trail. A sign warns you that the trail is steep and there are dangerous rocky cliffs. You will also learn that the trail is 1 mile long, one way.

The entire climb is a steady uphill grade, without relief; however, the trail is never really arduous or difficult. Most of the time it is wide, well-maintained, and weedless. Only in wet weather or subfreezing temperatures will you encounter poor footing.

In wet weather, the runoff from the mountain peak will continue to seep through the rocks and parts of the trail will be slightly muddy. In very cold weather there may be ice or snow left even several days after a storm. The peak of Table Rock is 4,000 feet high, and there is a considerable difference in temperatures at the picnic area and at the top of the hike.

A sign as you enter the parking area advises you that the area is a bear sanctuary. There are many deer here as well, and you will perhaps be startled as a grouse or a covey of quail erupt from the bushes only feet from you. Don't let these sudden explosions of noise and activity startle you into losing your footing.

At 0.4 mile you will be able to see, to your left, the Linville River Gorge. In all types of clear weather the gorge is spectacularly beautiful, and from your altitude the Linville River appears to be no more than a trickle. It is, in fact, a very powerful river, and if the wind is still, which is rare, you can hear the roaring of the rapids along the stream.

You climb steadily through a hardwood forest, and at 0.4 mile you will see a trail on the left that leads to Little Table Rock. (Just along the Little Table Rock Trail, a narrower path leads right to a spring and to Table Rock Gap.) Stay on the main trail which makes a switchback to the right at this junction.

When you reach the 0.8-mile distance, the trail sweeps to the right and sharply upward through a thick growth of laurel and rhododendron. There are huge rocks on both sides of you as you climb through a series of switchbacks and close in on the summit.

When you reach the 0.9-mile mark, you will have an unparalleled view of Linville Gorge, the endless peaks of the Pisgah National Forest, and some of the wildest country in the United States. In winter the distant peaks are often snow-covered. There are no trees now, and the thickets of laurel and rhododendron will be in full bloom in late May through June.

The trail is single-file width now, and you will need to pick your footing. At 0.1 mile from the peak there is a particularly impressive rock formation that lends the impression of having been carved and layered throughout the ages. The base of the rock is a soft gray, almost white, and at the top, added almost as an afterthought, is a larger, dark gray, lichen-covered rock that appears to be a cantilevered sample of modern architecture.

Thirty yards before you reach the summit another rock formation juts across the trail. The rock is tiered, with one perfectly flat and even lip extending until it hovers over the undergrowth on the opposite side of the trail.

At the peak itself you will witness huge expanses of white rock that look bleached by the wind and sun. Somehow small

Table Rock

growths of shrubs and wildflowers have found a foothold and have managed to endure the severe changes in climate.

At this point you have a complete 360-degree panoramic view of this section of North Carolina. On one side of the peak you see Linville Gorge again. On a clear day, other valleys and signs of logging roads can be seen in the distance. In late afternoon the sunlight on the evergreen foliage can be spectacular.

From another view you can see Lake James in the distance. This man-made impoundment is one of the finest outdoor recreation areas in western North Carolina, and its beauty has lured several Hollywood motion picture companies to do their location shooting here. In the early 1990s the fort scenes for *The Last of the Mohicans* were filmed at Lake James.

When you have enjoyed your fill of fresh air and scenery, you will backtrack down to the parking lot.

If you wish to add a fairly flat walk to your hike, you can cross the parking lot and follow the trail into the hardwood forest and out to the rim of the cliffs of Linville Gorge. The hike is 0.4 mile, one way, and can be made, round trip, in 45 minutes. From the rim of the cliffs you have a magnificent view of the valleys to the south, and you can climb out to a rock ledge where there is a superb view of Table Rock. This is one of the best photo opportunities you will have to capture the beauty and grandeur of the rock formation.

As you leave the picnic area, when you pass the gate and start the first switchback downward, you will also have a superior view of Table Rock. This too is a unique photo opportunity.

Best times to hike up Table Rock are in late April, May, September, and October.

37

Mount Mitchell Trail

Total distance (one way): 6 miles

*Hiking time: 5.5 hours or 3.5 hours
(depending upon direction)*

Vertical rise: 3,720 feet

Rating: Strenuous

*Maps: USGS 7.5' Montreat, USGS 7.5'
Mount Mitchell, and USGS 7.5' Celo*

In North Carolina there are several mountain ranges, including the Blue Ridge, Smokies (partly in bordering states), South, Uwharrie, Black, Balsam, Nantahala, Unaka, and Crowders Mountain areas. More than 40 peaks in the state have elevations of over 6,000 feet. Eighty peaks range in height from 5,000 to 6,000 feet, and several hundred peaks rise 4,000 to 5,000 feet above sea level.

In the Black Mountain area many peaks are 5,000 feet or higher, and the region contains a large number of excellent hiking trails, some of which will challenge the hardiest and most experienced hikers. One of these hikes is the Mount Mitchell Trail, which crosses through large portions of Mount Mitchell itself and the South Toe River area.

Mount Mitchell is the highest peak in the state and also the highest point east of the Mississippi. For years there was a running dispute over which peak was the highest in the East, with some insisting that Mount Washington in New Hampshire (6,288 feet) or various peaks near Mount Mitchell were the highest.

It was in 1835 that Dr. Elisha Mitchell, at that time 42 years old and a professor of science at the University of North Carolina (held by many to be the oldest state university in the nation by virtue of the fact that Harvard College was not state-operated), journeyed to the western part of the state and climbed several of the peaks.

By using mathematical computations and barometric pressure, Dr. Mitchell, who was also a theology scholar, determined

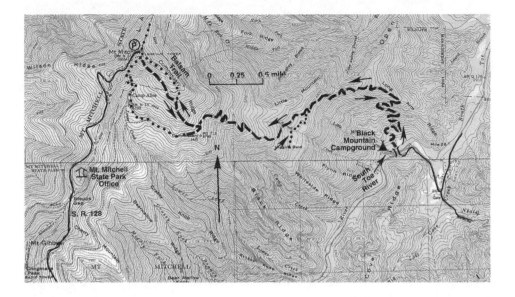

that Mount Mitchell was 6,476 feet high. He returned in 1838 and again in 1844; recalculating, he decided that the mountain was actually 6,672 feet high.

While he was still in error, it is astonishing that his calculation was in fact within 12 feet of the exact height of the mountain that bears his name.

Like most great thinkers and teachers, Dr. Mitchell produced students who were similarly if not equally great researchers and thinkers. One of Mitchell's former students, Thomas Clingman, who was at this time a United States senator, leaped into the fray and announced that Dr. Mitchell had erred and that the correct altitude of the mountain was 6,941 feet.

In 1857, at age 64, Mitchell returned to the area and set out to verify his contention that his earlier estimates were correct. He was hiking across the mountain when he apparently attempted to cross a small stream, lost his footing, and was swept over the 40-foot-high waterfall immediately below him.

Mitchell was knocked unconscious and drowned in the plunge basin below the falls. His body was recovered by a search group that included Zebulon Vance (whose home is a few miles south of Mount Mitchell), the legendary Civil War officer, governor of North Carolina, and United States senator.

Mitchell was buried in Asheville, where later the novelist Thomas Wolfe *(Look Homeward, Angel)*, short-story writer O. Henry, and Vance himself were buried. Mitchell's remains were later exhumed and transported to the peak of the mountain that bears his name—a fitting tribute to one of the leading scholars of his age, who brought the mountain to such public attention.

Later, Governor Locke Craig (1860–1924) campaigned vigorously to have the mountain preserved as a state park, the very first to be established in North Carolina. The mountain became a park in 1915.

To reach Mount Mitchell, the easiest and surest route is to join the Blue Ridge Parkway at Asheville and travel 35 miles north to NC 128. Follow the highway to the top of the mountain and to the parking lot. This route will be useful if you choose to start at the top of the Mount Mitchell Trail and hike downward to the Black Mountain Campground.

If you prefer to start at the campground and climb Mount Mitchell, you will need extra hiking time and greater endurance. In either event, you will need two vehicles, one to park at the campground and the other to leave at the top of Mount Mitchell—unless you prefer to backtrack, which will of course double your hiking distance and more than double the hiking time.

To reach the Black Mountain Campground, exit the Blue Ridge Parkway at Milepost 346 at Big Laurel Gap (Forest Road 2074). At 2.5 miles intersect with Forest Road 472. Continue on Forest Road 2074 for 0.8 mile and follow signs to Black Mountain Campground.

Because of the altitude of Mount Mitchell, you will find that the weather is invariably cool near the top. On our hike we left temperatures in the 90s, and hours later, in midafternoon, the temperature atop Mount Mitchell was a chilly 51 degrees. As always, stay alert for thunderstorms during the summer months. Lightning can be fierce and highly dangerous along the mountain ridges, and in June, July, and August you can expect rain or a storm virtually every afternoon.

Don't take chances with hypothermia at these elevations. You can become a victim in summer as well as during the cooler months. Often the temperature near the top of Mount Mitchell is in the low 40s, even in warmer months. Below-zero temperatures are common during cooler months, and if you are hiking in cool weather (in the lower areas) the temperature can be brutal atop the mountain. Dress appropriately and carry extra food and clothing.

If you start the hike from Black Mountain Campground, as you leave the campground you will cross over the bridge spanning the South Toe River and enter a forest of hardwood trees and a scattering of evergreens. The evergreens become thicker almost instantly, and you will start a series of severe switchbacks up the steep mountain.

At times the switchbacks are so curved that the trail very nearly doubles back to where you have just hiked; your natural temptation will be to leave the trail to take a quick shortcut to the next switchback.

You are urged to stay on the trail, which is at times highly strenuous. In warmer weather be alert for timber rattlesnakes and copperheads, which enjoy the cool shade of the many rock crevices along the trail. You will also encounter poison ivy.

At mile 1.5 the trail intersects with the Higgins Bald Trail. (If you wish you can hike this 1.6-mile spur trail and rejoin the Mount Mitchell Trail. If you stay on the original trail you will intersect with the Higgins Bald Trail again within 1.2 miles. The difference in distances is that the Higgins Bald Trail sweeps farther south and includes huge curves that add to the hiking distance.)

Where the two trails join a second time, you have hiked 3 miles, more or less, of the total distance. At the 3.9-mile point the trail elevation is about 4,500 feet.

At mile 4.0 you will reach the ancient Camp Alice, which in the 1920s was part of a logging camp. During this time period there was one large and very elaborate (for that time and place) lodge building that was later converted into a lodge for visitors to Mount Mitchell. Only the stone foundations remain today.

You will notice many dead trees, primarily balsam and spruce. These trees are victims, for the most part, of the balsam woolly aphid and acid rain. The effects and na-

Mount Mitchell as seen from the Blue Ridge Parkway.

tures of these two menaces are described in more detail in the hike description in chapter 38.

At mile 5.2 you will reach a junction with the Balsam Trail, which starts a few feet below the observation tower atop Mount Mitchell. Within 0.3 mile you will reach the trail that connects the observation tower and the parking lot. At this point you can retrieve the second vehicle or backtrack to the Black Mountain Campground.

If you choose the latter, allow at least 3.5 hours to make the descent.

Chapter 38 provides details for another hike you can make in the Mount Mitchell area.

38

Deep Gap Trail

Distance (backtrack): 6 miles

Hiking time: 5 hours

Vertical rise: 3,540 feet

Rating: Strenuous

Maps: USGS 7.5' Mount Mitchell, USGS 7.5' Montreat, and USGS 7.5' Celo

This hiking experience can involve taking a connecting trail from the Deep Gap Trail for a longer hike, or, if you prefer, you can hike only the Deep Gap Trail and backtrack to Mount Mitchell. If you choose a longer hike as part of one day's outing, you may wish to use two vehicles, with one at the parking area on Mount Mitchell and the second vehicle at your destination. (The other options are described below.)

To get to Mount Mitchell, drive north of Asheville on the Blue Ridge Parkway. The park is approximately 33 miles north of Asheville. When you reach NC 128, follow it to the parking area at the top of the mountain.

Along the way you will see striking examples of the changing face of the mountain. You will pass thick forests of balsam fir, some of which may attain heights of 75 feet and have trunks 2 feet in diameter. This is the tree that yields balsam oil, which is often used to cement lenses together, as an ingredient in medicines, and as a staple in artwork.

The resin from this tree, according to folklore, has major curative powers for sore throats and hoarseness. The seeds from this tree are eaten by quail and grouse, both of which inhabit the area.

You will also notice that there are numerous dead trees along the way and, indeed, almost everywhere you look along the slopes of the mountain. The major fatalities are among the Fraser fir and red spruce. The Fraser fir is the most abundant tree in the park and on the mountain. Named for the English botanist John Fraser, who explored the southern Appala-

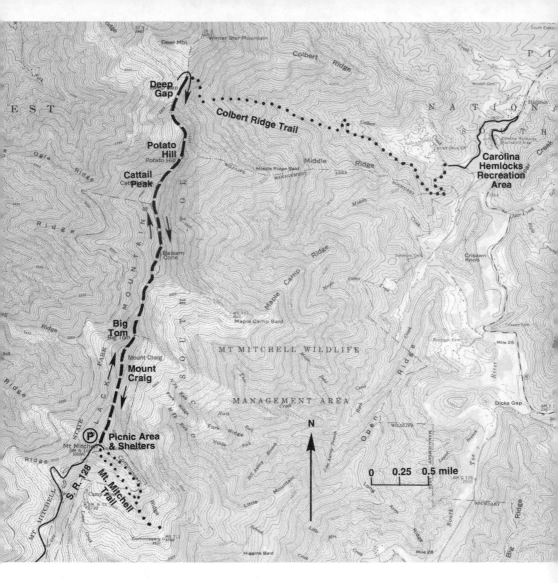

chians in the late 1700s, the tree is also known as the southern balsam. It is easily recognized by the wonderful fragrance of its needles and sap. The sap itself was considered for decades to be a panacea for rheumatism, dysentery, and wounds of all types.

The red spruce tree, which looks similar, can be distinguished by the stiffness and prickly characteristics of the needles and by the darker shade of bark than that of the Fraser fir. Balsam cones project upward, while spruce cones extend downward. The red-spruce wood is used for lumber and for musical instruments, and the smaller branches, when boiled in a potful of water, produce a drink that is known as spruce beer.

The cause of death of the many trees has never been verified by science, but all indications are that three major causes contribute to the decline of the forests: the balsam woolly aphid, acid rain, and stress of the severe weather.

In earlier years the logging industry reduced forests to a considerable extent, but logging has ceased in the area. The aphid is less than one-fourth of an inch long and has no natural enemies in the forests of North Carolina, so its growth is uncontrolled. This pest (Adelges picae) is composed entirely of females. These females reportedly can reproduce without mating or fertilization.

While the aphids are feeding, they inject a substance into the bark of the tree that keeps water and nutrients from entering into the tree's system. At the present time, no effective prevention has been found against this tiny creature, which has done more damage to one of the most beautiful forests in the nation than all other dangers combined, with the possible exception of acid rain.

Annually in the United States millions of tons of sulphur dioxide and nitrogen oxides are released into the air, and these chemicals form what is known as acid rain. Park officials report that in 8 out of 10 days the trees of Mount Mitchell are subjected to clouds and fog that at times are as acidic as vinegar. Thus the forests of Mount Mitchell are in serious trouble, but all known measures are being taken to protect what remains of the forests. Meanwhile, there is plenty left to be enjoyed by the hikers and other visitors.

When you reach the top of the mountain, you will find a wide, easy, gravel trail that leads 0.2 mile upward to the observation tower. At the base of the tower is the burial place of Dr. Elisha Mitchell, whose epitaph reads: "Here lies in the hope of blessed resurrection the body of the Rev. Elisha Mitchell, D.D., who after being for thirty-nine years a professor in the University of North Carolina lost his life in the scientific exploration of this mountain, in the sixty-fourth year of his age—June 27, 1857."

You can climb the observation tower, which is open year-round, for one of the finest and most awesome views anywhere east of the Mississippi. Climb the 47 steps and emerge onto a circular open area that provides a 360-degree view. At this point you are 6,719 feet above sea level.

To the north you can see Mount Craig and Mount Tom, sometimes referred to as the Black Brothers. The label is derived from the dark bark of the spruce trees, which also gave the Black Mountains their name.

The Black Mountain range near Mount Mitchell contains 6 of the 10 highest peaks in eastern America. Very small in length, the Black Mountain range is in the shape of the letter J, and the distance between the end points of the J is only 15 miles.

Near Mount Mitchell, on a clear day, you can see Green Knob (elevation 4,761 feet), Clingman's Peak (6,598 feet), and many nameless peaks well over 4,000 feet.

As you descend the tower steps, note the plaque marking the rededication of Mount Mitchell State Park in 1991, the ceremony marking the 75th anniversary of the establishment of the park.

Return to the parking area and descend the stone steps at the northern end for the Deep Gap Trail, one of the most strenuous trails in North Carolina. Cross NC 128 and enter the picnic area. Pass between two wooden shelters and proceed directly down a gravel trail, which quickly becomes a natural trail with rocks underfoot for long distances at a time.

Pass through a dense fir and spruce forest and immediately begin a sharp descent that at times is nearly vertical. After this descent, of 800 feet, you immediately start to climb Mount Craig.

You will hike along the surface of huge

boulders with occasional thin coverings of soil and vegetation. Along the trail there are blackberries, raspberries, fire cherries, and a wild array of flowers, many of them varieties of aster.

As you hike you will have superb views of Mount Craig, Mount Tom, the South Toe valley, and Roan Mountain, among other peaks. There are about 10 peaks over 6,000 feet high within a 5-mile hike.

The first peak reached after one mile of hiking is Mount Craig. At the very top is a plaque embedded in a huge boulder, and the inscription reads: "Mount Craig Altitude 6,663. Named for Locke Craig (1860–1924) who as governor of North Carolina (1913–1917) was largely responsible for the establishment of the Mount Mitchell State Park."

In another mile you reach Mount Tom, or Big Tom. This peak, along with Mount Craig, is one of the Black Brothers, as the locals refer to the mountains that are given their dark appearance by the dark bark of the spruce and balsams. Big Tom, named for Thomas Wilson, one of the leaders of the search party that found the body of Dr. Mitchell, is 6,558 feet high.

Other peaks along Deep Gap Trail include Cattail Peak and Potato Hill before you reach Deep Gap. At Deep Gap you have several choices. The most frequently used alternative is to backtrack to Mount Mitchell for a 5.4-mile hike. You can also continue straight ahead for 8 more miles and end the hike at the intersection of State Road 197 and State Road 1109. Or you can hike the Colbert Ridge Trail 3.7 miles into Carolina Hemlocks Recreation Area on NC 80 for a 6.4-mile hike. If you make any choice but the backtrack, a second vehicle is probably a necessity, but the remaining trails, while strenuous, are very rewarding.

If you are hiking very early or late, you may be treated to one of the most bone-chilling sounds on earth: the scream of a cougar or mountain lion, a creature which is officially considered to be extinct in North Carolina but which has been spotted on several occasions by reliable witnesses. Still others, including the authors of the book, have heard the unmistakable screams of the cougar, which is incredibly like the sound one would imagine a terrified woman would make. It is not a pleasant sound to the novice in the forest; it is a tremendously exciting one to veteran woodsmen.

You may also see foxes, bobcats, flying squirrels, and other animals among the forest of fire cherry, maple, hickory, laurel, and rhododendron.

When the hike is completed, you have finished one of the most memorable hikes in the state of North Carolina and one of the finest in the entire East.

39

Lake James State Park Trails

Total distance (backtrack): 2.7 miles

Hiking time: 1.5 hours

Vertical rise: 820 feet

Rating: Easy, handicapped accessible

Map: USGS 7.5' Marion East

For a hike that is easy, short, and quick, combining the Lake Channel Overlook Trail and the Sandy Cliff Overlook Trail at Lake James State Park is perfect, particularly for those hikers who are not physically able or inclined to undertake some of the more demanding hikes. This hike, like the Erwins View Trail at the Linville Falls Recreation Area, is one that can be made with relative ease.

To get to Lake James State Park, leave I-40 at the Lake James State Park–Nebo exit (Exit 90 in McDowell County between Asheville and Morganton) and drive north. You will cross US 64 and follow signs to the park. After you leave I-40 you will drive 0.4 mile to intersect with State Road 1760. Turn right and follow State Road 1760 to the park entrance.

Lake James is a man-made impoundment created between 1916 and 1923. The lake, named for James B. Duke, founder of Duke Power Company, was created by the construction of three dams, across the Catawba River, Linville River, and Paddy Creek.

The Linville River flows from the Linville Gorge and enters the lake some 12 miles from Linville Falls. The lake, which lies 1,200 feet above sea level, contains 6,510 acres and has a shoreline of 154 miles.

Part of Lake James became the newest member of the North Carolina state park system in 1987. The Lake James State Park offers fishing, hiking, camping, picnicking, and nature study.

Campsites are on a first-come, first-served basis at a fee of $9 per night per campsite. Sites include a cooking grill, pic-

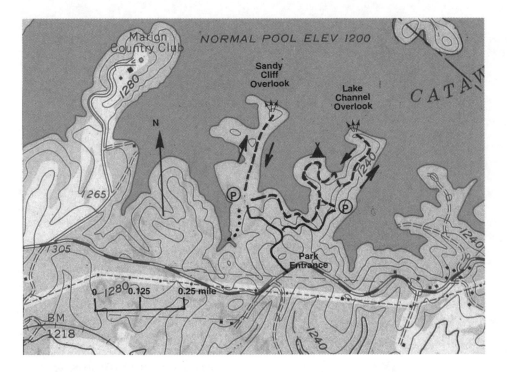

nic table, tent space, and water hydrants at every fifth site.

The state park has five miles of shoreline and approximately 564 acres. More than 220,000 persons visit the state park each year, primarily for fishing, camping, and swimming. Hiking trails, while neatly maintained, are seldom crowded.

They are so private that annually a pair of Canada geese nests on the shore only a few feet from the trail and the Lake Channel Overlook. The geese may use old nests of hawks and eagles, but they usually nest on the ground. The nest itself is made up of sticks and twigs that are lined or covered with down the geese pull from their bodies. These beautiful birds, which are unusually clever in using their coloration to elude their enemies, weigh up to 18 pounds. Wildlife authorities such as Laurence Palmer and Seymour Fowler say that the goose can fly up to speeds of 80 miles per hour.

Seeing the Canada goose (alternately known as cravat goose, wild goose, bay goose, Canada brant, and long-necked goose) can alone make the hike worthwhile. The best time to observe the nesting habits of the geese is in mid-April to early May. Five to nine goslings will be hatched in early June each year. The adult geese mate for life and demonstrate loyalty often absent in the wild—or tame—animal kingdom.

Other birds of interest that populate the park are the pileated woodpecker, which stands 19 to 20 inches tall and has a wingspan of 30 inches, kingfisher, yellow-shafted flicker, redheaded woodpecker, cormorant, screech owl, great horned owl, a variety of hawks, songbirds, and a wide range of waterfowl including mallards, green-winged teals, great blue heron, green heron, and others.

Larger animals in or near the park include black bear, white-tailed deer, bobcats, raccoons, muskrats, mink, and opossums. The snake population is made up largely of black rat snakes, king snakes, water snakes, garter snakes, hognose snakes, ring-necked snakes, copperheads, and other less common reptiles.

Rattlesnakes inhabit the area north of Lake James, but none have been spotted and identified in the park. A variety of lizards and skinks call the park home.

To start the hike, park in front of the park office building and walk eastward toward the picnic tables amid the cluster of tall pines. A maintenance road leads into the picnic area, and 50 feet down the road you will see two trail markers. One of these trails leads to the Sandy Cliff Overlook, 0.3 mile ahead. (Information in the park office states that the backtrack trail is 0.5 mile long, but may be somewhat shorter.)

The other trail, which leads to the right, is the longer Lake Channel Overlook Trail. This backtrack trail is 1.5 miles (total distance) and is a very easy, delightful trail to hike when time and energy are limited.

The Lake Channel Overlook Trail leads first around a narrow neck of the lake and through a forest of tall pines. At 330 feet there is an immense pile of stumps, log butts, root balls, and other debris left over from park construction work and left to decay and nourish the forest as well as to prevent against erosion on the hillside.

As you hike along the lakeshore, you will notice a number of huge trees that have fallen into the lake, partially because of high winds and partially from erosion. Park officials note that the park is losing one foot per year on the north side of the lake. As lake winds churn the water and boat wakes create a lapping effect, the water undercuts the bank until the tree roots cannot hold the tree upright.

Wind blows steadily from the Linville

Gorge–Shortoff Mountain area and is a constant factor in erosion and climate. If you hike in winter, the winds produce uncomfortably cold weather unless you are well protected against the chill factor.

At 0.2 mile, a break in the shoreline trees offers a superb view of the mountains beyond Lake James, with Table Rock clearly visible. Table Rock was a sacred mountain for the Cherokees. A superb hiking trail to Table Rock summit is described in chapter 36.

At 0.3 mile you will reach a concrete ramp built into the water and serving as a boat-landing area. The water is very deep around this area and the bottom of the lake is irregular, so no wading or swimming is permitted. In this portion of the lake the depth is up to 90 feet just offshore.

Immediately before you reach the concrete ramp you will cross a footbridge. The picnic-camping area is to the left and up the shore of the lake 30 feet.

At 0.4 mile the trail widens into an old logging road and then into a gravel road. Shortly past the 0.4-mile mark you turn right onto a very narrow trail, pass along a split-rail fence, and soon emerge into a clearing where there is another split-rail fence, a grassy slope on your right, and a flight of steps leading up to a clearing where there is a rest room (with facilities for persons with handicaps).

The road from the park office leads around the hardwood forest you passed through and reaches the rest-room area for campers. If you wish, you can drive to this point and hike the remainder of the way.

Keep the rest-room facilities on your right as you follow the walk and then in 30 feet turn sharply to the left and follow the gravel road again toward the lake. At 0.6 mile you will hike along the gravel road between beautiful dogwood trees (in full blossom in late April and early May) and through

The Linville Gorge area as seen from Lake James

Robert L. Williams

a forest of oak, hickory, poplar, maple, and a scattering of pine and cedar.

The lake is on both sides of you at this point. On the left, between the road and the lake, is a small outdoor theater or presentation platform.

Enter the deeper forest at the end of the gravel road and again hike along a narrow neck of land that juts into the lake. Stay on the trail. Some of the banks are severely undercut and may collapse if you try to hike too near the edge of the cliffs.

At 0.8 mile you will reach the Lake Channel Overlook. From the overlook you can see Table Rock clearly as well as the notch that is Linville Gorge, one of the wildest wilderness areas in the East. Once you have enjoyed the view, backtrack to the maintenance road in the picnic area near the park offices. At the sign you will turn to the right for the Sandy Cliff Trail.

The Sandy Cliff Trail is excellent for the total novice to learn the simplest fundamentals of hiking. It is also a superior trail for persons with physical handicaps to explore a natural world of beauty, tranquillity, and natural balance.

The trail proceeds along a wide strip of land in a nearly straight line until you reach the north end of the wide peninsula. The trail leads over gently rolling hills from which hikers can see wide expanses of Lake James, enjoy the songbirds that are numerous inside the park, and observe the waterfowl feeding along the banks.

Along the trail you will see, in season, a number of wildflowers, including but not limited to showy lady's slipper, cardinal flower, jack-in-the-pulpit, windflower or wood anemone, foam flower or false miterwort, wild field strawberry, wild morning glory, common morning glory, ox-eye daisy, and multitudes of other spring, summer, and fall beauties.

In addition you will find dewberries and blackberries. The dewberries, first cousins to the blackberries, are members of the rose family and grow very close to the ground. One of the special treats of the forests lining the Lake James State Park woodlands is the passionflower. This flower takes its common name because of the perceived similarities of the corona to the crown of thorns usually associated with the death of Jesus of Nazareth. The five sepals and the five petals are said to symbolize the ten faithful apostles (with Peter, who denied, and Judas, who betrayed, be-ing omitted). Other parts of the plant are said to symbolize the nails, or wounds, just as the dogwood tree is related in some parts of the country to the same historical event.

In 0.3 mile you reach the Sandy Cliff Overlook, an elevated platform large enough to hold a dozen or more people easily. The overlook provides a superb view of the dam to the right, a clear sight of Table Rock to the north, and the upper elevations of Linville Gorge.

Backtrack to the parking area. The return hike requires no longer than 20 minutes, unless you choose to linger to enjoy the vegetation and wildlife.

40

Cloudland Trail

Total distance (backtrack and loop): 5 miles

Hiking time: 2.5 hours

Vertical rise: 800 feet

Rating: Easy, handicapped accessible

Maps: USGS 7.5' Bakersville and USGS 7.5' Carvers Gap

Roan Mountain is located on the border of North Carolina and Tennessee. The mountain itself is known throughout the state and much of the South for the beautiful rhododendron gardens that are in full bloom in early summer, usually around the middle of June.

The blooming of the rhododendron attracts many thousands of people to the mountain, and there is a rhododendron festival nearby that attracts even greater crowds. In summer the hiking trails are rather crowded. The hikes at Roan Mountain are easy.

To get to Roan Mountain, leave I-40 at the US 226 exit at Marion, North Carolina, and follow US 226 until it intersects with NC 261 near Bakersville and Spruce Pine. Follow NC 261 to State Road 1348 (Roan Mountain Road) and follow the road to parking lot number one, partway up Roan Mountain.

From the parking-lot head you will find the trailhead for the Cloudland Trail at the far west end of the pavement. The trail begins in a high thicket of rhododendron and scattered hardwood trees. When you are 400 feet into the trail, you will see a trail split off to the left. Do not take this trail, which leads to the Rhododendron Gardens, which you will reach shortly. Remain on the trail to the right.

At 610 feet you will reach a short spur trail that leads to an overlook. This is a very short spur, and the overlook is well worth the few feet of hiking needed. From the overlook you can see the wide expanse of the valley on the Tennessee side of the

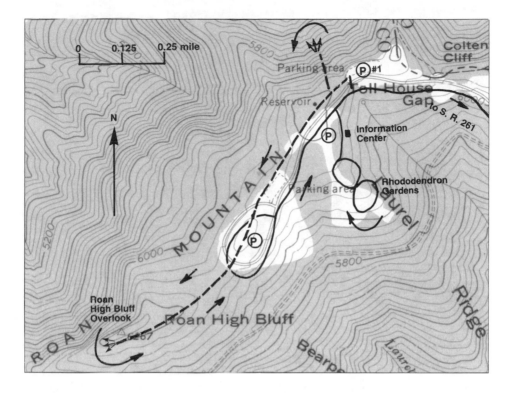

mountain, and some tiny settlements and farmsteads can be seen.

Return to the main trail (which you will reach at 727 feet) and continue westward. There are now many hemlock and fir trees along the trail and the rhododendron is more scattered. Occasional pines mark the forest on each side of the trail.

At 0.3 mile you will reach a sign pointing the direction to the Rhododendron Gardens. Do not take this direction but remain with the primary trail. At 0.5 mile the trail veers to the right. Do not continue straight ahead.

You will cross a gravel road at 0.7 mile and enter a thick forest of fir and hemlock. The trail, which started as a narrow trail and then widened into one that two could walk abreast, now narrows again into a single-file trail. The center portions of the trail have eroded because of heavy rains and you are,

for a short distance, walking in the ditch created by the erosion.

At 0.9 mile you will cross a second gravel road. There are picnic tables to the left, and heavy foot traffic from this point has resulted in a new widening of the trail, which now leads through a forest of huge hemlock trees with sporadic hardwood growths of hickory, oak, and ash.

You will reach the top of the mountain (6,267 feet elevation) and continue toward the overlook, which is the end of the trail. You have by this time passed two parking lots in addition to the one where the trail started. Anyone wanting to see the superior view but not having the physical capacity for the 3-mile round trip can park at the final parking lot and walk the remainder of the trail, a distance of less than 0.5 mile, to the overlook.

The trail is paved for approximately 300

Roan Mountain and Carvers Gap in winter

yards from the final gravel road crossing. The final 150 yards is the only part of the trail that could be considered moderately difficult. The upper portions of the trail tend to be wet much of the year, the result of heavy rains that occur with regularity in the higher elevations along the chain of mountains separating North Carolina and Tennessee.

In the final 100 yards of the hike the trail becomes rockier and the footing less certain. Huge oaks grow in the forests around the mountainside, and the trail itself is often a virtual tunnel of laurel and rhododendron.

Before you reach the overlook you will climb a short flight of rock steps (only five risers) and then you will step out onto the overlook itself, which is a wooden structure large enough to accommodate 15 to 20 persons. The platform is circled by a strong railing.

From this vantage point you can see some of the finest natural scenery in the mountains. The best time for photography from this vantage point is in mid morning or at noon. In mid to late afternoon the haze interferes with sight-seeing as well as photo work.

Backtrack, when you have had your fill of the view, to the sign directing you to the Rhododendron Gardens. You passed (at 1,417 feet into the trail) the sign on the way in. Now turn to the right and travel 60 feet to the road. Cross the road and travel to the information board in the parking area at the comfort stations.

You can now hike around a triple loop of paved trails (a total of 2 miles) that will lead you to every point of interest in the Rhododendron Gardens. These loop trails link with each other for easy transition from one trail to the other. One of the trails is designed for handicapped persons and can be easily handled by those with physical disabilities.

The lower trail has 16 stops on the self-guided nature trail. These stops include one overlook (with a virtual sea of flowering rhododendron starting yearly about June 19) spread out below the overlook itself. The best time to photograph the flowering shrubs is about 2 PM to 4 PM In the mornings the sun will be into the lens of the camera and will make good photos difficult.

The lower loop leads down the side of the mountain a short distance and then circles back to the comfort stations. The higher loop circles through a grassy bald and passes close enough to the rhododendron that you can get close-up photos of the blossoms.

Return to the Cloudland Trail and to the parking lot.

You have other excellent trail options while you are in the Appalachian Trail area. An Appalachian Trail Sampler is found in chapter 41.

41

Appalachian Trail Sampler

Total distance (backtrack): 7.8 miles

Hiking time: 4 hours

Vertical rise: 5,400 feet

Rating: Strenuous

Maps: USGS 7.5' Bakersville and USGS 7.5' Carvers Gap

The Appalachian Trail is known to almost any serious hiker. Of the 2,100 miles of this amazingly varied and scenic trail, many segments in North Carolina offer a satisfying one-day hike.

Of the more than 200 miles of the Appalachian Trail in North Carolina, nearly all the segments of the trail offer a unique experience and memories that are unforgettable. It is virtually impossible to select a sampler that will do justice to the most famous trail in the United States.

Because the Appalachian Trail crosses almost every imaginable type of terrain known to the eastern United States from Georgia to Maine, we tried to include a segment that contained some rugged forest miles, grassy balds, historical backdrops, lonely and solitary places as well as more populated areas, closed-in thickets and wide open spaces, and areas replete with wildflowers and wild animals, scenic vistas, and at least two shelters.

The selection we finally agreed upon was the hike from Roan High Knob to Roan Highlands Shelter. You can start atop the 6,285-foot peak and hike down to Carvers Gap at 5,512 feet, and from that point you can continue to Roan Highlands Shelter at 5,050 feet. This is a 4.8-mile hike. Then you can backtrack to Carvers Gap and add almost 3 miles to the total hike.

Make vehicle arrangements so that you do not have to backtrack up Roan High Knob once you have hiked down to Carvers Gap and across the balds on the opposite side of NC 261. Either park one vehicle at the top and another at Carvers Gap, or al-

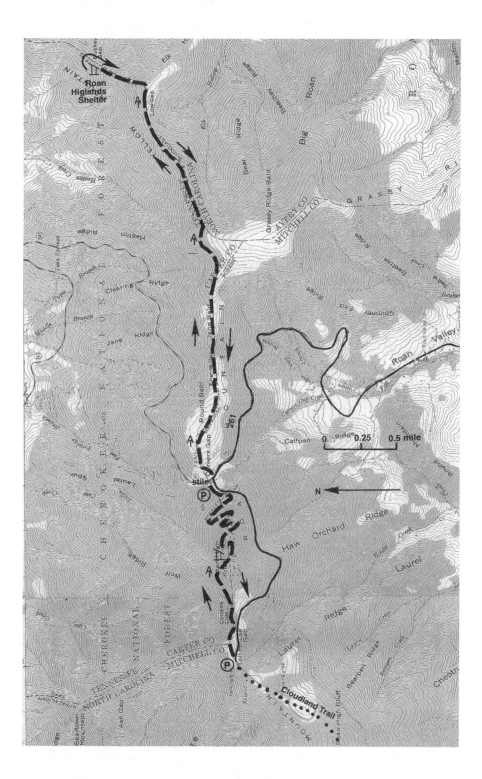

low one driver to drop off hikers at the top of the mountain and then wait to join them at the bottom.

The trail is rough, rocky, and often wet, particularly during the spring and summer seasons.Do not hike the segment in winter unless you are assured of good weather by an updated weather forecast.

Despite the moisture seeping across the trail, there are no streams along the hike. The one usable spring in the area is prone to run low because of dry weather across the state in recent years.

Start at the eastern end of parking lot #1 on Roan Mountain, the same parking lot used to hike the Cloudland Trail and the Rhododendron Gardens. (See chapter 40 for directions to Roan Mountain.) The only difference is that you strike the trail at opposite ends of the parking lot.

Leave the pavement and walk around the short barricade on the other side of the fence. You will plunge into a thick forest growth of oak, hickory, poplar, ash, hemlock, and fir. The laurel and rhododendron are virtually always present.

At times the descent of the trail is difficult. You will be losing almost 800 feet in elevation within 1.9 miles. Through a series of switchbacks and straight descents, the trail drops continually.

In 0.6 mile from parking lot #1, you will reach the Roan High Knob Shelter where, if you are hiking longer than the day hikes, you can spend the night. If you prefer to keep hiking, continue from the shelter for 1.3 miles to Carvers Gap.

At this point you are ready to tackle the balds ahead of you. When you stand at the parking area across the highway from the balds, the first sight you see is that of an old-fashioned stile and behind it a series of steps that reach three-fourths of the way to the top of the bald.

The stile is made up of four log steps leading on each side to the top of the fence. The stringers of the steps are also made of logs bleached white by age, wind, and sun.

Beyond the stile is a short stretch of wide trail (200 feet long and wide enough for two or three to hike abreast). Then you reach the log steps sunk into a bed of gravel to keep the hillside from eroding further.

You are urged to use the logs as stepping pads rather than using the eroded portions of the trail on each side of the logs. The hillside is very steep and erosion has been a problem for years in this area. The logs are eight feet long and ample for all hiking needs. Staying on the logs will help to assure that the trail will be usable for future generations of hikers.

As you cross the stile, you will see an information sign posted on one of the fence rails. The sign points out that you will find the Roan Highlands Shelter 2.9 miles straight ahead on the Appalachian Trail. (At 4.6 miles you would reach the Overmountain Shelter, and in 7.8 miles you would reach Hump Mountain.)

The Roan Highlands Shelter is not to be confused with the Roan High Knob Shelter on the south side of NC 261. As you hike this portion of the Appalachian Trail you will soon understand why there are several shelters within a short distance of each other. So many weekend and vacation hikers use this portion of the Appalachian Trail that the shelters tend to be more crowded than are many segments of the Appalachian Trail.

As you climb the log steps, if you turn and look behind you from time to time you will be rewarded by superb views of Roan Mountain. Look back every few minutes, because the view changes with each step, it seems, and changing light conditions present the mountain in different hues and shades within remarkably short time spans.

The colors on the trail are varied and impressive at nearly all times of the year. In spring the new foliage is a soft and delicate green; in late spring the hillside is dotted with wildflowers. In early summer the rhododendron is in full bloom, and in late summer the blueberry bushes are loaded with berries which attract many birds, deer, and other animals.

In early autumn the leaves are changing, lending their colors to an already magnificent scene; in late autumn the final wildflowers are in bloom and the wild strawberry plants have been turned a dark red by frost and time. In winter, the snows cover the mountains and add another dimension of beauty to the scene.

In truth, it would be difficult to find a spot more beautiful year-round than is Roan Mountain. And the hiking trails lead into the midst of all the beauty.

As the trail climbs the mountain, the rhododendron bushes line the log steps, and at the end of the logs there are huge rocks that stand out in stark contrast to the brilliant colors of the trail. At the top of the ridge, 0.5 mile from the highway, the trail narrows to a two-foot-wide path through the high grass of the bald.

As you hike along the top of the bald you will notice that the traditional footpath has been worn into a rut by water and by hikers' feet. Hikers have trampled out a new trail immediately adjacent to the old one.

The elevation at the top of Round Bald is 5,826 feet, and from the highway to the top the distance is 0.5 mile. From the top of the climb to the next bald, the distance is 0.6 mile.

Hike along the crest of the hill for 600 feet and then start downhill in a rapid descent that curves south and then east before it dips into a shallow valley and then starts up the next hill. The trail is now wide and covered with loose shale rock, which makes the trail from a distance look like asphalt.

As the climb begins, the trail narrows and becomes far more difficult. The footing is uncertain and the washouts have left makeshift steps ranging from rocks to dug-out steps in the sides of mud banks. At times you will have to pull yourself up by using branches of rhododendron shrubs for assistance.

As you climb, keep turning and looking behind you. At this point you have Round Bald and Roan Mountain outlined against the sky, which is often cloudy and menacing. You can see summer storms approaching for miles and sometimes an hour before they hit.

At the top of the second ridge there is another rock outcropping that provides an excellent place for a brief rest before hiking the rest of the way to Roan Highlands Shelter, 1.8 miles away. Allow enough time, if you are on a day hike, to get back to the highway before dark.

IV

Southern Highlands

42

Buck Spring Trail

Total distance (one way): 6.4 miles

Hiking time: 3.5 hours

Vertical rise: 2,600 feet

Rating: Moderate

Maps: USGS 7.5' Cruso, USGS 7.5' Dunsmore Mountain, and USGS 7.5' Shining Rock

To start the Buck Spring Trail, park either at the Mount Pisgah parking lot on the left side of the Blue Ridge Parkway at Milepost 408.5 or on the right side of the parkway (driving south) at 408.6. You can also hit the trail from the Pisgah Inn; however, parking is at a premium here and the spaces are needed for guests at the inn or restaurant. You may let someone drop you off in front of the inn, but do not leave cars parked there without permission.

You may need to set up a vehicle-shuttle arrangement before you begin the hike. The trail is long enough that backtracking will take a great deal of time that you may prefer to use on another trail. If you have two vehicles, park one at the gravel parking area on US 276. Driving south on the parkway, turn left on US 276 and travel four miles to reach the parking area. Then drive all hikers back to the Pisgah Inn.

Start the hike from the Mount Pisgah parking lot on the left side of the parkway (again, heading south). Go to the southernmost point of the parking lot and look for a large sign that shows the way to the Buck Spring Trail.

If you start from the parking lot across the parkway, cross the parkway and walk into the entrance for the parking lot. The trailhead will be on your immediate right as you face east. Follow the short trail through the rhododendron thicket to the Pisgah Inn. The trail begins at the northwest corner of the inn, or you can hit the trail at the southeast corner of the inn. Walk to the overlook and then take the trail to the right, off the overlook.

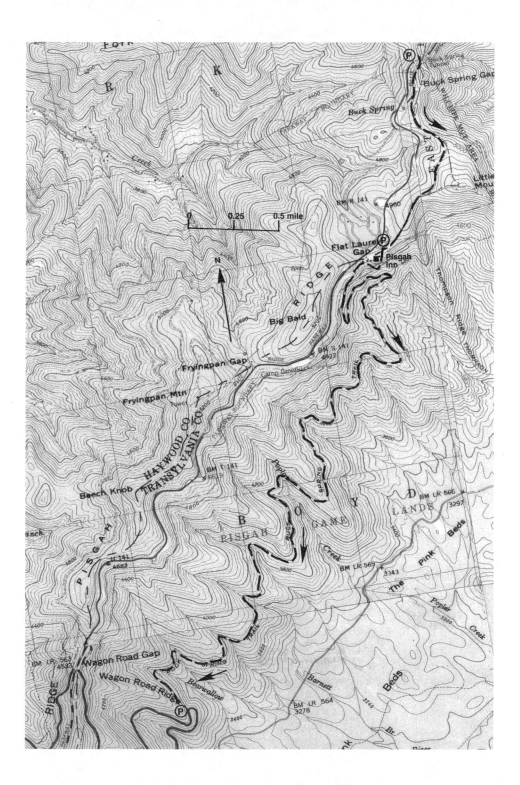

In warmer weather, you will hear two distinct sounds almost as soon as you start to hike the trail. The first of these sounds is a high-pitched, shrill whistle, very much like the frightened call of a bird. The second sound you hear will be that of leaves rustling virtually under your feet.

If you pause and watch carefully, you will see a number of chipmunks. These delightful creatures—or others like them—will accompany you along the entire length of the trail. An old woodsman's maxim is that if you hear the chipmunks whistle near you, there are not likely to be any snakes, poisonous or otherwise, in the immediate area. If you hear the tiny rodents whistle from a distance and there are no other hikers in the area, be alert for the presence of unseen and perhaps unwanted company in the forest.

While the maxim may not be totally reliable (and do not become careless simply because the chipmunks say all is well!), it is fascinating to see, hear, and enjoy the scurrying of these animals.

You will hike the first mile in approximately one-half hour, and you will likely keep this pace for the remainder of the hike. It is possible to hike much faster, but this trail, while missing the spectacular overlooks and waterfalls that grace so many other trails, is filled with tiny spectacles, such as brooks creeping from between rocks, interesting rock formations, an abundance of wild birds, including songbirds as well as game birds like wild turkey, grouse, and partridge.

The first mile of the trail is rocky underfoot, while the forest generally is clear of huge rocks. The forest growth is largely rhododendron and oak, and along the trail you will see rotted logs that were once magnificent chestnut trees, trees that were a staple growth for men, birds, deer, wild hogs, and other animals in a past time.

At 1.9 miles you will reach one of several springs along the trail. Typically, these springs are shallow and usually very slow-flowing, unless water tables are high and there has been plentiful rainfall in previous months.

Three hundred feet past the spring you will see another dead tree—yet another enormous chestnut tree that fell victim to the blight that almost completely destroyed all the chestnut trees once populating the midrange elevations of the mountains of the South. You will see other stumps and logs on an almost regular basis as you continue this and other hikes in the area.

When you reach the 2.4-mile point, there will be a huge rock cliff on the left of the trail and about 75 feet from the trail itself and above it. To your left the slope continues downward at a very steep angle for several hundred feet. This will be true of most of the entire hike.

You will remain closed in from the outside world by the thick foliage in summer months, and during the first 2.5 miles you will hear or see nothing except woodland sights and sounds. At 2.6 miles you will skirt a dense rhododendron thicket, and just above the topmost branches of the trees you will be able to see the ridge opposite you as well as a distant peak.

Take plenty of water with you, because there is a distinct scarcity of water along the trail, except in very wet weather when wet-weather springs feed the dry channels. The first of these channels occurs at 2.7 miles. The wash is clearly evident, but all that remains of the stream is a series of water-sculpted rocks dotting the dry streambed.

At 2.8 miles you will reach another streambed, one that is fed by a more dependable series of tiny springs. This one, while reduced to a mere trickle in dry weather, shows evidence that at times it functions as a genuine

A junction of the Mountains-to-Sea Trail.

stream. The primary evidence is the presence of a split-log bridge crossing the trickle.

The trail, which started as a one-foot-wide slash through the forest and remained as such for the first 3 miles of the hike, widens at 3.4 miles. From the beginning, the trail made a slow descent from the Pisgah Inn down the slope, and at this point it levels and you will enter a tunnel of rhododendron growth. The trail is wide enough that two can pass abreast here.

The only campsite along the entire trail is 300 feet past the 3.4-mile point, on the right and 25 feet from the trail. Remember that overnight camping on the trails of the Blue Ridge Parkway is not permitted, so before you make any plans to overnight there you should check with rangers.

At the 4.0-mile mark you will have crossed your third and fourth dry streambeds. However, at the 4.7 mark you will cross, via stepping-stones, a small stream that emerges from among a huge heap of boulders and forms deep pools under the miniature waterfalls. These small pools serve as homes for many of the frogs and other water-loving creatures along this part of the trail.

As you emerge from the rhododendron thicket and hike for another mile, you will reach a fork in the trail, with one fork leading to the left and down a steep incline 200 feet long. The other fork to the right leads you to the gravel parking area on US 276, where the Buck Spring Trail ends. This is where the second vehicle is parked.

43

Whiteside Mountain Summit Trail

Total distance (loop): 3.0 miles

Hiking time: 2 hours

Vertical rise: 610 feet

Rating: Moderate to strenuous

Map: USGS 7.5' Highlands

When you reach the Highlands, North Carolina, area, you are in some of the finest terrain east of the Mississippi River. The town of Highlands is reportedly the highest incorporated municipality not only in North Carolina but east of the Mississippi with an altitude of 4,118 feet above sea level.

Highlands has a population of 2,000 permanent residents and about 25,000 summer inhabitants. You can let these figures help you to determine when you want to visit the area.

One consideration is inclement weather. Highlands has perhaps the highest precipitation rate in North Carolina, with an average of 90 inches of rain, sleet, or snow falling each year. You cannot pick your time to visit if you are hoping for clear weather. The driest month of the year is July with 6.3 inches of rainfall, and the wettest month is March, with 8.9 inches of precipitation. There is no wet or dry season.

Here are a couple of other factors that may help you to decide when to hike. In the summer months some parts of the mountain (primarily the rock cliffs) are closed to climbers because of the nesting season of the peregrine falcons, a majestic but endangered bird that lives on the mountain. In summer you are also more likely to encounter snakes and pesky insects, including wasps and bees. So late September and most of October remain the best times to visit.

You will note that the loop distance of the hike is 3 miles. This figure will not agree with distances given in other sources. Here's why: if you start at the trailhead and take the left fork as you start the hike, and

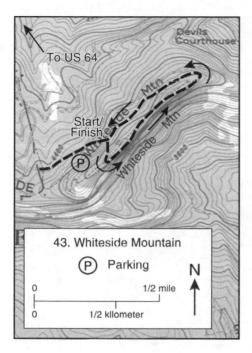

43. Whiteside Mountain

Ⓟ Parking

N

0 ————————— 1/2 mile

0 ————————— 1/2 kilometer

follow the trail straight up to the top, make your way around the crest, and then continue the loop back to the starting point, you will have hiked 2 miles. But if you take short spur walks, backtrack to re-inspect a peculiar rock formation or have another look at a spectacular view, you will hike 3 miles. On the other hand, if you take the right fork at the trailhead, hike to the top, and backtrack to the starting point, you will hike slightly less than 2 miles. We use the 3-mile figure because that's the distance we walked, and we are probably close to normal, in this respect at least.

To reach Highlands and the Whiteside Mountain Trail, follow US 64 from Brevard toward Highlands. You will pass through Cashiers (pronounced *Cash*-ers). Drive 5 miles east of Highlands and turn left (south) onto Whiteside Mountain Road. Go 3 miles until you reach a sign directing you to Whiteside Mountain. One of the first sights you see will be a notice that this is a fee

area. As of this writing daily permits are $2. The permit, incidentally, is good at any of the fee areas in the state, so if you choose to visit Whitewater Falls, Sliding Rock, or some of the other nearby attractions, you can use the same permit.

The only restroom facilities at Whiteside Mountain are of the primitive type. Parking is no problem. After you park, walk to the southwestern part of the parking lot, where you will find the trailhead. Almost as soon as you enter the forest, you will see a trail on your right start up a steep incline via a flight of stone steps. This is the direct route to the top, and while it is more strenuous, it will take you to the peak much faster, if you are in good shape to handle the climb. The trail to the left is more gradual and will take longer to reach the top.

Either way you choose to hike the mountain, you will make a loop by crossing the top of the mountain and then going down the other side to complete the loop. As you climb, you will be ascending, according to published reports, what may be the oldest mountain in the world, a peak that is more than 275 million years old. However, other sources estimate the age of Stone Mountain in North Carolina to be more than 300 million years.

Another claim made for the mountain (and this one has been reported widely) is that the first Kilroy in history visited here centuries ago. When DeSoto and his men made their trek through the mountains of North Carolina in search of gold, one member of the detachment reportedly scratched a message, possibly meant for later prospectors, deeply into one part of the rock cliffs. If the message is there, we did not find it on our hike.

As you climb you will pass through a forest that was once predominantly chestnut, back before the blight destroyed thousands of chestnut trees in the mountains of

An overlook on the Whiteside Mountain Trail with the headwaters of the Chattooga River below.

the Carolinas. You can still see the huge logs lying on the forest floor, and dead trunks still stand throughout the forest. The blight struck with ferocity in the late 1930s and 40s, and many local old-timers can recall a time before the blight when the chestnut yield was nothing short of astonishing, in terms of both lumber and nuts.

The remaining forest is composed largely of white pine, Canadian hemlock, oak, hickory, red maple, tulip poplar, magnolia, birch, ash, mountain laurel, rhododendron (both white and Catawba), and occasional dogwood and wild cherry trees. The laurel blossoms are at their peak in mid-May (depending upon how cold the spring is) at the lower elevations, and through June and into early July in many instances in the higher elevations. The Catawba rhododendron blooms from May until mid-June, and the white rhododendron blooms from late June until early July. Keep in mind that these plants are poisonous: bark, sap, leaves, and blossoms are all dangerous.

On the mountain there are about 180 species of birds, including many types of hawks, owls, and an occasional eagle. Songbirds are here in profusion, and you will see brown thrashers and mockingbirds in abundance. Other animal life includes white-tail deer, black bear, wild turkey, woodchuck, chipmunk, squirrel, rabbit, raccoon, and mice, among other small creatures. These animals do not present a danger under normal circumstances, but in May 2000 three black bears, including a mother and her cub, attacked and killed a hiker in the Great Smoky Mountains National Park. The attack was described as unprovoked, but you must keep in mind that a mother bear can be easily riled when she has her cub with her.

At the top of the mountain you can see

the headwaters of the Chattooga River (made famous in the movie *Deliverance*). The Chattooga, which is on the south side of the mountains, flows south into the Savannah River, while the Cullasaja River on the north side flows in the opposite direction and empties into the Tennessee River and then into the Mississippi.

Along the crest of the mountain you can see immense and sheer rock cliffs that range in height from 400 to 750 feet. There are rails along the trail near the cliffs, but you can see that some of the rail posts have been loosened over the years. So don't take chances: do not entrust your life to the rails.

During your climb you will start in the valley at an altitude of 2,100 feet above sea level and end the hike at 4,930 feet. Because this hike is somewhat short, you may wish to drive east toward Brevard and try the Whitewater Falls trails, which are also short but will, when combined with the Whiteside Mountain hike, add up to a satisfying and exhausting walk. Whitewater Falls hikes are found in Hike 45 in this book.

44

Mount Pisgah Trail

Total distance (backtrack): 3 miles

Hiking time: 2.0 hours

Vertical rise: 2,240 feet

Rating: Strenuous

Maps: USGS 7.5' Shining Rock and USGS 7.5' Cruso

If for no other reason, climbing Mount Pisgah would be worth the effort just to be able to see part of the estate once owned by George Washington Vanderbilt, grandson of the noted Cornelius "Commodore" Vanderbilt. The Biltmore Estate, including the mansion and surrounding grounds and forests, was in the early part of the twentieth century one of the largest privately owned estates in the nation and, perhaps, in the world.

Commodore Vanderbilt began his financial career at age 16, when he bought a sailboat and earned money by shipping produce and passengers between Staten Island and New York City. At the time of his death, in 1877, he had amassed a fortune conservatively estimated at more than $100 million.

George Washington Vanderbilt, grandson of Commodore Vanderbilt, came for a visit to North Carolina in the mid-1880s. So taken was he with the magnificent scenery around the city of Asheville (later the home of novelist Thomas Wolfe, and also home for a time to novelist F. Scott Fitzgerald and wife, Zelda, and other notables) that he rode through the hills around the city until he found a vantage point from which he had an outstanding view of all the countryside around the spot. He bought the spot for his retreat home, the Biltmore House, and then continued to purchase parcels of land until, at the time of his death, he owned about 125,000 acres of farmland and forest land.

Part of the property owned by Vanderbilt included the peak known today as Mount

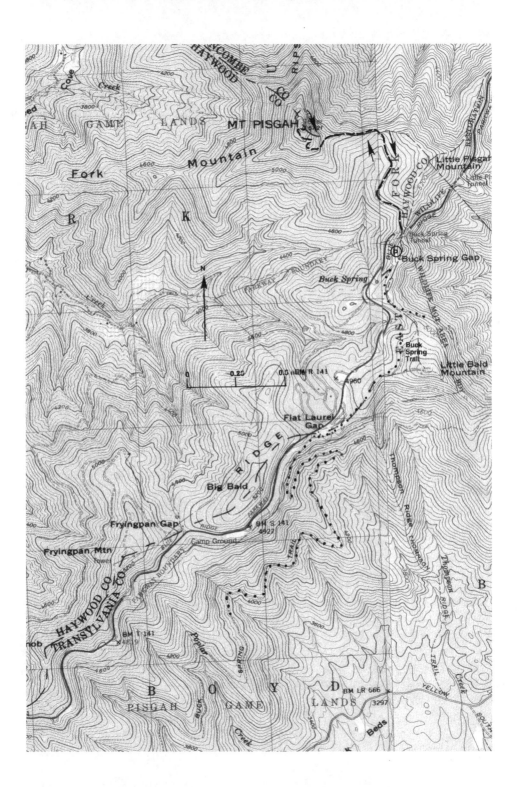

Pisgah. Vanderbilt himself had a hunting lodge built near Mount Pisgah, and trails were blazed through the mountains so that it was possible for horse traffic to reach the lodge.

After Vanderbilt's death in 1914, a large portion of the land was deeded to the United States government, and that land was to mark the beginning of the Pisgah National Forest. More land was sold, and the estate dwindled to about 8,000 acres. The sold land became, in part, the city of Biltmore Forest, sections of the Blue Ridge Parkway, and parts of I-26 and I-40.

Mount Pisgah, one of the highest peaks in the area, was named after the mountain (2,644 feet elevation) located in Jordan near the north end of the Dead Sea. The North Carolina Mount Pisgah rises to 5,721 feet elevation and to one of the finest panoramic views in the state.

To reach Mount Pisgah, drive south on the parkway 30 miles from Asheville. The Mount Pisgah parking lot is located on the left shortly before you reach the Mount Pisgah Inn. If the parking lot is filled, there is another parking lot across the parkway and south 300 yards. At the second parking lot rest rooms and picnic tables are available.

If you must park in the area across the parkway, you will add another 0.7 mile (round trip) to the hike by hiking across the parkway and then up the drive and into the parking area for the Mount Pisgah trailhead.

As you start the hike and pass the sign warning that the trail ahead is strenuous, you will hike along a wide, nearly flat trail for 0.4 mile and then the trail begins to climb relentlessly until you reach the top of Mount Pisgah. In the early stretches of the trail the forest is essentially hardwood (oak, ash, hickory, and an assortment of low-growing trees and shrubs), and the woods seem to be filled with the noise of wild animals, large and small.

The smaller animals you hear are very probably chipmunks and in all probability the eastern chipmunk (*Tamias striatus*), which as a rule would hibernate from the first frost in the fall until March. These chipmunks, perhaps largely due to handouts from the hikers, stay active until late in the autumn.

Another interesting specimen in the woodlands is the red squirrel (*Tamiasciurus hudsonicus*), which, unlike most squirrels, attacks and eats live prey. It is believed that the red squirrel may kill and devour as many as 200 birds in a year.

The largest animals in the forest in this area are probably the white-tailed deer, an agile animal that can leap 8 feet vertically, 30 feet horizontally, and attain a speed of 30 miles per hour when frightened.

As you begin the steep climb (you will ascend more than 720 feet within one mile), the trail narrows so that only single-file walking is comfortable, and the rocky footing becomes far more difficult and at times treacherous. You will step from rock to rock in many stretches of the trail, and at times you must step very high to make the next level or step. The closer you climb toward the top, the steeper the trail becomes.

As you approach the summit, the vegetation changes rapidly from hardwood forest to rhododendron and laurel, and the thickets along the trail are at points almost impenetrable. The trail moves along the southern slope and works upward at a seemingly slow rate. Near the top the trail switches back to a northerly direction and you can see the television tower that was erected many years ago atop the mountain.

At the very top you emerge from a rhododendron "hell," or thicket, and reach a platform overlook. From this vantage point you have a 360-degree panoramic view of the entire countryside. To the south you can see the Mount Pisgah Inn and beyond it the

A late autumn view of Mount Pisgah

mountains as they flatten slightly in the direction of Brevard. To the east you can see the ridges as they flatten into the foothills and then the Piedmont. To the west is ridge after ridge in clear view, and on some of them you can see roads and trails that have been cut into the undergrowth. Back to the north you can see Asheville and outlying areas.

It is much cooler at the top of the mountain than it was at the parking lot, and you are advised to wear warmer clothing if you plan to spend any time at the top. In warmer months it is also advisable to carry along rain gear, because thunderstorms on an almost daily basis sweep across the mountains. Be careful that you are not caught atop the mountain in a thunderstorm. The peak, the huge tower, and the bare rock surface at the top combine to make the location a highly undesirable one when lightning is in the area.

If you see a storm developing, leave the overlook and the peak as quickly as you can and start toward lower elevations. Once you are into the thick growth along the trail you will be relatively safer.

When you are ready to start down, be careful of the slick rocks, which are almost always slippery. In the early morning, dew or frost can make the rocks treacherous. In mid-afternoon and later, rain contributes to the problem. In the spring and early summer pollen gathers on the rocks to create insecure footing, and in autumn the falling leaves are ground underfoot and pulverized, and the result is another slippery mixture.

On most hikes you can assume that you will travel much faster downhill than you did going uphill. This trail may be the reverse. For this reason do not linger at the top, particularly in early spring and late fall, and let darkness catch you on the trail.

When you are back at the parking lot, you can find food and overnight accommodations (reservations are highly recommended) at the Mount Pisgah Inn. For overnight camping (none is allowed on Blue Ridge Parkway trails) you can drive 10 more miles to the recreation area known as Graveyard Fields and camp along the Yellowstone Prong River, or you can drive south to the exit for US 276 and drive to Brevard, which is about 16 miles away, to find food and lodging.

While you are in the area, you might wish to take advantage of the Buck Spring Trail, a fine hiker's delight that starts at the south end of the parking lot and crosses the southern portion of the Pisgah National Forest to emerge near the Pink Beds area north of Brevard.

45

Whitewater Falls Trails

Total distance: 2.6 miles

Hiking time: 3 hours

Vertical rise: 1200 feet

Rating: Moderate to strenuous

Map: USGS 7.5' Cashiers

The hiking trails around Whitewater Falls have one incredible characteristic: they are all centered around the Whitewater River, the gorge, and two of the most spectacular waterfalls you can see anywhere in the East. And, to make the trip a little better, you can add a third waterfall that, while not as stunning as the two major falls, is also superb.

These hikes, with one exception, are extremely steep. While they are strenuous and demanding at times, they are also short enough that you will not need to stop and rest.

The first hike is to the top of Whitewater Falls. To reach the falls from Greenville, South Carolina, you can follow US 276 north until you intersect with SC 11, and then follow SC 11 south to SC 130. Take SC 130 north for 10.5 miles until you pass the Duke Power Bad Creek Project on the right. As you cross the state line and enter North Carolina, watch for signs directing you to the Whitewater Falls recreation area, which you will reach within five minutes. When you see the entrance sign, turn off the highway to the right and enter the parking lot. Here you will pay a $2 per vehicle use fee, but you can also use the stub to visit other attractions on the same day.

To reach Whitewater Falls from the north, follow US 64 west from Brevard. This highway is known as the Waterfall Highway, and if you follow it long enough, you will soon see why the road is so named. However, you will leave US 64 when you reach the Rosman-Cashiers area. As you

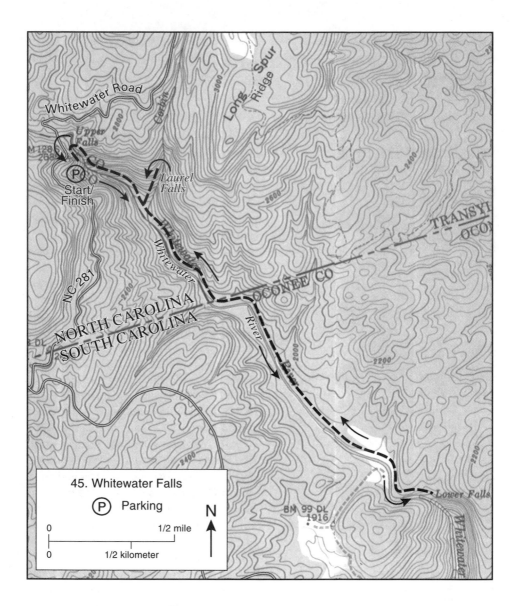

45. Whitewater Falls

Ⓟ Parking

N

0   1/2 mile

0   1/2 kilometer

go through Oakland, watch on the left for a highway called Whitewater Road (NC 281). Turn left onto the Waterfall Highway and follow it for 9 miles, until you see the signs directing you to the Whitewater Falls parking area, where you'll pay a $2 fee. Along the way you will cross the Horse-pasture River, which has some of the best waterfalls in the state (Transylvania County alone has well over 200 waterfalls).

From the parking lot, walk 0.5 mile north on the paved walk until you reach the first Whitewater Falls overlook. Plan to spend a few minutes here just so you can enjoy the waterfall. You are looking at the highest waterfall east of the Mississippi. It is also one of the most beautiful waterfalls you will find anywhere in the East. If you want photos, you will need a wide-angle lens.

The best time to visit the waterfall is from 9–2. The best time of year is October, when the autumn foliage turns gold, red, and orange, or in winter when the leaves are off the trees, and you get the finest look at the falling water. If you visit after a heavy rain, you will see an even more spectacular sight. Sometimes in late summer, particularly if the summer has been a dry one, the volume of the Whitewater River is reduced significantly, and the waterfall is less impressive.

After you have enjoyed the view sufficiently (actually, there is seldom enough time for looking at the falls), you can walk to the left of the overlook and see the trailhead for the hike to the top of the falls. The hike is easy and enjoyable. As you walk you will pass through a forest of evergreens with occasional hardwood trees. The ascent is gradual, and you will hike along a trail that is soft dirt one minute and unrelenting rocky trail the next. The hike to the top of the falls is little more than a mile, although you can continue past the river if you wish. Most people, however, stop at the river and enjoy the quiet and beautiful stream that becomes a torrent a few feet downstream, where the water suddenly plunges down a series of cliffs and then crashes into the rocky valley below. The total plunge of the waterfall is 411 feet.

A word of warning here. At the overlook you saw signs informing you of the number of people who have died from falls as they wandered around the cliffs and lost their footing. You will also see people climbing out onto the rocks at the top of the falls. Do

not attempt to do this. If you lose your footing, you also lose your life. There is no way you will survive the fall. Do not risk becoming a statistic.

As you reach the Whitewater River, you can make your way along the rocks that have been carved by the water over the centuries into fantastic designs. There are superb places for you to take photos of the river, but you cannot photograph the falls from this point.

As you backtrack, you will find yourself once again at the overlook. Notice the flight of steps leading down the mountainside. If you want to descend the stairs, you will soon reach an excellent overlook that affords an even better look at the falls. There are 154 steps and platforms that you will descend and then ascend before continuing.

If you choose, you can hike past the overlook to the Foothills Trail at the bottom of the gorge. At the bottom of the gorge you will reach a steel and concrete bridge over the river, and when you cross the river you will reach Corbin Creek, which flows into the Whitewater River. It is a rough and undeveloped trail, but a short distance up Corbin Creek you will see Laurel Falls, which is also close to 400 feet high.

After you leave the falls, follow the Foothills Trail downstream until you reach a spur trail that leads to a point near the Lower Whitewater Falls, which is in South Carolina. This waterfall, like its predecessor, is also about 400 feet high, making a total of almost 1,200 feet of waterfalls visible on one relatively short hike.

This trail is steep and difficult at times, and it will take you about an hour to reach the overlook, one of the finest such construction projects you will find. Keep one eye on the time of day, because you will need at least another hour to climb back to

Whitewater Falls

Robert L. Williams

the parking lot. Take along rain gear as well, particularly in the hot summer months. Afternoon thunderstorms are fairly regular, and you will be a long way from the car. Remember that when the trail is wet the hiking is a little more treacherous, so take extra care. When you complete the hikes, you are close to other waterfalls and to other excellent hiking trails. Plan to enjoy them while you are in the vicinity.

46

Horsepasture Waterfalls Trail

Total distance (backtrack): 3.1 miles

Hiking time: 3 hours

Vertical rise: 1,280 feet

Rating: Moderate

Map: USGS 7.5' Reid, NC/SC

One of the most rewarding hikes in the entire state of North Carolina (and there are hundreds of delightful trails) is the Horsepasture Waterfalls Trail, a 3.1-mile moderately difficult hike through the dense woodlands of the Pisgah Forest and along the Horsepasture River. What makes the hike so fascinating is the series of especially interesting waterfalls in a part of the state known nationally for its waterfalls.

In Transylvania County alone there are more than 200 notable waterfalls, some of them more than 400 feet high: Whitewater Falls is the highest waterfall east of the Mississippi, and Toxaway Falls, only a few miles away, is also 400 feet high. But the waterfalls along the Horsepasture River are not known for their height as much as they are for their beauty, majesty, unique qualities, and number.

The Pisgah Forest itself was once part of a 100,000-acre tract of land owned by George Vanderbilt, who also owned the magnificent Biltmore House in nearby Asheville. The Horsepasture River flows out of western Transylvania County and south into South Carolina. The major waterfalls accessible along the Waterfall Trail are in North Carolina.

The name Transylvania County, (trans meaning "across," and *sylvan,* "forested") was not derived from the legendary home of Count Dracula (although there is in fact a Halloweenfest held on the last Saturday in October each year in the county) but from the beauty of the countryside forests, which are among the finest anywhere.

To reach the Horsepasture River recre-

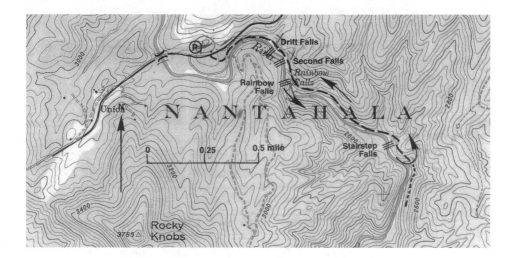

ation area, drive down US 276 to Brevard, and then take US 276S and US 64 through Brevard and south through Rosman, Lake Toxaway, to Sapphire. Stay on the same highway until you reach the NC 281 junction. This latter highway is also known as Whitewater Falls Road.

Keep on NC 281 1.7 miles south until you see a small parking area that is unmarked except for the highway railing, the wide shoulders, and evidence of a great deal of use. There are no signs or other indications of an official parking area. You will be very near a bridge, under which the Horsepasture River flows.

To reach the actual hiking trail, you cross the highway from the parking area and walk along the highway railing until you see the paths leading down to the major trail. There are a number of pathways, some very easy and others rather troublesome. The best paths are back toward US 276 and US 64.

Hike back along the highway 50 to 100 yards until you see the broadest, most used, and shortest path. The river curves slightly and flows very near the highway at this point.

When you reach the end of the access path, you will be on the Waterfall Trail, and within 50 yards you will reach the first of a series of waterfalls. This is Drift Falls, which is not a true waterfall but rather is a cascade, as the water flows over a gigantic rock and then drops into a deep pool at the base of the falls.

In summer months the river is used frequently by both trout fishermen and swimmers or tubers. College students (from nearby Brevard College) and local high schoolers congregate after classes in early spring and again in the fall. During the summer swimmers come from hundreds of miles to enjoy the river.

At Drift Falls you can leave the major trail and pick your way down to rocks that jut out into the river. You can stop here for as long as you wish to enjoy the waterfall and the swimmers, if any. In cooler months the trail is virtually deserted and you have a much better chance of observing wildlife.

The major forms of life here include black bears (seldom seen but to be avoided, particularly if the bear is a mother with cubs), deer, bobcats, rabbits, squirrels, woodchucks, and a wide variety of birds, ranging from hawks and owls to finches and woodland birds.

Wildflowers grow in profusion along the trail, at the river's edge, and in the dense hardwood forest that lines the river banks. The major trees are oak, hickory, poplar, beech, maple, dogwood, sourwood, fir, pine, and cedar.

After you leave Drift Falls, you will hike for approximately 15 minutes (0.3 mile) to a second waterfall, this one spectacular but unnamed. Again, you can sit on rocks, photograph the falls and the swimmers, or simply enjoy the scenery.

Hike another 0.3 mile and you will arrive at one of the finest waterfalls in the state: Rainbow Falls. This is a high waterfall (more than 100 feet high) that crashes loudly to the deep pool below. When the sun is overhead, the mist rising from the waterfall creates a splendid rainbow, from which the name is derived. The considerable volume of the river makes these waterfalls even more spectacular. Many of the mountain streams are thin ribbons of water that create pretty but unimpressive waterfalls, but the Horsepasture River is powerful enough that it is unparalleled in this part of the state.

In fact, the power of the river virtually ended the beauty of both river and waterfalls in the mid-1980s. A power and electric company tried to buy the land along the river and to cut the timber, build a dam, and essentially destroy the grandeur of the forest and waterfalls.

Several state politicians, along with newspaper editors, students, interested citizens, and influential businesspeople interceded on behalf of the environment. As a result, the efforts to commercialize the river were thwarted, and, following lengthy discussions, the federal government agreed to designate the river as part of the National Wild and Scenic River program.

Today, the 400-plus acres of the area is devoted to the recreational enjoyment of all people. The work is appreciated, apparently, because this is one of the most thickly populated recreation areas in the North Carolina mountains.

If it had not been for the efforts of state leaders, the waterfalls and the hunting and fishing territory, as well as the hiking and camping opportunities, would have been destroyed.

Rainbow Falls is one of the most convincing arguments to support the Wild and Scenic River program. This is a superb place to savor the moments of beauty before moving on to new territory.

Again, you can hike down to the falls for a close-up look, or you can enjoy the waterfall and the wildflowers that grow along the grassy bank near the falls. For the safety of visitors, the Forest Service has constructed a sturdy railing. This is one of the best places along the river for you to photograph the waterfalls.

The next waterfall is more difficult to locate. When you leave Rainbow Falls hike another 15 minutes (0.4 mile) along a clearly marked trail until you reach a creek that is approximately 10 feet across.

The trail then leads up a rather steep incline of about 850 feet. Here the trail becomes confusing and difficult to follow. The trail that leads to the left quickly narrows and becomes more and more difficult to follow. Do not take it.

Instead, turn to the right and proceed down the river. Follow the river approximately 0.2 mile until you see the justly famous Stairstep (or Staircase) Falls.

This waterfall is so named because the water descends in a series of cascades, like gigantic steps. Here you have more great opportunities to photograph the falls and to rest.

Although this trail is rather short, it is not one of the easier ones to hike. The trail

Summer fun at one of the waterfalls on the Horsepasture River

Robert L. Williams

stays wet much of the time, partly because of the frequent rains and partly because of the mist from the waterfalls. Often the trail is not level but sloped, and it is often difficult to keep your footing.

You may wish to end your hike at this point and backtrack to the highway. There is one more waterfall farther down the river, but the trail is exceptionally rough and at times quite dangerous.

Because of the frequent rainfall, it is wise to take along rain gear during the spring and summer months. Make plans as well to waterproof your camera, if photography is part of your agenda.

This hiking trail is one of the most enjoyable you are likely to find in this extreme southern and western part of the state. And if you like waterfalls, you will find several other hiking trails that lead to other falls, some of them nearly as impressive as those along the Horsepasture River.

V

The Great Smokies

47

Clingman's Dome and Silers Bald Trails

Total distances: 1 mile (backtrack); 7.2 miles (backtrack)

Hiking time: 6 hours, or overnight

Vertical rise: 5,760 feet

Rating: Moderate to strenuous

Maps: USGS 7.5' Silers Bald and USGS 7.5' Clingman's Dome

A hiking trip to the Great Smoky Mountains National Park is one of the rarest of outdoor treats for experienced hikers and novices alike. The area is unquestionably one of the most varied of all North Carolina mountain terrains and one of the most scenic and interesting in the entire nation.

The park itself consists of more than 520,000 acres (275,895 of which are in North Carolina), and the terrain includes beautiful waterfalls, numerous peaks of 5,000 to 6,000 feet, an astonishing variety of plants and animals, and hiking trails to meet every taste.

The animal life in the park includes deer, bobcats, black bears, several species of owls, dozens of varieties of songbirds, snakes, opossums, raccoons, and many other animals that frequent higher elevations, cold streams, and deep valleys.

The Great Smoky Mountains National Park has more visitors each year than any other national park, with more than 10 million tourists arriving annually, predominantly in the spring, summer, and fall months. During the winter many of the roads are closed, and hiking, like auto travel, can be hazardous.

The highest peak in the Great Smokies is Clingman's Dome (not to be confused with Clingman's Peak, near Mount Mitchell) at 6,642 feet above sea level. More than a dozen other nearby peaks have elevations greater than 6,000 feet.

There are two major tourist or resort towns very near the Smokies park, and numerous campgrounds are available to visitors. Inside the national park the nightly rate

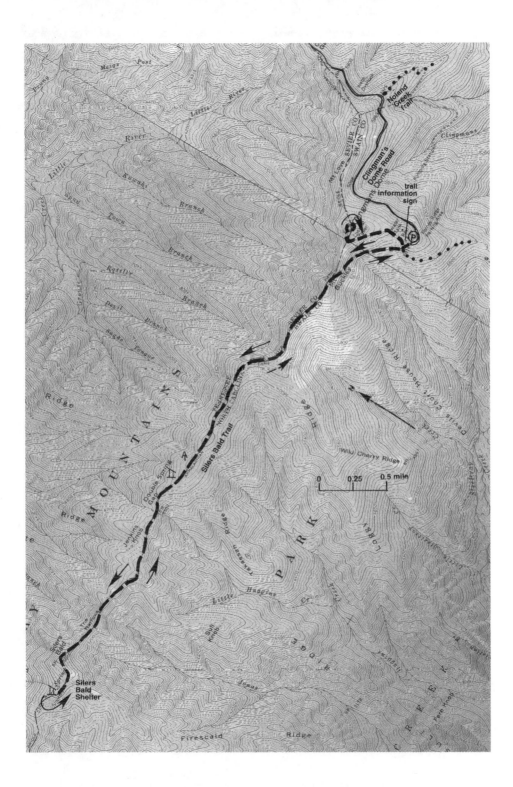

for family camping (occupying one campsite) is $11. The campground can accommodate recreational vehicles, tent campers, and trailer campers.

Numerous trails in the park have backpacking campsites, and a large number of the campsites are shared by horseback riders who also use the trails. All overnight campers are required to secure a permit from the park office before spending the night. Campers are also advised to take every precaution against unintentionally attracting bears into the campsites.

Many of the backcountry campsites are rationed, which means you must obtain permission to use the camping facilities. If you use these campsites without reservations, you are subject to a fine and in addition your hiking permit will be invalidated at the moment you are discovered.

To reach the Great Smoky Mountains National Park, one of the easiest routes is via I-40 to the US 74 Exit. Follow US 74 until it junctions with US 441, which leads into the town of Cherokee at the Cherokee Indian Reservation. As you pass through Cherokee you will reach the national park within three miles. The Oconaluftee Visitor Center, on the banks of the Oconaluftee River, is an important stop for those persons wishing to obtain hiking trail maps of the national park or other brochures detailing the major attractions of the area.

One brochure designates 51 "favorite hiking trails," with hiking distances ranging from 0.5 mile up to 16 miles. Difficulty ratings vary from easy to strenuous, and the hikes may climb from 120 feet to 3,562 feet.

There are other much longer trails in the park, one of them nearly 70 miles long. This is the portion of the Appalachian Trail that crosses the Great Smokies.

One of the most popular short hikes in the park is the Clingman's Dome Trail, a 0.5-mile climb from the parking lot near the top of Clingman's Dome to the observation tower on the peak. While the hiking trail is paved all the way and the climb to the top of the observation tower is a concrete ascending ramp, the one-mile round trip is nevertheless rather strenuous. The trail is a constant ascent from the parking lot to the tower, and there is never a respite from the climb.

The tower affords a spectacular panoramic view from the circular overlook, and the temperature is invariably several degrees lower than at the Oconaluftee Visitor Center. On a day in which the visitor center temperature may be in the 40s or even 50s, there may be two-foot icicles hanging from the rocks on the shady side of the top of Clingman's Dome. Because of the severe temperature fluctuations, it is wise to dress for the colder weather at the top.

The road to the top of Clingman's Dome may be closed when the weather is bad, and it is closed during winter months. Other parts of the park remain open. If you drive to the top of the mountain, the hike consists simply of following the paved trail on the north end of the parking lot. When you reach the base of the observation tower, follow the trail to the top of the observatory.

At the observatory you will find information plaques that identify all of the major peaks and other landmarks within the panoramic vistas. For the clearest viewing opportunities, make the trip in October or April. The summer haze, which provided the name for the mountain range, is at its worst in July and August. Early morning is the best time of day for maximum visibility.

As you descend the trail, at the point where the information signs are located and where the asphalt meets the concrete, you will see on the west side of the trail and at the north side of the parking lot a trail information sign that directs hikers to the

Clingman's Dome Overlook

Noland Creek Trail (3.6 miles, backtrack), Pole Road Creek Trail (3.8 miles, backtrack), and Deep Creek Trail (11.8 miles, backtrack).

These trails, like most trails in the Great Smokies, junction with other trails along the way, so that you are free to make up loops or backtrack trails to suit your needs. There are more than 500 miles of hiking trails in the North Carolina portion of the park and more than 400 additional miles in the Tennessee portion of the park. We have chosen to describe the Silers Bald Trail as a sampler of the numerous possibilities.

When you leave the paved area at the Clingman's Dome parking lot, you will follow the Silers Bald hiking trail down a very steep incline with treacherous footing. You step from stone to stone and often the stones are unstable and wet.

The trail starts in a northerly direction and within 30 feet curves abruptly southwest. You descend a long hill (slightly more than 1 mile) along a very narrow trail with continued treacherous footing. At 200 feet there will be a huge rock ledge on the left as you enter deeper into an evergreen forest with laurel or rhododendron undergrowth, or both.

At the 0.5-mile point the trail veers northwest and becomes very moist, even in the driest weather, and the footing worsens. The trail essentially follows the North Carolina–Tennessee state lines as you descend gradually and constantly into a cove. Two mountain ridges converge at the 1.7-mile point, and the trail leads near the headwaters of several mountain streams.

Two miles from the Clingman's Dome parking area you will reach Double Spring Gap, a backcountry shelter that will accommodate 12 persons. Other shelters are located in the area and will be noted in this and the following trail descriptions.

The elevation is 5,507 feet at the Double Spring Gap shelter. You have descended 1,135 feet at this point in the hike.

The next shelter is 1.6 miles farther down the trail. This is the Silers Bald backcountry shelter, which, like the first shelter, will sleep 12 persons and will also accommodate 12 horses. It is a good idea to plan to spend the night at the Double Spring Gap shelter, if you are ready to stop, so that equestrians may have access to the second shelter.

At several points along the trail, openings in the forest permit exceptional views of the ridges and valleys in the area. The trail terminates at a point 900 feet lower than the starting point of the hike. The final elevation is due to the fact that the trail descends sharply at first and then climbs near the end of the hike.

The trail is rocky and the footing is somewhat precarious throughout the trail, and the vistas are essentially the same because you remain on one side of the mountain with the same valley and coves before you.

To complete the suggested hike, backtrack from Silers Bald to the parking area at Clingman's Dome. Other trails in the Smokies are described in later chapters of this book.

48

Chasteen Creek Trail and Hughes Ridge Trail

Total distance: 10 miles (backtrack) or 14.8 miles (loop)

Hiking time: 5 or 7.5 hours, or overnight

Vertical rise: 6,240 feet

Rating: Moderate to strenuous

Map: USGS 7.5' Smokemont

Start and end the Chasteen Creek Trail and the Hughes Ridge Trail at the Smokemont Campground just off US 441 north of Cherokee, North Carolina. To reach Cherokee from I-40, take the US 74 Exit and travel US 74 until it junctures with US 441. The Smokemont Campground is an excellent headquarters for hikers if you choose to stay overnight in the area.

For those camping in the area, a few details might be helpful. Fees per night in the campground are $11 per site, with registration and checkout time at noon. Campsites may be reserved from May 15 through October 31. For the rest of the year the campsites are on a first-come, first-served basis.

Campers cannot stay more than 7 consecutive days in peak months or 14 consecutive days during slack months. No more than six persons can occupy a site, and no more than two vehicles can be parked at the site. Hikers are asked to remember that some of the hiking trails are also used as horse trails and to show consideration for riders.

When you hike the Chasteen Creek Trail, which, like so many other trails in the Great Smokies, traverses bear habitat, you are urged to follow some simple precautions. First, do not feed the bears or any other wild animals. Second, when you sleep, if you intend to hike an overnight trail, prepare to store food outdoors in a safe manner.

Under no circumstances should you sleep with food in your tent or near your sleeping bag. Bears too often are attracted to a campsite because of the odor of food and will invade without warning. Keep all food wrappers and other items that may

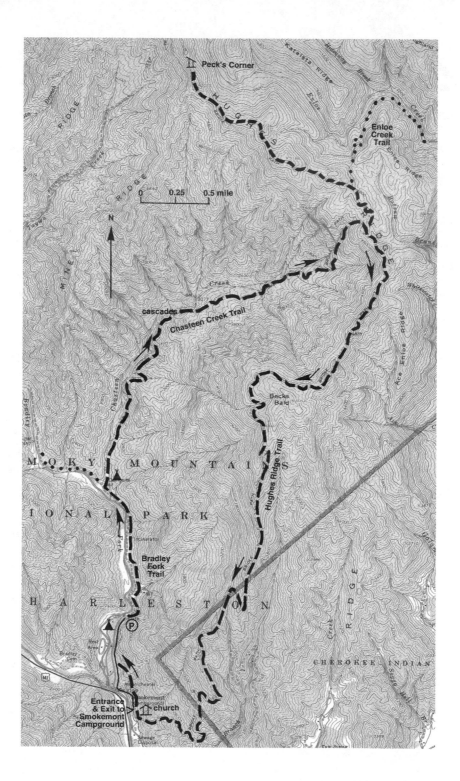

hold food odors, such as pots used in cooking, in the pack.

To store food at night, choose trees 10 to 20 feet apart. Tie a rope around the trunk of one tree and throw the rope over a limb of the second tree (high enough that a bear cannot reach it while standing upright). Then tie the rope to the pack.

Pull the rope until it raises the pack at least 10 feet off the ground and then retie the second end securely around the tree. By doing so, you can lower the pack when you need it and raise it to keep food out of harm's way. The pack should also be at least 4 feet from the nearest limb, trunk, or other support the bear could use (see page 234).

Remember that a backcountry permit is necessary if you plan to make an overnight hike. For overnight hikes, the maximum size for any party is eight; you may stay no more than one consecutive night in a shelter; you must stay in designated areas and you must adhere to the itinerary included on the backcountry permit. Park rangers cannot afford the risk of having an undetermined number of persons hiking or sleeping randomly throughout the area.

When you start the Chasteen Creek Trail, follow the maintenance road at the upper end of the Smokemont Campground (see chapter 50 on the Smokemont Loop for further details) to the junction, at mile point 1.2, of the Smokemont Loop Trail and the Chasteen Creek Trail.

Where the Smokemont Loop Trail proceeds to the left, the Chasteen Creek Trail veers sharply to the right. From the campground to the footbridge crossing Chasteen Creek, where it flows into the Bradley Fork, you will hike 1.8 miles. As you hike into the deep forest northeast of the confluence of the two streams, you will find a campsite at mile 2.1. The campsite is on the right, on the banks of Chasteen Creek.

About 80 feet past the campsite you will cross Chasteen Creek again, and at 2.3 miles you will reach a hitching post for horses and a mounting platform. Within another 100 feet you will reach the Chasteen Creek cascades, which drop 15 feet from the rocky streambed above to the shallow pools below.

From this point the trail climbs through a dense hardwood forest and junctions at mile 5.0 with the Hughes Ridge Trail. Along the trail you will pass through one continuous hardwood forest composed of poplar, ash, chestnut oak, and, around the stream or wet areas, sycamores.

From the 2.4-mile point, starting at the cascade, you will follow the channel of Chasteen Creek, working your way along a very narrow, often very rocky, and sometimes fairly strenuous trail.

The elevation of the ridges and coves will vary from the 2,400 level at the Smokemont Campground to more than 4,500 feet near Hughes Ridge Trail junction. In warmer months you will have the opportunity to see any of some 200 species of birds, and more than one thousand species of wildflowers, shrubs, and flowering trees.

Along the creek, which at the time it flows into Bradley Fork is 10 feet wide in many places but at the top of Hughes Ridge is only a bold rill, there are dozens of species of moss, lichens, ferns, and fungi. If you travel slowly you will also have a good chance of seeing deer as they come to the creek to drink.

The best places to spot and observe deer are in the laurel and rhododendron growths along the creek and along the lower elevations of the ridges reached by the trail. Often the rock cliffs are barely obscured by the thick vegetation, which is green all year, and if you will wait patiently and watch carefully you will perhaps catch glimpses of the deer as they move silently among the thick cover.

During the 3.3-mile hike from the confluence of Chasteen Creek to the junction with the Hughes Ridge Trail, you will find that the Chasteen Creek Trail lies in a northeasterly direction that seldom changes. Rarely are you more than a short distance from the stream and its dense vegetation.

At the 2.6-mile mark (from the bridge over Chasteen Creek) the trail bends almost due north for 150 feet and then swings back in a southeasterly direction. At 2.8 miles the trail again veers due north and in the final 0.2 mile before it junctions with the Hughes Ridge Trail it shifts back to its original northeastern direction.

At this point you can backtrack to the Smokemont Campground. By backtracking, you will hike a total of 10 miles. If you wish to add more distance to the hike and convert the backtrack trail into a long loop (the total hike is highly suitable for an overnight trip), at the junction with the Hughes Ridge Trail turn to the right, which will lead you in a southeasterly direction back to the Smokemont campground.

The total hike from the time you join the Hughes Ridge Trail, which is a forest hike through magnificent hardwood forests alternating with spruce and hemlock, is 9.8 miles. Such a hike, when added to the Chasteen Creek mileage, will be 14.8 miles.

The Hughes Ridge Trail is one of the few trails in the area that can be classified as really strenuous. There is an elevation change of slightly more than 3,300 feet.

If you plan to spend the night on the trail, the only campsite that is handy will be Peck's Corner, which is an elevation of 5,280—exactly one mile high—and has sleeping accommodations for 12 persons. This is also a bridle trail shelter and is used often enough to be occupied throughout most of the warm months. Do not plan to overnight at this shelter unless you have made reservations well in advance. Using this shelter will lengthen the hike by more than 4 miles since it is slightly more than 2 miles northwest of the junction of the Hughes Ridge Trail and the Chasteen Creek Trail; your hike would be 7.2 miles to the shelter on the first day and 12 miles to Smokemont on the second day.

If you plan to hike 12 miles on the second day, be certain that you get an early start. The descent is rather difficult because of the slippery rocks and often wet weather. Keep rain gear handy at all times on all Smoky Mountain trails.

When you emerge from the Hughes Ridge Trail, you will see a quaint chapel nestled among the trees only 0.3 mile from the entrance to the Smokemont Campground. This is Lufty Baptist Church, which was established in 1836 by the hardy pioneers who settled the Smokemont area. It was reconstructed in 1912. The church remains open for visitors at all times.

When you have completed either the Chasteen Creek backtrack hike or the combined Chasteen Creek and Hughes Ridge hikes, you will perhaps be ready for shorter, more restful hikes. If such is the case, you may be interested in the Smokemont Self-Guiding Nature Trail and the brief pioneer village trail at the Oconaluftee Visitors Center (see chapter 49).

49

Smokemont Nature Trail and Pioneer Farm Trail

Total distance (two loops): 1.5 miles

Hiking time: 1 hour

Vertical rise: 480 feet

Rating: Easy; Pioneer Farm Trail, handicapped accessible

Map: USGS 7.5' Smokemont

The 11 self-guiding nature trails in the Great Smoky Mountains National Park range in length from 5 miles down to 0.3 mile. While most of the trails are very short, they can be combined into a 14.3-mile hike or to any shorter length that you prefer.

These shorter trails can also serve well as the topping-off of a longer hike. If there is still daylight and energy, you can hike one or more of these trails easily. Younger hikers, especially those in grade school, will find the trails educational as well as relaxing.

One of the most popular of these shorter trails is the Smokemont Self-Guiding Nature Trail. If you are camped at Smokemont, located on US 441 three miles north of the Cherokee Indian Reservation, the trail will be very handy. (To reach Cherokee from I-40, take the US 74 exit and travel US 74 until it junctures with US 441.)

Park in the hikers' spaces across from campsite B-15 in the Smokemont Campground. You will cross a one-railed footbridge that spans Bradley Fork immediately and enter a thick growth of laurel and rhododendron. In the course of the hike you will reach 12 special-interest locations that show man's impact on Nature and the harm that can be done from injudicious use of the woodlands. The various stops include observation points showing how the streams of the forest have contributed so greatly to the wide variety of plant and animal life. One stop details how the yellow poplar quickly populates scarred, burned, or otherwise desolated areas of a forest. The yellow poplar will begin to appear within two or three seasons, and it plays a

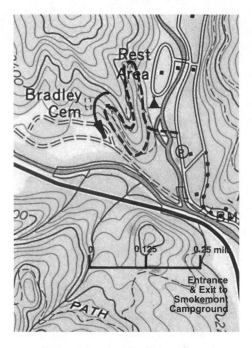

vital part in the succession stages of a forest that is starting anew.

At the third stop there is a small Norway spruce tree, a foreigner to the Great Smokies. It is impossible to determine how the tree reached the area, but best guesses are that loggers may have introduced it. Another guess is that the tree somehow made its way to the Smokies through the work of the Cradle of Forestry (see chapter 43), the first true forestry school in America, which is located at Brevard, across the southwestern tip of the state. The tree was part of experiments there, and it is possible that specimens from the Brevard area were taken to nearby regions for growth testing.

Other stops include information on how to recognize various important trees and shrubs, including laurel, rhododendron, and hemlock, in the area. One stop depicts the trunk of a dead chestnut tree and explains how the fungus that destroyed the tree was introduced from abroad.

The remainder of the hike leads through laurel slicks and across ridges populated by scarlet oak (one of the 10 species of oak trees in the Great Smokies) and monstrous white pines, a once-bountiful tree that has been reduced alarmingly by lumbering and insect damage, coupled with the effects of acid rain.

A second short hike leads around the Pioneer Farmstead at the Oconaluftee Visitors Center. Both the farmstead and the center are 2.9 miles south on US 226 from the Smokemont Campground. This hands-on sample of a mountain farmstead shows how the early settlers of the area, Scotch-Irish from the mountains of Virginia and Pennsylvania, entered the Smokies in search of a better way of life and found a mountain paradise, which the settlers shared with the native Cherokee Indians.

The land was one in which the slogan "make do or do without" was a literal way of life. The farmstead, which can be reached by a paved walkway from the parking lot, is a clear and austere example of how three basic needs—water, shelter, and food—were at the core of the farmsteader's universe.

The farmstead, which is not one actual farming endeavor but collects relics from a

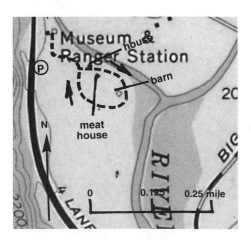

Pioneer Farmstead

variety of local sources, includes the farmhouse, bee gum stands (hives), woodshed, meat house, springhouse, blacksmith shop, chicken house, apple house, pigpen, sorghum mill, corncrib, barn, garden, and toolshed.

The house itself was built in 1901 by John E. Davis, who "matched" the logs in the house by splitting one log and using each of the halves to make a log so that on opposite walls the same size log was used to guarantee trueness in height and other important considerations.

Davis's sons, ages eight and four, helped to build the house by using a team of oxen and a sled to haul the stones they found and loaded for later use in building the chimneys, one on two walls of the house, so that there would be heat in the kitchen and in the family living room.

Near the house stands the inevitable meathouse, where the family hung venison, wild-turkey carcasses, and bear meat, along with the domestic meats that would feed the family. It is worthy of note that the delectable tenderloin of venison, one of the most desired meats anywhere, graced the tables of mountain settlers, alongside the rougher fare.

To tour the Pioneer Farmstead, drive to the Oconaluftee Visitors Center and park in the larger parking lot to the south of the main building. From the edge of the parking lot you can walk on a paved lane down to the Pioneer Farmstead, and the remainder of the hike, which leads alongside the Oconaluftee River, is self-guiding. You are free to wander about the farmstead, examining (with ordinary consideration of property and others) the relics of a bygone day.

While it may seem strange to think of wildlife among such a crowded atmosphere (and the crowds are huge during all but the worst of weather days), if you take the time to look carefully you will see woodchucks or groundhogs galore. In fact, primarily because of the almost-constant presence of people, the groundhogs are not nearly as timid as they are in the wild.

On a recent walk through the farmstead, the authors witnessed the woodchucks playing like so many kittens. At least a dozen were visible in one small field near the farm buildings, and virtually no one seemed to be aware of the presence of these interesting mountain (and flatland) animals.

The woodchuck may weigh from 5 to 12 pounds and a large male may reach 27 inches in length, including its 6-inch tail. This creature is very active during the day throughout the warmer months, but in winter the woodchuck hibernates, during which time its body temperature may drop from 98.9 degrees to 37.4 degrees, and his heart rate may decrease from 80 beats per minute to only 4 or 5 beats per minute.

The groundhog, which is a cousin of the marmot, has edible flesh, and often this burrowing animal, a great destroyer of some farm crops, provided meat for the table.

Another animal likely to be visible on any of the nature trails is the eastern chipmunk. A variety of squirrels may be seen if the hiker is patient and relatively silent.

Many other short, educational, and scenic hikes in the area are described in a pamphlet called *Walks & Hikes* that may be bought at the Oconaluftee Visitors Center and at other locations inside the Great Smokies National Park.

50

Smokemont Loop

Total distance (loop): 6 miles

Hiking time: 3 hours

Vertical rise: 2,720 feet

Rating: Moderate

Map: USGS 7.5' Smokemont

The Smokemont Campground is one of the most popular in the Great Smokies National Park. The area is quiet, serenely lovely, and bounded on three sides by tall peaks that are exceptionally beautiful in the spring and early summer, when the rhododendron and laurel and other flowering plants are in bloom, and in the fall when the leaves are changing.

A delightfully picturesque stream, the Bradley Fork Creek, flows through the campground, and other creeks feed into the Bradley Fork in the forests outside the campground. The Oconaluftee River flows in front of the campground, which is on US 441 three miles from Cherokee Indian Reservation. To reach Cherokee from I-40, take the US 74 exit and travel US 74 until it junctures with US 441.

To start the Smokemont Loop, walk or drive to the extreme northeast end of the campground, past D loop, and enter a maintenance road that is blocked to vehicle traffic except for park vehicles. There are parking spaces near the road, and if these are taken, others are available along the northern or exit side of the campground. These are all labeled as parking for scenic trails. Do not park in spaces numbered for campsites.

To provide some idea of the size of this campground, from campsite B-15, which is located near the center of the camping area, to the maintenance road, the distance is 2,102 feet. This campsite is mentioned in particular because there is a parking space for hikers just across the campground road from it, and the parking space is ideally located for starting three separate and delightful trails.

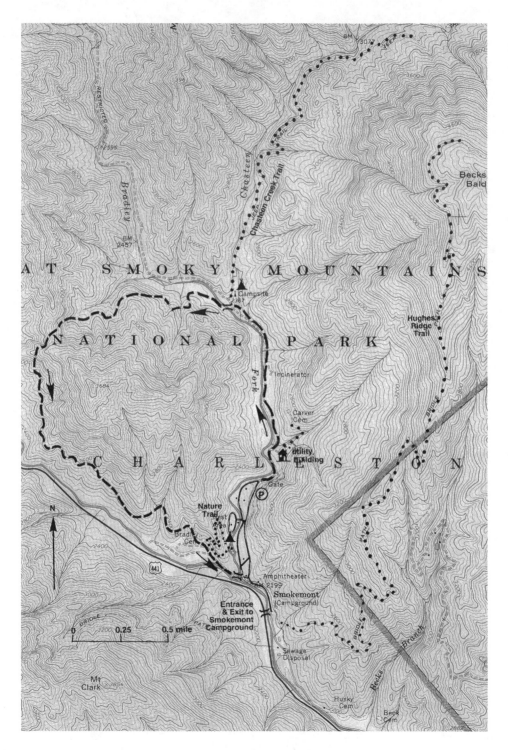

As you start up the maintenance road, you will begin a very gradual ascent that will continue for 1.3 miles. At no time is the climb steep or difficult; it is only gradual and very smooth. The maintenance road leads into the forest and continues until you reach the junction with the Chasteen Creek Trail.

As you hike the Smokemont Loop, you will parallel virtually at all times the Bradley Fork, which can be viewed as either a very small river or very large creek. The stream, whatever its label, is clear, broad, rocky, and impressively scenic at all times. It varies from a smooth flow to deep pools, myriads of ripples, and occasional wider expanses that are dappled with smooth, round boulders.

At 0.7 mile you will reach a utility building on the right, and 20 feet uphill from the building is a service road leading to a part of the water system for the park. This road is marked with a No Admittance sign, but you will see that hikers have made trips past the sign.

One ranger in the park stated that it was permissible for hikers to travel the road, as it leads to junctions with other trails, but it would be prudent to ask for permission before making the trip.

The trail along the Bradley Fork is bounded by a series of ridges on the right, in addition to the stream on the left. These wooded mountains are the home of plentiful deer and bears, and it is advisable to stay on or near the trail at all times.

At mile 1.6 you will cross a footbridge over Chasteen Creek, and 315 feet farther you will reach a signpost that gives the following distances to other trails: Chasteen Creek Trail—0.1 mile; Hughes Ridge Trail—4.1 miles; Smokemont Loop—0.5 mile; Cabin Flats Trail—2.9; return to campground—1.2 miles.

Continue straight ahead and you will junction with the Smokemont Loop. The maintenance road provides the first part of the loop, but the trail proper begins 0.5 mile ahead.

The area you will now enter is part of what was once a huge lumbering endeavor. Around 1918, almost at the point of the entry of the United States into World War I, the Champion Fibre Company purchased a series of smaller wood-cutting operations, fused them into one giant logging operation, and made Smokemont the central location for the corporation's entire logging work.

In the area were constructed a boarding house, or hotel, and the commissary, or company store. Today, nearly all evidence of the existence of the lumbering operation has disappeared; however, the effects of the operation will remain in the Smokemont area for decades to come.

After you cross the footbridge (at mile 1.7) you will see thick growths of poplar interspersed with the hemlocks, firs, sycamores, and sporadic hardwoods such as oaks, hickories, cherry, dogwood, and the ever-present thickets or growths of rhododendron and laurel, particularly around the stream banks and on the lower slopes of the mountain ridges.

The Smokemont Loop Trail wends around the lower slopes of Richland Mountain as the trail leaves the Chasteen Creek Trail and leads first west, then sharply to the southeast, then sharply again westward in the first half-mile of the hike. From this point and for the next mile the trail leads in a generally westward direction.

The final 3 miles of the trail lead down from the slopes of Richland Mountain and back toward Bradley Fork. The final mile of the trail is a series of twists and turns that lead back to the north, then northeast, almost due south, and then southeast. The trail culminates in the crossing of a bridge over the Bradley Fork. The bridge was constructed in 1921, and this date coincides with the early years of the establishment of the Champion Fibre lumber operations in the area.

From the bridge you will hike back up the campground exit loop road to the parking space in the B loop. Note that along the trail there were many large, tall yellow poplars, often referred to as the tulip poplar. This tree occasionally attains a height of 200 feet (although the average height is 100 feet) and may have a trunk diameter of 12 feet (but, again, the average diameter is 4 feet).

The yellow poplar was often used for log cabins by the mountain folk, because the wood was easily worked and resisted decay well as long as it was kept dry. The poplars along the trail are often very tall and thin, signs of rather young trees of the species. Poplars are often the first trees that invade areas made barren either by forest fires or by intensive harvesting of the mature trees.

The poplars along the trail are thought to be about half a century old, which would mean that the trees sprouted in the early 1940s, around the time that President Franklin D. Roosevelt dedicated the Great Smoky Mountains National Park.

The terrain around Bradley Fork and other streams in the area typically consists of relatively new forest growth. Here the railroad system penetrated the forest for miles upstream in order to haul the logs from the forest to the mills.

The harvested trees numbered in the thousands as hemlock and red spruce were cut to ship to the paper mill in Canton, North Carolina, on the outskirts of Asheville. Sparks from the locomotives started slash or brush fires that denuded the railroad right-of-way and slopes nearby, and the heavy rains that typify the Great Smokies eroded the barren land and drastically changed the entire face of the mountains.

Between 1918 and 1925 more than 115 million board feet of lumber had been cut and shipped from the area, and the fact that the Smokies are once again reforested, luxuriant, and beautiful is a living testimonial to the wisdom and care exerted by officials of the park and government.

When you hike the Smokemont Loop, keep in mind that in the early part of this century the total devastation of the forest was horrendous, but consider also that what has been accomplished here can easily be destroyed by carelessness with fires and cigarettes. If you camp in the Smokemont Campground you will be warned by park rangers that you *must* extinguish campfires at night (or any other time) not only by permitting the flames to burn down or by covering the coals but also by watering down the fire so that not one spark is left alive.

Despite the fact that the Great Smokies receive more precipitation (as rain, snow, and sleet) than virtually any other land area in the contiguous United States, the area also has long dry periods, particularly in August and October (the latter month historically one of the driest in the state) and the high winds that prevail so often dehydrate surface dead leaves so that the threat and danger of a forest fire is virtually constant.

When you have completed the Smokemont Loop Trail, you have a choice of several other trails close enough that you need not drive any considerable distance. These trails include Chasteen Creek Trail and Hughes Ridge Trail (see chapter 48), and the shorter but interesting Smokemont Self-Guiding Nature Trail (see chapter 49).

Suggested Books for Further Reading

Blackmun, Ora. *North Carolina: Its Mountains and Its People.* Boone: Appalachian Consortium, 1977.

Dean, Jim, and Lawrence Earley. *Wildlife in North Carolina.* Chapel Hill: University of North Carolina Press, 1987.

Homan, Tim. *Hiking Trails of the Joyce Kilmer, Slick Rock, and Citigo Creek Wilderness Areas.* Atlanta: Peachtree Publishers, 1990.

Jacobs, Jimmy. *Trout Streams of Southern Appalachia: Fly-casting in Georgia, Kentucky, North Carolina, South Carolina, and Tennessee.* Woodstock, Vermont: Backcountry Guides, 2001.

Joseph, Catherine. *North Carolina: Four Seasons of Splendor.* Charlotte: Aerial Photography Services, 1989.

Justice, William S., and C. Ritchie Bell. *Wildflowers of North Carolina.* Chapel Hill: University of North Carolina Press, 1987.

Kuralt, Charles, and Loonis McGlohan. *North Carolina Is My Home.* Old Saybrook: Globe Pequot Press, 1986.

Lefler, Hugh Talmudge, and Albert Ray Newsome. *North Carolina: The History of a Southern State.* Chapel Hill: University of North Carolina Press, 1963.

Lord, William G. *The Complete Guide to the Blue Ridge Parkway.* Conshahocken: Eastern Acorn Press, 1990.

Mullet, Rosa. *Fall and Winter in North Carolina Forests.* Crockett: Rod and Staff Publishers Inc., 1982.

____. *Spring and Summer in North Carolina Forests.* Crockett: Rod and Staff Publishers Inc., 1982.

Wenburg, Donald C. *Blue Ridge Mountain Pleasures.* Old Saybrook: Globe Pequot Press, 1988.

Index

A

Acid rain, 180, 182, 185
Alder Trail, 28–31
Alligator Back Overlook, 87
American chestnut trees, 43, 108, 135, 204, 207–8, 234
Anticlinorium, 65
Appalachian Trail, 196–99
Apple trees, 87, 102, 104
Art Loeb Trail, 139
Attic Window Peak, 125
Avery County, 13
Azaleas, 146

B

Backpacking, 16, 226
Backside Trail, 23
Balanced Rock, 66
Balsam Cone, 99
Balsam firs, 183
Balsam oil, 183
Balsam Trail, 182
Balsam woolly adelgid, 97–99
Balsam woolly aphid, 180, 182, 185
Barkhouse Picnic Area, 166
Basin Creek Trail, 80–83, 86
Beacon Heights Trail, 118
Bean Shoals Canal Trail, 53, 56
Bears, 208, 220, 229, 231

Beavers, 95
Bee Tree Creek, 91
Benn Knob, 37
Big East Trail, 139
Big Sandy Creek, 75, 76
Big Sandy River, 70
Biking, 49
Biltmore Estate, 210
Birding, 22, 30, 43, 50, 60, 64, 95, 188–89, 190, 204, 208, 231
Black Balsam Knob, 139
Blackberries, 99
Black Bottom Road, 103
Black Brothers, 185, 186
Black locust tree, 115
Black Mountain Campground, 180
Black Mountains, 185
Blue Ridge Mountains, 14
Bluff Mountain Trail, 80, 84–88
Bluff Ridge Primitive Trail, 80
Bluff Ridge Trail, 84–87
Boating, 35, 93, 95–96
Boone, Daniel, 94
Boone Fork Creek, 91–92, 94, 95
Boone Fork Loop Trail, 89–92, 113, 122
Bradley Fork, 231, 233, 239, 240
Bradley Fork Creek, 237
Brahm, Geraud de, 164–65
Brinegar Cabin, 84, 87–88

Let Backcountry Guides Take You There

Our experienced backcountry authors will lead you to the finest trails, parks, and back roads in the following areas:

50 Hikes Series
50 Hikes in the Adirondacks
50 Hikes in Connecticut
50 Hikes in the Maine Mountains
50 Hikes in Coastal and Southern Maine
50 Hikes in Maryland
50 Hikes in Massachusetts
50 Hikes in Michigan
50 Hikes in the White Mountains
50 More Hikes in New Hampshire
50 Hikes in New Jersey
50 Hikes in the Hudson Valley
50 Hikes in Central New York
50 Hikes in Western New York
50 Hikes in the Mountains of North Carolina
50 Hikes in Ohio
50 Hikes in Eastern Pennsylvania
50 Hikes in Central Pennsylvania
50 Hikes in Western Pennsylvania
50 Hikes in the Tennessee Mountains
50 Hikes in Vermont
50 Hikes in Northern Virginia

Walks and Rambles Series
Walks and Rambles on Cape Cod and the Islands
Walks and Rambles on the Delmarva Peninsula
Walks and Rambles in the Western Hudson
     Valley
Walks and Rambles on Long Island
Walks and Rambles in Ohio's Western Reserve
Walks and Rambles in Rhode Island
Walks and Rambles in and around St. Louis

25 Bicycle Tours Series
25 Bicycle Tours in the Adirondacks
25 Bicycle Tours on Delmarva
25 Bicycle Tours in Coastal Georgia and the
     Carolina Low Country
25 Bicycle Tours in Maine
25 Bicycle Tours in Maryland
25 Bicycle Tours in the Twin Cities and Southeast-
     ern Minnesota
30 Bicycle Tours in New Jersey
30 Bicycle Tours in the Finger Lakes Region
25 Bicycle Tours in the Hudson Valley
25 Bicycle Tours in Ohio's Western Reserve
25 Bicycle Tours in the Texas Hill Country and
     West Texas
25 Bicycle Tours in Vermont
25 Bicycle Tours in and around Washington, D.C.
30 Bicycle Tours in Wisconsin
25 Mountain Bike Tours in the Adirondacks
25 Mountain Bike Tours in the Hudson Valley
25 Mountain Bike Tours in Massachusetts
25 Mountain Bike Tours in New Jersey
Backroad Bicycling on Cape Cod, Martha's
     Vineyard, and Nantucket
Backroad Bicycling in Eastern Pennsylvania
Backroad Bicycling in Connecticut

Bicycling America's National Parks Series
Bicycling America's National Parks: Arizona &
     New Mexico
Bicycling America's National Parks: California
Bicycling America's National Parks: Oregon &
     Washington
Bicycling America's National Parks: Utah &
     Colorado

We offer many more books on hiking, fly-fishing, travel, nature, and other subjects. Our books are available at bookstores and outdoor stores everywhere. For more information or a free catalog, please call 1-800-245-4151 or write to us at The Countryman Press, P.O. Box 748, Woodstock, Vermont 05091. You can find us on the Internet at www.countrymanpress.com.